A Short History of Sociological Thought

Also by Alan Swingewood

The Sociology of Literature (co-author)
Marx and Modern Social Theory
The Novel and Revolution
The Myth of Mass Culture

A Short History of Sociological Thought

Alan Swingewood
Lecturer in Sociology, London School of Economics

MACMILLAN

First published 1984
Reprinted 1988, 1989

Published by
MACMILLAN EDUCATION LTD
Houndmills, Basingstoke, Hampshire RG21 2XS
and London
Companies and representatives
throughout the world

Printed in China

British Library Cataloguing in Publication Data
Swingewood, Alan
A short history of sociological thought.
1. Sociology—History
I. Title
301'.09   HM19
ISBN 0-333-31078-0
ISBN 0-333-31079-9 Pbk

Contents

Contents

Contents

HISTORY OF SOCIOLOGICAL THOUGHT

Origins

Eighteenth-century social thought (Vico, Montesquieu,
Smith, Ferguson, Rousseau)

The development of nineteenth-century sociological
positivism (Comte), sociological evolutionism (Spencer) and
Marxism (Marx and Engels)

↓

Classical Sociology

Weber, Simmel, Pareto
(the tradition of *verstehen*
sociology and critique of
positivism and evolutionism)

Durkheim's critique of the
positivist tradition

The development of Marxism after Marx involving a critique of materialism
and evolutionism: Labriola, Gramsci, Sorel, Lukács

↓

Modern Sociology

Phenomenological Sociology (Schutz)
Freud, Mead, Mannheim

Functionalism
Systems Theory and Action Theory
(Parsons)
Structuralism

Introduction

This book is neither a history of sociology nor of sociological theory but a selective history of sociological thought from its origins in eighteenth-century philosophy, history and political economy. By sociological thought is meant an awareness of society as a distinctive object of study, as a system or structure objectively determined by laws and processes. Eighteenth-century social thought was sociological in this sense although it failed to develop an adequate sociological concept of the social, too often assimilating it to political and economic elements. In effect eighteenth-century social thought posed many of the critical issues of sociology without resolving them sociologically. In contrast, early nineteenth-century sociological thought (specifically Comte, Spencer, Marx) sought to define the social both in terms of society as a complex structural whole and in its relation with specific institutions, notably the division of labour, social classes, religion, family and scientific/professional associations. Society was industrial society and the broad themes of the early sociologists were those of social conflict, alienation, community, social cohesion and the possibilities of evolution and development. The task of social science was to identify the forces promoting historical change. Early sociological thought was concerned with the separation of an autonomous social sphere (or 'civil society') from centralised state institutions (or 'political society'). It is this notion of 'finalisation', that history has a meaning apart from the actions of everyday life, which differentiates early sociological thought from later, classical sociology and the various schools of 'sociologised' Marxism.

Early sociological thought was broadly optimistic: the

certainties of the natural sciences could be applied to the social sciences unproblematically. Classical sociology emerges as a reaction to this form of positivist scientistic thought. The broad themes of classical sociology were pessimistic: industrialisation produces social structures which alienate the individual from the community, transform cultural objects into commodities, rationalise human life into bureaucratic systems of domination and effectively strip the individual of autonomy. Classical sociology becomes centred not on large-scale changes but on the human subject: 'voluntarism' and action replace the historical determinism of nineteenth-century systems theory. It is this distinction which sets the agenda for the later development of modern sociology.

Modern sociological thought begins with the breakdown of the classical, voluntarist model. The dominant paradigm becomes functionalism, its pre-eminence bound up with the emergence of American sociology in the years following the Second World War. Classical sociology had been almost entirely European: the rise of European Fascism, Communism and the Second World War shifted the focus of sociological thought across the Atlantic. And it was not until the 1960s that new schools of sociology – phenomenology, action theory, structuralism, Marxist humanism – which drew much of their inspiration from classical sociology, emerged.

In this book I have attempted to describe these developments. In particular, there is extended discussion of Marxism both as a distinctive theory of society and for its influence on classical and modern sociology. It has become fashionable to argue that Marxism is a sociology. I suggest that Marxist thought is certainly sociological and as such has been absorbed into sociology itself and, increasingly, that Marxism assimilates sociological concepts and thought in order to offer adequate accounts of modern industrial society and historical development. Many of the crucial differences between sociology and Marxism resolve themselves around the relation of centralised state structure to decentred social structures. By defining its object of study as civil society sociology developed theories which emphasised the differentiated and potentially autonomous nature of modern industrial society. In contrast, Marxist thought articulated a theory of the social formation built around a deterministic relation of economic 'base' to socio-cultural 'superstructure'. It is this decentred, sociological concept of the social which links together the various schools of sociological thought. This does not imply a single sociology. Since the rise of classical sociology there have been many different sociologies but they share a common object of study and their focus is broadly similar.

Part I examines the historical rise of sociological thought and its development into positivism, evolutionism and Marxism. Part II describes the complex reaction to positivist social science and Marxism by classical sociologists such as Weber, Durkheim, Sombart and Simmel. Because Marx's thought played such an important role in the formation of classical sociology I have discussed his theory of class and power in Part II contrasting it with Weber's work on social stratification. This is not an argument that sociology developed through a 'debate with Marx's ghost'. Indeed, classical sociology 'debated' with Kant as much as Marx. Kant's epistemology and moral philosophy played as vital a role in the development of classical sociology as Hegelian dialectics in the development of Marxism. Part III explores the development of modern sociology, first in the form of sociological functionalism, and then in its attempts to rediscover the insights of classical sociology. It is the depth of this renewal which suggests a convergence of sociological thought in the midst of apparent fragmentation and diversity.

The development of sociological thought is the result of collaborative, communicative and dialogic interaction involving individuals, social groups and communities. Of all areas of the history of sociology this is perhaps the most complex and neglected although there have been valuable contributions by Coser, 1971; Jay, 1973; Clarke, 1973; Schwendinger, 1974 and Therborn, 1976. Certain themes – race and gender, for example – are not discussed, largely because they have not been in the forefront of sociological thought. This book is, as I have said, a selective history. At the end I have listed a number of works by chapter which refer the reader to further general discussion as well as more specialised studies. A history of sociological thought – from Vico to Bakhtin – can easily become a 'shopping list' of great names: I have tried to avoid this by concentrating in some detail on major themes of sociological relevance as well as significant thinkers.

November 1983   ALAN SWINGEWOOD

PART I
FOUNDATIONS

1
Origins of Sociology

There was no sociology before the advent of the nineteenth
century, if by sociology is meant a systematic corpus of
knowledge, specific methodology and conceptual framework
which clearly differentiate it as a distinctive discipline, with its
own object of study, from the related studies of economics,
history, philosophy and law. The term sociology was coined by
Auguste Comte in the early nineteenth century although the
study of society as an historical and empirical object had begun
much earlier, especially in eighteenth-century France and
Scotland, where a commitment to historical and scientific
modes of thought and inquiry shifted the prevailing discourse
of political and moral philosophy away from traditional
concerns with the universal and the transhistorical to a grasp of
the specificity of the social. This is not to suggest that
eighteenth-century social theory constituted a sociology, rather
it remained a peculiarly invigorating mixture of political
philosophy, history, political economy *and* sociology.

The work of Montesquieu, Ferguson and Millar exemplified
a sociology in the making. In discussing the development of
sociology it is crucial to distinguish between those writers who
discussed broad sociological themes within a non-sociological
discourse (Aristotle, Plato, Hobbes, Locke) and those genuine
precursors who defined both a method of inquiry and a concept
of society as a distinctive object of study, a dynamic structure of
institutions and processes analytically separate from political
society.

Human nature and social order

Two pre-sociological theories – those of classical Greek thought and the Social Contract – are sometimes regarded by historians of sociology as laying down the foundation for a science of human society. Both Plato (427–347 B.C.) and Aristotle (384–322 B.C.) defined society in holistic terms as an organism in which the constituent parts were necessarily related to the whole. Plato particularly emphasised the unity of the social organism, the parts defined in terms of their subordination to the whole. In contrast, Aristotle conceived society as a differentiated structure in which separate elements, while contributing to the whole, remained independent of it. Thus Plato analysed society as a unified system, structured around the division of labour and social inequality. Social health, or social order, was the product of 'wise legislation' in which the interests of the whole exerted priority over those of the individual parts. Plato's ideal state has thus been described as a form of communism in that the separate elements, such as private property and the family, functioned in relation to the higher unity of the whole.

Aristotle's concept of society was equally anti-atomistic: as a complex, differentiated structure the social whole consisted of groups not individuals. For Aristotle, the origin of society lay in human nature; humanity was by nature social and political and thus destined to live with others in communities. Social structure consisted of social groups based on function and social wealth (food-producers, warriors, tradesmen; the rich, the poor, the middle class). Aristotle's *Politics* is full of sociological insights into the nature of human society and contains one of the first systematic attempts to analyse and classify social phenomena, such as government, into ideal types (tyranny, oligarchy, democracy). Yet Aristotle's social thought remains within the framework of traditional political philosophy. As with Plato, there is no clear distinction between the state and society. And for Aristotle social institutions are derived from basic human instincts such as sexual desire which predispose individuals to form groups and associations which then function to further develop essential human nature. Society was thus the expression of an inherent sociability with social relationships the culmination of this instinct. Aristotle's formulations blocked the possibility of defining society in terms of objective laws and historical processes.

Aristotle's static world view was not challenged until the sixteenth century. Medieval social organisation did not generate a philosophy oriented to problems of social change and secular political obligation. Social contract theory developed as an alternative world view rejecting notions of Divine Law and religious conceptions of sovereignty. Social contract theory sought the origins of society in a structure of contractual obligations and reciprocal social relationships. Human nature was still an important component of the theory but Aristotle's essentialist sociability was replaced, in the work of Thomas Hobbes (1588–1679), by an asocial, egoistic and individualistic humanity. In the pre-social state of nature, Hobbes argued, there was an absence of social bonds and a condition of permanent warfare. A peaceful and unified civil society was made possible only through the renunciation of certain individual rights: a contractual obligation linked the individual with a sovereign state that guaranteed order and harmony under the rubric of positive law.

Social contract theory prepared the way for the secular social theory of the eighteenth century even though it remained tied to asocial notions of human nature. Society was conceived as partly the product of human and not divine action. Not all social contract writers were as pessimistic as Hobbes: John Locke (1632–1704) argued that the state of nature was rather a state of peace, good will and reciprocal relationships, the development of social conflict and diverging interests the result of the growth of private property and thus of social inequality. Both Hobbes and Locke grasped the secular historical nature of human society but assimilated this notion of the social to an underlying concept of a pre-social, transhistorical human nature: egoism for Hobbes, sympathy for Locke. In the eighteenth century Jean Jacques Rousseau (1712–78) further developed Locke's dichotomy of a sociable humanity existing in a state of nature and the corrupt, egoistic humanity of modern civil society; humanity as the product of nature versus humanity as the product of society and culture.

In the writings of Aristotle, Plato, Hobbes, Locke and

Rousseau there are numerous sociological themes relating to problems of social differentiation, inequality, social conflict and social cohesion, the development of the division of labour and private property – but this does not make these theorists sociologists. Locke is more sociological than Aristotle in his analysis of property and social differentiation; Rousseau is more sociological than Locke in his awareness that society creates more complex needs and therefore a more complex humanity than that found in the state of nature. Pre-eighteenth century philosophy, however, was largely dominated by a weak, not strong concept of the social: society was not defined as an objective structure of secular institutions and processes, but the product of asocial forces and the voluntary acquiescence of pre-social individuals in the formation of modern states and political obligation. The emphasis on human nature as the basis of human society and social order led to the view of the social as the expression of an immanent transhistorical process. There was no conception of society as a complex structure of different levels – the economic, political, cultural – dependent for their functioning on specific, objective laws. In this sense the true precursors of sociology are Giambattista Vico and Baron de Montesquieu.

Vico: science and history

The New Science of Giambattista Vico (1668–1774), first published in 1725, is one of the most remarkable works of early eighteenth-century social thought; a vast comparative analysis of the history of human culture which discusses the rise of property, religion, and the development of language, art and literature. The third edition of 1744 preceded Montesquieu's *Spirit of the Laws* by four years and together they stand as the first major attempts to theorise society as an organic whole and relate its varying cultures, values and institutions to a specific stage of historical development.

Vico's *New Science* sought to make history intelligible by defining it as a process characterised by three distinct stages of development – the age of the Gods, the age of the Heroes and finally the age of Men – and thus invested with immanent meaning. The theory itself is perhaps less significant than Vico's attempt to apply scientific concepts to the study of human history. His starting point was the affirmation of humanism – the creative, active role of the human subject. 'In the night of thick darkness', he wrote, which envelops the remote past 'there shines the eternal and never failing light of a truth beyond all question: that the world of civil society has certainly been made by men' (Vico, 1948, Section 331). Vico thus rejected the fixed concept of human nature which had characterised the social thought of Aristotle, Hobbes and Locke: the general argument of the *New Science* was that human society was historical, social institutions and human relationships defined as the product of action. For Vico, society and human nature were dynamic categories: he accepted that human nature rested on certain principles to be unfolded and revealed in the historical development of institutions such as the family. Vico's dynamic sense of history contrasts sharply with the anti-historical rationalism of social contract theory which, assuming society as the expression of an unchanging human nature, postulated a static notion of the social which failed to account for the richness and variety of traditions and customs and the ways in which elements of the past survived actively into the present.

Vico's concept of history as an active, creative process made by humanity, clearly differentiates his social thought from the mechanistic materialism of Hobbes and Locke with their emphasis on the determining influence of the environment on human action. Vico was also opposed to the scientific rationalism associated with the natural sciences: the *New Science* rejects many of the assumptions of Newton, Galileo and the philosophy of Descartes. Cartesian rationalism, a potent influence on philosophy and science at this time, assumed that the only certain knowledge was derived from principles and concepts drawn from mathematics and physics. Descartes advanced what he called the 'geometrical method' as the basis for understanding both the natural and the social worlds. True knowledge, therefore, was essentially deductive, the application of rules that were universal and timeless. But mathematics itself, Vico argued, was man-made and the knowledge derived from mathematical propositions was true knowledge only

11

because humanity itself had created it. Here Vico states one of his revolutionary new principles, that humanity can know only that which itself has created: the true (*verum*) and the made (*factum*) are convertible. It was not, therefore, a question of passively recording, classifying and observing an external reality in the manner of the physical sciences, for 'the world of human society has certainly been made by men, and its principles are therefore to be found within the modifications of our own human mind'. Vico's distinction between 'inner' and 'outer' knowledge derived from his humanist, anti-mechanical and anti-determinist standpoint: factual knowledge of the external world was clearly inadequate as the basis for human science since it eliminated the active core of human culture, diminishing the making in favour of the made.

For Vico, then, the subject matter of the natural sciences differed from that of the human sciences. Social theory must be based on the human subject as an active agent, on human experiences and mental states. But for all its revolutionary implications, perhaps because of this, the *New Science* found little response among the major philosophers and political theorists of the eighteenth-century Enlightenment. It was not until the nineteenth century that Vico's work was given its true recognition. His concept of society as an organic whole was clearly opposed to the atomistic individualism of French philosophical materialism. Yet Vico's work was typical of one important strand of eighteenth-century thought which culminated in the holistic theories of society and culture advanced by Hegel, and later, during the nineteenth century, by Comte and Marx. Vico's humanist historicism is important here for the argument, central to both Hegel and Marx, that human action has meaning only in terms of the whole. History is conceived as a process which succeeds in binding together the often contradictory and chaotic actions of individuals in such a way that they form a coherent whole. At the end of the *New Science* Vico restated his 'first incontestable principle' but added that

this world without doubt has issued from a mind often diverse, at times quite contrary, and always superior to the particular ends that men had proposed to themselves . . . Men mean to gratify their bestial lust and abandon their offspring, and they inaugurate the chastity of marriage from which the families arise. The fathers mean to exercise without restraint their paternal power over their clients, and they subject them to the civil powers from which the cities arise (Vico, 1948, Section 1108).

This notion of the unintended effects of social action is developed by Vico as part of his general theory of historical change. As we shall see it was to exercise a great influence on eighteenth-century social theory.

Montesquieu

Eighteenth-century philosophy remained unreceptive to Vico's humanist historicism. When Montesquieu visited Venice the *New Science* was recommended but there is no evidence that he either read or acquired the work. It was Montesquieu, not Vico, who influenced the sociological writings of the Scottish School of Ferguson, Smith and Millar. Like many other eighteenth-century intellectuals, Montesquieu (1689–1755) was not a specialist but a man of letters trained in classics and philosophy. His work combined the study of history, political science, criticism, political theory and sociology, but he has been described as the first, and greatest sociologist of the Enlightenment. In the 'Preface' to *The Spirit of the Laws* (1748) he emphasised his scientific intent: 'I have not drawn my principles from my prejudices but from the nature of things.' Such was his reputation that in 1767 a despairing Adam Ferguson noted that 'when I recollect what . . . Montesquieu has written, I am at a loss to tell why I should treat of human affairs'.

Montesquieu, employing a richer and more detailed mode of historical analysis, more extensive and systematic than anything found in previous social theory, was able to define society as a structural whole and, more significantly, attempt to locate the specific causes of different social phenomena. The laws of society, although the embodiment of human reason, must nevertheless suit the physical context and its social institutions. Legal codes and customs are discussed from the perspective of their relationship with social structure; the role of the legislator is one of balancing the requirements of an 'ideal' constitution with the situation or 'milieu'. It was this aspect of Montesquieu's thought that Emile Durkheim regarded as significant for the development of sociology: to accept the view that legislators alone framed constitutions and social customs was tantamount to denying 'any determinate order in human societies, for if it were true laws, customs and institutions would depend not on the constant nature of the state, but on the accident that brought forth one lawmaker rather than another' (Durkheim, 1965, pp. 11–12).

Montesquieu's point of departure is clearly indicated in the 'Preface' to the *Spirit of the Laws*:

> I have first of all considered mankind, and the results of my thoughts has been, that midst such an infinite diversity of laws and manners, they were not solely conducted by the caprice of fancy.

And in the first book he writes:

> They who assert that a blind fatality produced the various effects we behold in this world talk very absurdly; for can anything be more unreasonable than to pretend that a blind fatality could be productive of intelligent beings? (Montesquieu, 1949, Book 1, Section 1).

Montesquieu is arguing that although society presents itself as a chaotic and diverse phenomenon, there exists beneath the surface a definite structure comprising regularities of behaviour, institutions and laws. Social institutions and processes are thus the product of definite material conditions which can be discovered by empirical and historical analysis. Regular relationships exist between these objective forces. In his study of the Roman Empire (1734) Montesquieu wrote:

> It is not chance that rules the world. Ask the Romans who had a continuous sequence of successes when they were guided by a

certain plan, and an uninterrupted sequence of reverses when they followed another. There are general causes, moral and physical, which act in every monarchy, elevating it, maintaining it . . . All accidents are controlled by these causes (Montesquieu, 1965, p. 165).

All social phenomena are interconnected, 'every particular law is connected with another law'. Montesquieu's concept of society is thus couched in holistic, not atomistic, terms; societies are self-contained, integrated wholes.

Montesquieu's main concern was forms of government. But his types of government are effectively types of society. Law must accord with social context, but Montesquieu attempts to define context more precisely as a structure consisting of soil and climate, occupations, religious institutions, 'commerce, manners and customs'. His analysis of law is far from narrowly political, for as laws express the 'spirit' or inner essence of society as a whole, the distinction between the political and the social is purely formal. Thus although adhering to Aristotle's classification of government – republics which include aristocracy and democracy, monarchy and despotism – Montesquieu concentrates his analysis on the distribution and exercise of power within them and the principles or 'spirit' binding them together – virtue, honour and fear.

Montesquieu emphasises that his classification is of ideal rather than real types: the fact that a republican government exemplifies virtue (through the frugality and equality within its city states) does not imply that all republics express virtue only that they 'ought'. Montesquieu's forms are effectively ideal types, logical constructs, abstracted from the rich and varied historical details of reality to facilitate analysis, a methodological standpoint which clearly differentiates his thought from the classic Aristotelian political tradition. Aristotle's governments were essences – timeless, universal abstractions based on a limited historical experience. Montesquieu's awareness of the relation of the social to the political effectively yielded a classification of governments and societies.

But in making this break from political philosophy Montesquieu failed to develop a theory of social change; he did not analyse the ways in which one type of society passed into a different form. His typology was broadly synchronic, concerned with describing the typical elements of different formations as they unite in a coherent unity; Montesquieu's sociological 'formalism' is thus insensitive to the problems of genesis and change. The important question of transition is never raised and in this sense Montesquieu was not historical enough, his formal classification, although of great significance for sociological method, blocking the development of a dynamic concept of civil society. The writers of the Scottish Enlightenment, while indebted to Montesquieu's typology and formal historical sense, were more concretely aware of social change and the transition from one type of society to another. Thus they attempted to identify those elements within society which led to social change.

Montesquieu's synchronic approach led him to define society as a system in which the various elements had meaning only in terms of the whole. The basic elements comprising this system were climate and geography: other writers had advocated physical factors as the basis of social analysis but Montesquieu was the first to analyse their contribution to the structure of society as a whole. Montesquieu's concept of environment, or milieu, implied the concept of a system in which the political 'superstructure' and culture express the spirit of the whole. Of course, Montesquieu overstates his case: suicide, slavery, marriage are all mechanically and causally related to specific climatic conditions and peculiarities of geography. But there can be no doubting the scientific spirit behind these arguments. Also Montesquieu did not suggest a totally monistic view: there are moral, as well as physical causes, and in Book XIX of *The Spirit of the Laws* he argued that

Mankind are influenced by various causes: by the climate . . . religion . . . laws . . . maxims of government . . . morals and customs; whence is formed the general spirit of nations. In proportion as, in every country, any one of these causes acts with more force, the others in the same degree are weakened. Nature and climate rule almost alone among the savages; customs govern the Chinese.

The structure of any society thus hinges on the workings, not of

16

one single factor but of many factors; society is the product of an equilibrium between a multiplicity of elements. Social development gradually weakens the influence of purely physical elements and strengthens the moral. The role of the legislator is to discover a balance between physical and moral forces, the latter by their nature more amenable to human manipulation. The milieu is thus the framework in which physical and moral factors operate, a structure of multi-causality which allows Montesquieu to adopt a voluntaristic position, the legislator mediating between the emerging influence of the moral and the weakening influence of the physical. Nevertheless, the broad implications of Montesquieu's concept of society is that the individual is merely the instrument of historical change, a passive element within a system conceived as the ceaseless interaction of moral and physical forces that climaxes in the spirit of the nation. Virtue, honour and fear function to create social unity and maintain social order.

The sociological core of Montesquieu's thought is undoubtedly the attempt to discover an underlying pattern of relationships between the different elements of society; beneath the apparent diversity and chaos of empirical reality exists a structure and system which, once clarified, illuminates the cause of diverse phenomena and thus generates meaning. His comment on the feudal system is apposite:

> The feudal laws form a very beautiful prospect. A venerable old oak raises its lofty head to the skies; the eye sees from afar its spreading leaves; upon drawing nearer it perceives the trunk but does not discern the root; the ground must be dug up to discover it (Montesquieu, 1949, Book XXX, Section 1).

It was this task which fell to Adam Ferguson and John Millar.

The Scottish Enlightenment

As I have suggested earlier, the atomistic individualism of the French Enlightenment prevented the further development of Montesquieu's sociological conceptions, especially the notion of society as an integrated, systemic whole. Thus Diderot's project, the *Encyclopedia* contains no entry for society; Voltaire, like Diderot, remained firmly within the individualistic rationalism and philosophical scepticism of post-1750 French thought. Rousseau is one exception, for as I have noted earlier, in the discussion of social contract theory, sociological themes saturate his works. In *The Social Contract* (1762) and the *Discourse on the Origins of Social Inequality* (1755) Rousseau analysed the rise of property and its relation with the division of labour, inequality and social conflict. And like Montesquieu, he grasped both the distinctiveness of the social and society as an organic whole in which individual interests were assimilated into a common, general will. Society was not a collection of atomised individuals. But unlike Montesquieu, Rousseau was concerned with origins: for him society was the result of a contract, an act of association which generated a moral and collective order greater than the individual wills comprising it. Society was thus the product of both the principles of nature (the original state of nature and natural man) and those of reason. There is here a sharp distinction between the concept of society in Montesquieu and Rousseau. For Montesquieu, society was a system built around objective structures or elements; for Rousseau, society was an organism based on individual wills collectively organised into a quasi-mystical general will.

In the development of sociology Montesquieu was the more potent force. During the second half of the eighteenth century a group of intellectuals working in Glasgow and Edinburgh advanced the scientific study of human society in directions opposed to social contract theory. Such were the achievements of David Hume (1711–76), Adam Smith (1723–90), Adam Ferguson (1723–1816), John Millar (1735–1801) as well as the historian William Robertson (1721–93) that Edinburgh became known as the Athens of the North, compared only with Paris as the major centre of learning during the latter half of the eighteenth century. For this group of intellectuals society as a distinctive object of study could not be assimilated to a contractual relation between individual and government, but defined empirically, as a distinctive structure with a natural or 'theoretical history'.

While there has been much comment on the intellectual

achievements of the Scottish Enlightenment, there has been a tendency to concentrate on its contributions to philosophy and economics and to underemphasise the sociology. Smith, Ferguson and Millar raised critical sociological issues and problems analysing the social role of property, forms of government, the development of the division of labour, the alienation of industrial work and the development of language: these were not mere themes within their work but constituted a core of sociological thought and theorising within the broad framework of economics, philosophy and history.

Of these intellectuals the least sociologial was David Hume but his influence on Smith and Ferguson was crucial. Hume was an empiricist: experience, fact, utility constituted the backbone of his epistemology and social philosophy. He rejected the social contract theory of society arguing that to locate the origins of political society in the voluntary acquiescence of individuals was to ignore the real historical world of human experience and facts. Social contract theory was effectively dismissed for its lack of sociology. Society could not be deduced from universal principles of human nature, for although characterised by uniformity it is moulded by the social context especially education, custom and habit. Hume emphasised the role of social factors which affect human character. One of the most important is sympathy which is defined socially in that 'the mutual dependence of man is so great in all societies that scarce any human action is entirely complete in itself, or is performed without some reference to the actions of others, which are requisite to make it answer fully the intention of the agent'. Writing of justice Hume remarked that it is established by common consent 'and where every single act is performed in expectation that others are to perform the like'. Sympathy is social because 'the propensity to company and society is strong in all rational creatures'. In a similar way he argued that custom and habit were not irrational forces but elements essential for the proper workings of society. Hume failed to develop a conception of society as a structure, and in general his model remained atomistic and his method deductive. Thus although human association was the product of human nature, Hume's concern lay with the forms of sociability which human nature takes within society. He continually defined human action as social because it is oriented towards the actions of others: 'Reduce a person to solitude and he loses all enjoyment except either of the sensual or speculative kind; and that because the movements of his heart are not forwarded by correspondent movements in his fellow creatures.' A non-social man, like the state of nature, is a mere 'philosophical fiction'.

Hume's essays are full of proto-sociological themes. Authority, he notes, is always a 'mixture of force and consent' made generally acceptable by its practical utility. He argues for the close relation of property and power, advocating a functional balance between them. But the existence of sociological themes does not make a philosopher into a sociologist; nor do they necessarily cohere into a theory of society as an independent object of study. Unlike Hume, Ferguson, Smith and Millar defined the basic unit of analysis as groups – Ferguson's 'troops and companies' – which thus constituted a definite patterned structure. Hume followed Aristotle in defining society as coeval with the human family, a social group which unites and preserves sexual union until 'a new tie takes place in their common concern with their offspring'. From sexual desire Hume deduced the universality of the human family and therefore society. Ferguson, while agreeing with Hume on the importance of sexual desire in the process of family formation, and noting the existence of human instincts, was more concerned with the institution of the family and its contribution to socialisation and forging the necessary bond between parent and child. This distinction, however, between Hume's deductive approach and Ferguson's inductive, empirical standpoint is by no means clear-cut, but the tendency towards a sociological analysis of the institutional and structural basis of society is markedly present in Ferguson, Smith and Millar. Ferguson's *Essay on the History of Civil Society* (1767) marks a distinct advance on Hume's more speculative essays of the 1740s.

Problems of method

As I have suggested, there was no sociology that can be separated from economics, philosophy and history until the nineteenth century. A distinctive sociological framework, or perspective, did not exist in eighteenth-century thought, but rather a core of sociological concepts and an empirical methodology subsisting within economic, political and historical perspectives. In the writings of Adam Smith three distinct, although related levels of analysis can be identified: the economic, the philosophical and the sociological. In *The Wealth of Nations* the emphasis falls equally on the economic and social consequences of the division of labour. What is significant about the contribution of the Scottish Enlightenment to sociology is the clear awareness that society constituted a process, the product of specific economic, social and historical forces that could be identified and analysed through the methods of empirical science. Society was a category of historical investigation, the result of objective, material causes.

The Scots rejected both the theory of the 'divine origins' of society and the theory of the great legislator. Theoretical, or 'conjectural history', as the approach was termed – misleadingly since the intention was a science of history and society, positive not conjectural knowledge and therefore theoretical in the best sense – was superficially similar to Montesquieu's broad comparative perspective. But the Scots were concerned above everything else with the problem of social change and the causes which lead to the transition from one type of society to another. As Millar wrote:

> In searching for the causes of . . . systems of law and government . . . we must undoubtedly resort . . . to the differences of situation . . . the fertility or barrenness of the soil, the nature of its productions, the species of labour requisite for procuring subsistence, in the number of individuals collected together in one community, their proficiency in the arts . . . The variety that frequently occurs in these and such other particulars must have a prodigious influence upon the great body of the people; as, by giving a peculiar direction to their inclinations and pursuits, it must be productive of corresponding habits, dispositions and ways of thinking (Millar, in Lehmann, 1960).

Social diversity is thus explicable in terms of an underlying structure consisting largely of economic factors. Millar's

comparative approach, however, sought to analyse diversity
and uniformity in terms of the change from 'rude' to 'polished'
society. Similarly, Ferguson related forms of government to
property, social stratification, division of labour and social
conflict. Ferguson's standpoint was civil not political society.
Thus the Scots' typology of societies: savage, barbaric and
polished (Ferguson), hunting, pastoral, agricultural and commercial (Millar, Smith), constituted forms based on the
dominant mode of production in each. And having defined
societies in these terms the Scottish writers analysed their
dominant institutions and mechanisms leading to social
change. One institution which occupied much of their thought
was social stratification.

The emergence of class

Neither Hume nor Montesquieu discussed social stratification
in any depth. Montesquieu's concerns lay with societies as
organic wholes and not with possible sources of conflict and
differentiation. Montesquieu lacked a theory of transition, his
synchronic model of society eliminating the sources of energy
and thus of structural change.

For Adam Smith, the development of a commercial society
produced a social structure divided into three clear classes,
landowners, capitalists and labourers, 'the three great and
constituent orders of every civilised society'. Like Ferguson and
Millar, Smith did not employ the concept of social class, but
there can be no doubt that in his work, and that of Millar
particularly, a theory of class as a sociological category is
articulated. The relation between Smith's three social 'orders'
and the economic elements is unambiguous: the three groups
derive their revenue from rent, from stock, and from wages.
Property forms the basis of social differentiation, 'the natural
source of influence and authority' closely bound up with social
change and pervading 'every corner of society'. Millar argued,
indeed, that social development necessarily engendered social
inequality ceaselessly introducing 'corresponding gradation
and subordination of ranks'. An economic interpretation of
history is suggested:

The distribution of property among any people is the principal circumstance that contributed to reduce them under civil government, and to determine the form of their political constitution. The poor are naturally dependent on the rich, from whom they derive subsistence; and, according to the accidental differences of wealth possessed by individuals, a subordination of ranks is gradually introduced and different degrees of power are assumed without opposition, by particular persons (Millar, in Lehmann, 1960).

In pre-industrial society, Millar argued, social stratification was based largely on function: in fishing and hunting communities, for example, outstanding personal accomplishments, such as courage, strength and military skill, constituted the basis of authority. But distinctions hinging on function are unstable and 'cannot be productive of any lasting influence and authority'. But with the growth of agriculture and settled mode of subsistence property became increasingly accumulated in private hands and thus a permanent differentiation of ranks emerged: authority became stabilised and institutionalised.

For Millar, commercial society produces damaging effects through the division of labour. Both Millar and Ferguson, aware of the relation of social stratification to the division of labour, treated work specialisation sociologically. Their analysis represented a sharp break from previous discussion, for although Montesquieu and Hume had noted its economic significance they minimised the division of labour's social effects and failed to grasp its broad, structural significance. Thus Ferguson pointed out that the division of labour was a social as well as an economic institution separating those whose function commanded skill from those for whom work required neither thought nor the exercise of 'ingenuity'. Work thus becomes more efficient 'under a total suppression of sentiment and reason' and where 'ignorance is the mother of industry as well as of superstition'. In a famous passage Ferguson wrote:

Manufactures . . . prosper most where the mind is least consulted, and where the workshop may, without any great effort of imagination be considered as an engine, the parts of which are men (Ferguson, 1966, pp. 182–3).

23

As mechanical labour is divided so too are other activities: 'In the progress of society, philosophy or speculation becomes, like every other employment, the principal or sole trade and occupation of a particular class of citizens . . . subdivided into a great number of different branches.' Division of labour is a total process; Ferguson has outlined, indeed, the basis of sociology as a distinct and separate field of study. The norms of efficiency and dexterity apply equally to philosophy and industry, 'more work is done . . . and the quantity of science is considerably increased by it'. Specialisation, Ferguson suggests, leads to a loss of the whole. Manufacturing occupations, unlike the occupation of philosopher, stultify the human intellect; the more minute the task, the fewer the ideas; the more that men work the less time they have for thought and study. Social development is indeed double-edged. As Millar wrote:

> As their employments require constant attention to an object which can afford no variety of occupations to their minds, they are apt to acquire an habitual vacancy of thought, unenlivened by any prospects, but such as are derived from the future wages of their labour or from the grateful returns of bodily respose and sleep (Millar, in Lehmann, 1960).

One of the unintended effects of industrial development, the consequence of a 'polished' society, is that humanity increasingly resembles machines, stripped of its mental powers and 'converted to a mere instrument of labour'.

The dialectics of social change

The concepts of class and industrial society are implicit in the Scottish analysis although remaining untheorised in comparison with later nineteenth-century sociology. Ferguson and Millar identified industrial change as a source of progress in human culture but which, inevitably, brought with it dehumanisation and alienation. Social development was contradictory. It is the analysis of the transition from one stage of social development to another which lies at the heart of the Scottish contribution to sociological thought.

24

Social development occurred both through economic forces as well as the combined efforts of groups and generations. Social change was grasped as a collective not individual phenomenon involving physical situation, economic and political organisation and the division of labour. Property was the key factor. Such a rigorously deterministic concept of social development circumscribes the activity of the human agent, and while Millar introduced accidental causes and personalities into his historical schema, the basic tendency is mechanistic. Yet Ferguson continually emphasised the active nature of the human agent, the natural disposition to 'remove inconveniences' and improve the situation. Man, he wrote, was 'not made for repose . . . every amiable and respectable quality is an active power . . . and all the lustre which he casts around him, to captivate or engage the attention of his fellow-creatures . . . shines only while his motion continues'. In opposition to the utilitarian concept of humanity as pleasure seeking, Ferguson noted that 'the most animating occasions of human life, are calls to danger and hardship, not invitations to safety and ease', while Robertson argued that 'no small part of that fertility which we ascribe to the hand of nature, is the work of man'.

Vico's 'voluntarism' thus finds an echo in these formulations, but the dualism implied in the concept of an active agent and determining environment was never adequately solved. The important point is the way in which social change was conceived, as a process with both an objective structure – especially the mode of production – and active subject. Change is dialectical in that it emerges as the largely unintended result of human action. 'Every step and every movement of the multitude', Ferguson wrote, 'are made with equal blindness to the future; and nations stumble on establishments, which are indeed the result of human action, but not the execution of human design' (Ferguson, 1966, p. 210, 45). Vico's 'incontestable truth' takes on a sociological meaning in Ferguson's analysis; while in Smith's *The Wealth of Nations* private and egoistic interests are converted into the collective social good by an 'invisible hand' which advances 'the interest of society' without intending or knowing it. Smith's conception is similar to Vico's in that the historical process rectifies and corrects human selfishness and failings: there is, in other words, a logic to history which escapes its active agents. Smith's theory of unanticipated effects of human action is implicitly historicist; Ferguson's, by contrast, is empirical and anti-historicist. Thus discussing the development of commercial society, Smith described initially the structural forces which led to the decline of feudal society and property and the necessary evolution of trade and manufacture. The key to understanding this transition, Smith argued, was the actions of two contending social groups, the rich barons whose concern with social status and ornament led to their gradual impoverishment and the more secular, and efficient, merchant class whose manufactured goods brought the ruin of the great landowners. The rising merchant class replaced the landed groups, buying their agricultural holdings and making them efficient and profitable. Smith's assumption here was that wealth from agriculture was more durable than that derived from commerce, but his more significant point is that social change was unconsciously effected by social groups pursuing their own interests and without the slightest regard for the public good:

> To gratify the most childish vanity was the sole motive of the great proprietors. The merchants and artificers, much less ridiculous, acted merely from a view to their own interests, and in pursuit of their own pedlar principle of turning a penny wherever a penny was to be got. Neither of them had knowledge or foresight of that great revolution which the folly of the one, and the industry of the other, was gradually bringing about (Smith, 1970).

Smith's 'hidden hand' – an historicist and religious notion ultimately – succeeds in regulating the centrifugal tendencies of civil society, the complex structure of property ownership, division of labour and social classes, into a harmony of interests and equilibrium. Smith's conception is basically optimistic: the bad effects of the division of labour can be mitigated by education and religion and the collective workings of market forces.

Ferguson, in contrast, developed no link between the social actions of individuals, as members of social groups, and the wider, collective historical process. Indeed, for Ferguson the individual, as with the state of nature, was merely a fiction. Man is a member of a community, 'part of a whole', his actions social because they are collective. There is nothing of Smith's individualism in Ferguson's concept of the unanticipated effects of social action, or the facile optimism that separated historical meaning from the human subjects which themselves constituted history. Of course there was harmony but also conflict within society, a conflict not to be assimilated to an underlying historical process. Without conflict there was no society, no structure, no process. Without the 'rivalship of nations and the practice of war', Ferguson wrote, 'civil society itself could scarcely have found an object or a form'. Conflict functions to strengthen social bonds and the sense of community. The state itself was founded in war becoming institutionalised in those 'polished' societies characterised by 'collisions of private interest'. It is precisely in these formulations that Ferguson, of all the eighteenth-century writers, approaches a modern sociological standpoint.

The atomistic individualism of the post-Montesquieu French Enlightenment blocked the development of a genuinely sociological concept of society. For Ferguson, society was conceived as a definite structure in which the relation of part to whole constituted the 'principal object' of social science. Like Montesquieu, the writers of the Scottish Enlightenment emphasised the structural nature of social phenomena rejecting the view of society as the product of a haphazard and accidental process. In their notion of the unintended consequences of social action Ferguson and Smith went beyond the static limitations of Montesquieu's synchronic, systemic definition of society to embrace a concept of society as both structure and process. It is this complex relation between human agent and structure which lies at the heart of the Scottish contribution to social theory and not, as some historians of sociology have argued, their emphasis on the social aspects of humanity and their analysis of the social effects of specific material forces. Many of the insights developed in the work of Ferguson, Millar and Smith would be lost in the subsequent emergence of nineteenth-century sociology. But Vico, Montesquieu and Ferguson had laid the foundations and posed the essential problems of a science of human society, culture and historical change, of the relationship between human action, objective social structures and historical evolution. The concept of society as an organised system developing through definite laws and stages had been established. The real history of sociology begins at this point with the work of Saint-Simon, Comte and the positivist tradition.

2
Industrialisation and the Rise of Sociological Positivism

The social thought of Vico, Montesquieu and Ferguson is characterised by a profound belief in humanist values, the application of science to the study of human culture and history and to humanity's control over the environment. The eighteenth-century Enlightenment had produced what David Hume termed the moral sciences – psychology, political economy and a nascent sociology – all of which argued a common theme, that social development brought with it increasing sociability: industry, knowledge and humanity, Hume wrote in his essay, 'On Refinement in the Arts', were linked together by 'an indissoluble chain'. The emergence of these separate, but related sciences was in part the product of the development of a new reading public which, while remaining relatively insignificant in relation to the widespread illiteracy of the great mass of the population, was nevertheless a real and an important element in the secularisation of culture and the emancipation of the writer from patronage. In Diderot's novel, *Rameau's Nephew* (1779), the first ambition of the artist is stated as securing 'the means of life without servitude' an attitude widely shared by contemporary composers, philosophers and economists. A prosperous, liberal middle-class reading public encouraged the growth of literary institutions, clubs and societies; publishing, as a trade, further encouraged the growth of a secular humanism. Man, wrote Diderot, is and will always be at the centre of things for his presence makes existence meaningful. Ferguson expressed this humanist core of Enlightenment thought in his rejection of all biological or organicist metaphors: the proper study of humanity is man 'and we can learn nothing of his nature from the analogy of other animals' (Ferguson, 1966, p. 6).

The relation of the Enlightenment to the development of sociology, however, goes beyond the mere assertion of humanism: the Enlightenment involved the philosophical emphasis on reason, freedom and individualism and emphasised the concepts of society and social development as objective, collective forces. Three broad streams of thought can be identified as contributing to nineteenth and early twentieth-century sociology: first, the humanist historicism of Vico with its emphasis on the creative and active human subject and rejection of any simple application of natural science methods to cultural analysis; secondly, the mechanistic social theory of Montesquieu, Millar and, to a lesser extent, Ferguson, concerned with objective facts and the relevance of natural science to the study of society; and finally, the *philosophes*, Voltaire, Diderot and Rousseau, whose critical rationalism was dedicated to a scientific understanding of the social world, a rationalism that would free the individual from superstitious beliefs and intellectual error. Both the Scottish and the French Enlightenment were built around the principles of modern science, the rejection of metaphysics, the separation of facts from values, and a belief in the possibility of objectivity. Science was positive based on facts not conjecture: the origins of nineteenth-century positivism can thus be traced to the work of Montesquieu and Ferguson, a positivism which was critical and, given the historical context, revolutionary.

Empiricism and positivism

Positivism formed an integral part of the Enlightenment tradition: science and facts opposed metaphysics and speculation; faith and revelation were no longer acceptable as sources of knowledge. Positivism in this extremely general sense must, however, be distinguished from empiricism although both are closely connected historically and theoretically. Sociological positivism dates from the early nineteenth century in the work of Auguste Comte (1798–1857) whose attack on metaphysics was as sharply drawn as that of Hume who had described all forms of metaphysical philosophy as containing no 'reasoning concerning matters of fact and existence' but pages of mere 'sophistry and illusion'. Hume's philosophy was essentially empiricist committed to the concepts of experience and objective facts a standpoint common to sociological positivism.

Eighteenth-century empiricist philosophy, deriving from the work of Bacon, Locke and Descartes, developed an epistemology which located the foundation of human knowledge in experience and the basis of science in experiment, induction and observation. Empiricism assumed the existence of an external world made known through the senses; only that knowledge which could be tested against experience was genuinely scientific. Knowledge was thus defined as a social product, useful and functional, secular and innovating. The transformation of the raw data of experience into knowledge, however, was not a simple mechanical process; it was the function of the human mind to process the data through immanent categories such as judgement, measurement and comparison. Thus although Descartes had argued for the importance of sensory experience in the formation of knowledge, he advanced the view that knowledge equally developed from principles derived from mathematics and logic. Empiricism was in effect an inconsistent doctrine, a materialist epistemology which declared that there existed, independent of experience, laws of mind and laws of thought. It is this dualism between the active and passive properties of cognition which positivism developed by strengthening the mechanical, passive aspects of the subject's relation to experience. As empiricism sought the laws of mind, so positivism established the external laws of historical change and defined society as an external datum, a structure of facts known and verified through observation and experiment.

Positivism, therefore, developed a concept of society while empiricism a theory of concepts. Both empiricism and positivism tended to minimise the active element in human consciousness: some Enlightenment philosophers, for example, sought to eradicate the emphasis which Locke and Descartes had accorded to the innate activities of the human mind thus defining the human subject as the product of an external environment. At the heart of Enlightenment philosophy lay a contradiction: on the one hand, the concepts of human perfectability and progress, the triumph of reason over ignorance and superstition, the belief in the role of ideas in the education of humanity; on the other, the theory that ideas themselves were largely the necessary results of the external situation and of experience. Thus the human subject was conceived in passive terms: both subject and ideas constituted epiphenomenal forces, their existence dependent on the operations of other, different elements. This is not to suggest that every Enlightenment philosopher accepted this mechanical form of materialism: others argued that knowledge flowed from deductions based on *a priori* categories and that human reason, once liberated from mystical and religious thought, would be free to develop objective knowledge.

The *philosophes* in particular developed an extreme form of philosophical dualism arguing that on the one hand material conditions determined forms of human consciousness and modes of action, and yet, on the other, advancing the voluntaristic view that through notions of freedom and reason humanity would be educated out of ignorance and servitude to traditional ideologies. The rationalist optimism of Enlightenment philosophy was thus built around the free individual who, guided by the precepts of science, could reconstruct society through the principles of human reason. In effect, reason was higher than empirical reality.

The French Revolution and sociology

As we have seen, positivism originated in the materialist philosophy of the Enlightenment. As a philosophical and sociological movement positivism embraced a number of different meanings which included a belief in science as the foundation of all knowledge (scientism as it has been called), the employment of statistical analysis in social theory, the search for causal explanations of social phenomena and the fundamental laws of historical change or of human nature. But eighteenth-century Enlightenment positivism was essentially critical and revolutionary, its fundamental tenets of philosophical individualism and human reason largely directed against the irrational powers of the Absolutist state, organised religion and residual social institutions. Institutions, it was argued, should accord with the principles of reason. Knowledge is acquired only through experience and empirical inquiry: reality cannot be comprehended through God.

The transformation of this critical positivism into nineteenth-century sociological positivism occurred in post-revolutionary France. From its beginnings it opposed the individualistic atomism of Enlightenment philosophy. It needs emphasising that with the exception of Montesquieu and Ferguson eighteenth-century social thought had failed to develop a theory of society as a system and objective structure. A theory of society as a totality is fundamental to sociology as an independent empirical science; the relation of parts to whole constitutes the methodological axiom guiding research into the social role and functions of institutions such as religion and the family. It was precisely this concept which could not develop within a rationalist atomistic framework. Enlightenment philosophy had effectively minimised the significance of institutions which the *philosophes* had labelled irrational. In particular the problem of continuity within change could not be posed adequately given the prevailing emphasis on human perfectability and progress. So-called irrational institutions, such as religion, formed in the historical past, could not be conceptualised in their active relation with the present: lacking a concept of society as a whole, rationalist thought defined religious ideas as peripheral and residual exercising no significant and *positive* role in the maintenance of society.

The French Revolution had the effect of challenging these rationalist assumptions. Enlightenment philosophy was judged deficient in its analysis of those traditional institutions which effectively create the social bonds necessary for a functioning society. Edmund Burke (1729–97), Louis de Bonald (1754–1840) and Joseph de Maistre (1754–1821) were three influential critics of philosophical rationalism who rejected the individualistic concept of society developed by the Enlightenment philosophers, identifying its 'negative' and 'critical' principles with the collapse of traditional modes of authority and the organic nature of social bonds.

Society was defined as an organic whole in which 'irrational' and traditional elements played an active, constitutive role. Religion and the family were integral parts of the whole. The Enlightenment slogan of the natural rights of man and the rational principles enshrined in the social contract theory were rejected in favour of a concept of society which emphasised hierarchy, duty and the collective good. As Bonald expressed it: 'The schools of modern philosophy . . . have produced the philosophy of modern man, the philosophy of I . . . I want to produce the philosophy of social man, the philosophy of we.' As an organism, society was defined in terms of its inner 'spirit' or 'soul', an essence fundamentally religious in nature. Bonald and Maistre thus developed a concept of expressive whole, the various parts manifesting the inner essence and spirit. All elements of the organic whole were integrally linked as expressions of an irreducible essence.

Linked with this organic notion of totality was the rejection of empirical science as the means of analysing social forms. For Maistre and Bonald society was apprehended through intuition, not reason or science. This belief in intuition and feeling is linked with attempts to discover a new source of political authority in the post-revolutionary world that followed the collapse of the old regime. Revolution and industrialism were creating a new kind of society, one in which the old traditional values no longer held sway. The result was a concept of society which emphasised the creative role of the family, corporations and a hierarchical structure of authority similar to the rigid estate system of feudalism. It was through these institutions that the individual participated in the social whole, the 'I' transformed into a 'We'. The post-revolutionary critique of emerging industrial society was thus couched in terms of pre-industrial organic values: modern society was conceived as a calculating, individualistic system built around pragmatic, material values and interests with authority vested in formal rules and written contracts. Such a society could eventuate only in the collapse of social bonds and render problematic the organic relation of the individual to the collective.

For Maistre and Bonald society did not consist in an

aggregate of individuals: society was the expression of a whole culture, a collective concept which decisively influenced the sociological positivism of Auguste Comte. Equally important was the emphasis on the positive role of traditional institutions and the problem of authority in the post-revolutionary world of the early nineteenth century. Burke, Bonald and Maistre mourned the passing of the traditional legitimacy of the old society and in their work posed the question of new modes of political obligation. It was in this spirit that Saint-Simon wrote of the eighteenth century as critical and negative, while the nineteenth would be positive in laying the foundation for social reorganisation. Only positivism, wrote Comte, provided the necessary basis for the new society pointing the way forward from 'the critical condition in which most civilised nations are now living'. Ideas were of paramount importance either governing the world or throwing it into chaos:

> The great political and moral crisis that societies are now undergoing is shown by the rigid analysis to arise out of intellectual anarchy . . . whenever the necessary agreement on first principles can be obtained, appropriate institutions will issue from them, without shock or resistance; for the causes of disorder will have been arrested by the mere fact of the agreement. It is in this direction that most must look who desire a natural and regular . . . state of society (Andreski, 1978, pp. 37–8).

Comte's preoccupation with social order and progress developed within a sociological framework that owed much to the work of Bonald and Maistre notably their emphasis on the nature of the social bond. But in the development of sociological positivism the irrational and negative view of science advocated by these philosophers was rejected: the moral crisis of the post-revolutionary age could be resolved only through the application of positive science and the principles of industrial organisation derived from the empirical study of social development. The work of Henri Saint-Simon was decisive in this process.

The concept of industrial society: Saint-Simon

Saint-Simon (1760–1825) introduced the term industrial society into European social theory. He defined the process of industrialism as essentially pacific in contrast to the militaristic spirit of feudal society. Saint-Simon was particularly concerned with the transition from feudal type societies, structured around consumption, to industrial societies centred around production. Saint-Simon's status in the history of sociology has always been ambivalent: on the one hand his concept of industrial society emphasised the centrality of social classes, the importance of property and the structural significance of the division of labour in the process of class formation. His collectivist notion of society was broadly socialist and materialist; but on the other hand, Saint-Simon's analysis of technology and the role of science and intellectual élites – mostly composed of scientists and industrialists – combined with his theory of moral crisis suggests a conservative standpoint close to the sociological positivism of Comte. In a very general sense Saint-Simon can be claimed as an influence on both nineteenth-century sociology and the development of socialism and Marxism. What is not in doubt, however, is that Saint-Simon's work represents a theorisation of the emerging separation of state and civil society, the development of a public sphere consisting of economic, political and cultural institutions independent of centralised, bureaucratic administration. More emphatically than Adam Smith, Saint-Simon defined the state administration as parasitic and hostile to the needs of production and the newly emerging social classes engendered by the process of industrialism. By its nature, he wrote, mankind was destined to live in society, first under governmental or military regimes and then, with the triumph of the positive sciences and industry, under an administrative and industrial regime. The administrative institutions of industrial society would no longer be centralised in the state but rather in the institutions of civil society.

Saint-Simon's basic argument is of the necessary relation between property and power. Political constitutions should express the state of society itself; they must be structured firmly in social reality. In his *Industrial System* (1821) Saint-Simon argued that society could, and should be organised on scientific, positive principles with the economic and political systems working in harmony with each other. The study of politics was transformed from the conjectural to the positive, from metaphysics to physics. For Saint-Simon, science was positive, and therefore, through its principles of prediction and verification, formed the basis of practice. Like Adam Smith, Saint-Simon's model of society was based on astronomy: 'The astronomers only accepted those facts which were verified by observation; they chose the system which linked them best, and since that time, they have never led science astray' (Ionescu, 1976, pp. 76–8).

Saint-Simon coined the terms 'social physiology' and 'social physics' and, following Maistre and Bonald, defined society as an organic unity. The positive stage of development was dominated by the centrality of science and the growth of systematic social knowledge especially in relation to the laws which regulated the social whole. Saint-Simon's model of society was thus holistic: he defined a 'healthy' society as one in which the various parts subsisted in a state of functional harmony with the whole. Social health was closely identified with production and the role of the productive social classes. Industrial society, in contrast to all previous forms of social organisation, was not based on a centralised power structure but rather built around the institutions of civil society. Saint-Simon did not argue for the abolition of political institutions only that decision-making must increasingly devolve on the institutions associated with science and technology. Politics does not express the 'good will' but an equilibrium subsisting between economic and political structures. Saint-Simon described industrial society in terms of collaboration and consensus: under the old system force constituted the means of social cohesion, but industrial society creates partners not subjects and associated modes of co-operation involving labourers and the wealthiest property owners. The principles of free production generate moral solidarity. Saint-Simon contrasted the authority structure of feudal society, in which corporations symbolised coercion, with the unequal, hierarchical nature of industrial society arguing that industrial institutions were, by their nature, both functional and spontaneous.

Society would become a vast workshop organised around the production of goods, and authority transformed from authority over individuals to authority over things.

Saint-Simon's social theory was thus a theory of the rising bourgeoisie and he emphasised the class struggle between the industrial classes and the old feudal classes. 'The entire history of civilised mankind', he wrote, 'is inevitably divided between these two great systems of society.' The French Revolution had not completely destroyed ecclesiastical and feudal power but merely 'diminished confidence in their basic principles' as the basis of social order. Only industry which embraces all forms of useful work, theoretical and practical, intellectual and manual, can produce the values that will hold modern society together. Industry has ushered in 'a new era' signalling the end of government by force in favour of consultation and consensus. In effect, what Saint-Simon calls 'administrative action' comes to replace feudal–military action so that administrative power finally dominates military force:

> In the end soldiers and jurists must take orders from those most capable of administration; for an enlightened society only needs to be administered . . . The guiding principles of social force should be supplied by the men who are most able to administer; now, as the most important industrialists are those who have given proof of the greatest administrative ability, since it is their competence in this sphere that they owe what importance they have acquired, in short, it is they who should necessarily be given the direction of social interests (Ionescu, 1976, p. 188).

But the nineteenth century was still dominated by the 'critical' spirit of the Enlightenment and was failing to adopt the organisational character organic to it. A disjunction existed between the institutions of industrialism, especially administrative action, and the broader culture. Saint-Simon's writings during the 1820s point to a major issue which had largely eluded the eighteenth-century philosophers and social theorists of progress: in the past, civil society and the state were bound together with social regulation flowing from traditional institutions and the structure of traditional values. But with the separation of the state from civil society the problem of social regulation was posed in an acute form. Traditional modes of authority, and their associated values, had collapsed in the face of a triumphant critical philosophy with its beliefs in the rights of the individual over that of the collectivity. Traditional authority could no longer legitimise political forms: a moral vacuum therefore arose within modern society. Saint-Simon rejected the view of the political economists that the market worked to harmonise different and often conflicting interests into a social and therefore moral unity. Social cohesion would not flow from the free play of purely economic forces. Industrial society required a strong moral centre which he described in his last work, *The New Christianity* (1825), as a secular religion opposed to the egoism of philosophical individualism and functioning through a priesthood of artists, scientists and industrial leaders whose interests were identical with those of the masses.

Social regulation is thus described as a process directed from above by an élite of intellectuals. Although Saint-Simon's image of industrial society was one of co-operative enterprise, he defined industrial society as a system organised around the principles of functional hierarchy, rational discipline and selective leadership. Saint-Simon, however, was not advocating a new form of centralised authority; authority is returned to civil society and vested, not in control over individuals but within the institutions of planning, co-operation and production. Industrial society was not a communist Utopia but a hierarchical structure which had produced a new governing class of scientists and industrialists. Scientists were associated with the spiritual realm, industrialists with the temporal: together they would create the leadership and the values necessary for a functioning modern society.

There is, here, an authoritarian strand to Saint-Simon's thought, a distrust of democracy and representative institutions, a lack of confidence in the masses, or the people, to create for themselves a culture of self-government. His distinction between productive and non-productive, or 'idle' classes is polemical rather than scientific. Saint-Simon failed to develop a sociological theory of class: his main concern was always with those who produced and those who consumed, industrial proprietors, investors and bankers were productive, the military, nobility, lawyers and those living off profits were the idlers. Those producing 'useful' things were the only valuable members of society and for this reason politics was defined as the science of production and the new society, emerging from the ruins of post-revolutionary Europe, industrial, technocratic and undemocratic.

Comte and positive science

Saint-Simon did not develop a distinctive sociology. Auguste Comte (1798–1857) who, at one time, acted as Saint-Simon's secretary publishing his early works under Saint-Simon's name, founded the first comprehensive system of sociology, one that was strongly influenced by the work of Saint-Simon and his belief in science and technology (elements found in eighteenth-century philosophers of history and champions of progress such as Turgot, 1727–81 and Condorcet, 1743–94), and 'that immortal school' of Bonald and Maistre with their concept of society as an organic, harmonious whole composed, like medieval society, of different and static social orders. Comte attempted to reconcile the anti-atomistic theories of Bonald and Maistre with the rationalist concept of progress and notion of the perfectability of man. Like Saint-Simon, Comte's work was produced at a critical period of French history, the period following the revolution in which the old regime had disintegrated and a new industrial regime was in the process of formation. Comte's sociological positivism was forged at the same time as Balzac was describing in fictional form the irresistible rise of the industrialists and the bankers within a French culture still permeated by the old aristocratic values.

Comte never held a full-time academic position. Sociology was not yet institutionalised; Frederic Le Play, who wrote a massive study of the European family during the 1850s and the leading French sociologist before Durkheim attained an academic position but only as a Professor of Mining. Comte remained a marginal figure in French intellectual culture, ridiculed in academic circles, suffering from periodic bouts of madness and suffering the indignity of being listed as deceased in a contemporary bibliography. J.S. Mill, who corresponded with Comte, argued that his influence in the development of social science was greater than his actual achievements and that while not creating sociology as a science Comte's work nevertheless made it possible. Thus although Comte's interpreters note his strong conservative bias and deprecate the influence on his sociology of Maistre and Bonald as well as 'the illustrious Gall' (1758–1828), as he described the founder of phrenology, his place within the history of sociology is guaranteed by his attempts to explain the origin and growth of industrial society and his analysis of the social effects of the division of labour, increasing wealth and development of individualism and his rejection of metaphysics in favour of positive empirical methods in the study of social facts. Yet these elements had already been widely discussed by eighteenth-century writers such as Ferguson, Millar and Montesquieu: the Scots especially had provided a detailed empirical account of the emergence of industrial society, social class, social conflict, the division of labour and the mechanics of social change. Since Comte knew the work of Adam Smith and Ferguson, as well as minor writers such as Lord Kames, it is obviously important to grasp the ways in which his own approach differs from theirs and assess the extent to which Comte's sociological positivism assimilated and developed this proto-sociology.

Comte's attitude to the Enlightenment was, of course, negative: although he accepted the theory of progress, especially Condorcet's notion of social evolution developing through the workings of specific natural laws, he rejected the critical positivism of eighteenth-century philosophic rationalism abhoring its 'negative' attacks on the values of traditional authority and morality, on religious institutions and the family. In particular he rejected the Enlightenment view that pre-industrial society, especially the Middle Ages, constituted the dark age of civilisation. For Comte, Condorcet's one-sided devaluing of the past, in his *Sketch for a Historical Picture of the Progress of the Human Mind* (1794), was rounded out by the positive approach of Maistre and Bonald:

Right views upon the subject were impossible . . . until full justice had been rendered to the Middle Ages, which form at once the

41

point of union and separation between ancient and modern history. Now it was quite impossible to do this as long as the excitement of the first years of the revolution lasted. In this respect the philosophical reaction organised at the beginning of the century by the great de Maistre was of material assistance in preparing the true theory of progress. His school was of brief duration, and it was no doubt animated by a retrograde spirit; but it will always be ranked among the necessary antecedents of the positive system (Comte, 1875–6, Vol. 1, p. 50).

Comte's *Cours de Philosophie Positive* (1830–42) is essentially an attack on the 'negative' philosophy developed by eighteenth-century individualistic philosophy. He agreed with Saint-Simon that the eighteenth-century had only destroyed rather than provided the foundations for a 'new edifice'. This new structure was to be directed exclusively in the interests of social order and social consensus. The 'essential aim of practical politics', he wrote, was 'to avoid the violent revolutions which spring from obstacles opposed to the progress of civilisation'.

From the beginning, the *Course* set itself the task of social reorganisation: writing from within a society which appeared close to anarchy it seemed obvious to Comte that 'true science' was nothing less than 'the establishment of intellectual order, which is the basis of every other order'. Comte's positivism, a science of stability and social reconstruction can thus be seen on one level as a response to the negative and critical traditions of Enlightenment philosophy by seeking to unite the notions of order and progress. The task of social physics would be wholly positive:

> Under the rule of the positive spirit . . . all the difficult and delicate questions which now keep up a perpetual irritation in the bosom of society, and can never be settled while mere political solutions are proposed, will be scientifically estimated, to the great furtherance of social peace . . . the positive spirit tends to consolidate order, by the rational development of a wise resignation to incurable political evils. A true resignation . . . can proceed from a deep sense of the connection of all kinds of natural phenomena with invariable natural laws. If there are political evils which . . . cannot be remedied by science, science at least proves to us that they are

incurable, so as to calm our restlessness under pain by the conviction that it is by natural laws that they are rendered insurmountable (Comte, 1896, Vol. 2, pp. 185–7).

On this definition, therefore, sociology prescribes a wholly passive and fatalistic orientation to the social world and contrasts sharply with Vico's injunction that the social world was the work of humanity. The active relation of human labour and thought to the development and transformation of social forms is effectively assimilated to a theory of objective, determining facts. The polemical thrust of Comte's positivism is thus clear: but what of his concept of science?

Sociology was defined in its relations with other sciences and Comte's stated aim was the synthesis of all available knowledge, a task facilitated by the law of three stages and hierarchical classification of the sciences. Both these conceptions had been stated by previous writers notably Turgot, Condorcet and Saint-Simon: in their beginnings all the sciences, wrote Saint-Simon, are conjectural but end by being positive, developing from the simple to the complex. Comte systematised these arguments tracing the evolution of the sciences in great detail. All human thought, he argued, has passed through three separate stages, the theological, the metaphysical and the positive. In the theological state the human mind seeks for origins and final causes analysing all phenomena as the result of supernatural forces; feelings and imagination predominate and Comte divided the theological state into three separate periods of fetishism (nature defined in terms of man's feelings), polytheism (a multitude of gods and spirits) and finally, monotheism (the existence of one God and the gradual awakening of human reason with its constraint on the imagination). For Comte, each stage and sub-stage of evolution necessarily develops out of the preceding one: the final sub-stage of monotheism prepares the way for the metaphysical stage in which human thought is dominated by abstract concepts, by essences and ideal forms. In the final stage of evolution thought abandons essences and seeks laws which link different facts together through the methods of observation and experiment; absolute notions of causes are abandoned and the emphasis shifts to the study of facts and their invariable relations of succession and resemblance. Each science develops in exactly the same way passing through these separate stages, but they do so at different rates: knowledge reaches the positive stage in proportion to the generality, simplicity and independence of other disciplines. As the most general and simple of the natural sciences astronomy develops first, followed by physics, chemistry, biology and sociology. Each science develops only on the basis of its predecessors within a hierarchical framework dominated by the law of increasing complexity and decreasing generality.

Sociology is particularly dependent on its immediate predecessor in the hierarchy, biology. The science of biology is basically holistic in character beginning not from isolated elements, as in chemistry and physics, but from organic wholes. The distinctive subject matter of sociology is society as a whole, society defined as a social system. Sociology is thus the investigation of the action and reaction of the various parts of the social system. Individual elements must be analysed in their relation to the whole, in their mutual relation and combination. As with biological organisms, society forms a complex unity irreducible to its component parts: society cannot be decomposed into individuals any more than 'a geometric surface can be decomposed into lines, or a line into a point'. Knowledge of the parts can flow only from knowledge of the whole, not vice versa.

Society was defined, therefore, as a collective organism characterised by a harmony between its individual parts and whole. The analogy between biology and sociology is constantly reiterated:

> . . . in biology, we may decompose structure anatomically into *elements*, *tissues* and *organs*. We have the same things in the social organism . . . forms of social power correspond to the *tissue* . . . the *element* . . . is supplied by the family, which is more completely the germ of society than the cell or fibre of the body . . . *organs* can only be *cities* the root of the word being the nucleus of the term civilization (Comte, 1875–6, Vol. 2, pp. 223–6).

Although Comte warns against pushing the analogy too far – cities are organic wholes themselves or aspire to be so – his theory of social order derives almost entirely from biology especially his concepts of harmony, equilibrium and social pathology. Pathological situations develop within the social organism, for example, when the natural laws governing the principles of harmony or succession are disturbed by elements analogous to diseases in the bodily organism. Social evolution proceeds in accordance with biological laws and the general intent of Comte's positivism is to subordinate the study of society to biological concepts. The absence of a spontaneous harmony between the parts and the whole of the social system indicates the existence of social pathology. Harmony is consensus; conflict is equated with pathology. While Ferguson had rejected the biological analogy, Comte assimilated biological terms and models to his sociology arguing that the distinction between anatomy and physiology enabled sociology to differentiate structure from function, dynamics from statics, social order from social progress. All living beings exist under dynamic and static relations: statics investigates the laws of action and reaction of the different parts of the social system which 'normally' produce an equilibrium between parts and whole, a functional interrelationship of social institutions. Comte's notion of statics is concerned with clarifying the interconnection between social facts functional for a social system such as the division of labour, the family, religion and government and is clearly synchronic in nature. Dynamics is the empirical study of these interconnections as they change in different types of society and Comte describes this aspect of sociology as the historical method.

Comte describes the historical method as specific to sociology. It is clearly important to grasp what Comte meant by this term, since it suggests a movement from analogical representations of societies to empirical analysis of social processes. 'If the historical comparisons of the different periods of civilization are to have any scientific character', he wrote, 'they must be referred to general social evolution' (Comte, 1896, Vol. 2, pp. 252–7). The comparative method belongs to statics, the historical method to dynamics. He defined the comparative method as

The comparison of different co-existing states of human society on

45

the various parts of the world's surface – those states being completely independent of each other (Comte, 1896, Vol. 2, p. 250).

The historical method links these states of society with evolution through the dynamic laws of social development which effectively relate to the growing solidarity and unity of society structured in the co-operative functions of the division of labour and the universal principles enshrined in religion and language. Social evolution, in other words, works through the existence of certain invariable laws which synthesise order and progress. It is in this sense that Comte repudiates empiricism. Sociology is not a science which accumulates mere desultory facts but seeks to interpret and connect them with each other through theory: facts are not strictly speaking based on observation but are constructed by the guiding hand of theory. Real knowledge can never be based on observed facts alone but on laws which connect all social phenomena through resemblance and succession. No real observation is possible, wrote Comte, 'except in as far as it is first directed, and finally interpreted, by some theory'. Observation and laws are 'indispensably connected' (Comte, 1896, Vol. 2, p. 243).

Comte's awareness that facts and theory are mutually connected suggests that sociology is an interpretative science, a formulation which goes beyond the critical positivism of the Enlightenment. Comte was the first theoretical sociologist who was thoroughly sceptical that observed facts will, as it were, speak for themselves. But the theory which Comte developed was essentially a speculative theory of historical change, a philosophy of history. The result was a conception of the historical method extremely abstract and non-historical: specific historical events, and the specifically historical character of institutions, fell outside the framework of sociological positivism. States of development are abstractly conceived, the sequences are conceptual and ideal, neither empirical nor chronological. One result of Comte's abstract formulations of the historical method and the distinction between static and dynamics was to separate the study of concrete events, or facts, from the study of social change as an historical category.

Positivism and determinism

All social phenomena are subject to invariable laws and once these have been scientifically established humanity must, from necessity, submit to their dictation. Science makes possible social control and Comte defined 'true liberty' as the 'rational submission' of the individual to the laws of nature. Positivist sociology effectively abolishes 'the absolute liberty of the revolutionary school . . . and, by establishing social principles, will meet the need at once of order and progress'. From science comes 'prevision' and from 'prevision comes action', for 'to see in order to foresee is the business of science'. Eighteenth-century philosophy had laid the foundations of social science through the law of human progress, while the French Revolution had generated the need for order.

What Comte's 'wise resignation' means in practice is a submission to the facts of inequality within the emerging industrial society. The law of progress, as Comte described it, clearly affected social groups differently. Thus in his discussion of the role of the working class Comte described their 'inevitable lot' as existing on the 'precarious fruits' of labour and to suffer constant deprivation. Positivist sociology, while recognising this as a 'great social problem', would seek to ameliorate the workers' condition, but not at the cost of 'destroying its classification and disturbing the general economy' (Comte, 1896, Vol. 3, pp. 36–7). In his early writings of the 1820s Comte agreed with Saint-Simon's argument that the aftermath of the French Revolution had created a spiritual vacuum and absence of 'any moral discipline whatsoever'. The result was a state of 'anomie', a state of normlessness, of deregulation. Saint-Simon's solution was an ethic of universal love – a new Christianity – which in Comte's work became the Religion of Humanity interposing itself as a remedial agency between the working class and the governing classes. In this way the economic and political 'imperfections' of modern society, the products of 'intellectual and moral disorder' and the prevailing states of consciousness, were solved. What particularly concerned Comte was the maldistribution of wealth since it provided 'a most dangerous theme to both agitators and dreamers'. Only by convincing humanity of the superiority of

moral over political solutions would these 'quacks and dreamers' relinquish their 'dangerous vocation'. The solution to
inequality and class differences and interests was the organic
society in which the positive concept of 'duties' replaced the
negative concept of 'rights'. A moral education would inculcate
an awareness of the individual's rightful social status: the
subordination of the working class to their employers would be
seen as resting wholly on their less 'extensive actions' and
responsibilities. And once established this gradation would be
acceptable because of its clear principles and awareness that
the working class are 'privileged in that freedom from care . . .
which would be a serious fault in the higher classes, but which
is natural to them'. Following Saint-Simon, Comte conceived
industrial society as a system dominated by the moral influence
of a 'Speculative' stratum of scientists and philosophers, in
which capital is 'useful to society at large' thus rendering the
distribution of property unimportant to 'popular interests'
(Comte, 1896, Vol. 3, pp. 313–35).

Like the socialists of his day, therefore, Comte accepted the
structural significance of the industrial working class but
differed from their analysis by his stress on the inevitable laws
of social evolution which point to their integration into an
unequal society. There was no question of class organisation
and practice: the individual might 'modify' the course of social
development and assert a freedom of action over 'blind
fatality', but ultimately the natural laws of society are higher in
their practical efficacy than human action. Social evolution,
which for Comte was the progressive development of the
human mind as it finds its expression in the three stages, is thus
a process without a subject, a universal history of humanity
which claims the importance of knowledge for the ends of social
reorganisation, but subordinates the individual to the inevitable 'realities' of social life: the needs of order and progress.

Sociology, political economy and the division of labour

Comte defined the social as the only universal point of view, the
only perspective which grasps all scientific conceptions as a

whole. The relation of the social to the political is described as one of 'spontaneous harmony'. Comte separates the social both from the political and the economic arguing that in modern society social cohesion – social authority – flows essentially from moral and intellectual, not political or economic, forces. Government fulfils its obligations not by exercising force but through moral and intellectual leadership. Comte was particularly critical of previous social theorists who had minimised the crucial, constituting role played by these 'spiritual' elements. Only morality provides an adequate regulation of economic activity, only morality can sustain social harmony. For Comte, the 'essential vice' of political economy was its tendency to define social order in natural terms as the expression of market forces and thus free of regulation by artificial (positivist) institutions.

Yet although Comte disagreed with the *laissez-faire* principles of classical political economy, he accepted its pessimistic and largely negative conclusions on the social consequences of an advanced division of labour. Specialisation of work, while an essential element of an advanced society, tends to 'restrict human understanding' and promote ignorance and squalor among the working classes. Comte cited the example of pin manufacture: workers engaged in this tedious and routine labour cannot develop their faculties to the full with the result, 'a miserable indifference about the general course of human affairs' and a fundamental 'dispersion' of ideas, sentiments and interests. Comte drew a radically different conclusion from the political economists, arguing that the division of work necessarily entails moral regulation by external institutions.

Comte's solution to the problem of the division of labour was the institution of 'wise government' with its principles fundamentally religious and universal thus consecrating and regulating command and obedience. Civil society itself is judged incapable of generating from within its own spontaneously developed institutions the values necessary for social cohesion. Comte's distrust of democratic institutions is explicit; society is to be regulated from above. Humanity must learn to accept inequality and the natural laws of social subordination. Fortunately the masses recognise the intellectual superiority of their rulers and thus experience the sheer 'sweetness' of consigning 'burdensome' responsibilities to 'wise and trustworthy guidance'. The division of labour creates the intellectual and moral skills on which all systems of government and stratification rest: 'Thus do individual dispositions show themselves to be in harmony with the course of social relations as a whole, in teaching us that political subordination is as inevitable . . . as it is indispensable' (Comte, 1896, Vol. 3, pp. 294–8).

Comte's sociological positivism strips the division of labour of its *negative* effects and transforms it into an agency of social harmony although regulated by an élite of positivist intellectuals. Conflict relations engendered by the division of labour as constituting a source of social change was simply unthinkable. By emphasising the essentially religious nature of social bonds Comte advocated moral solutions that were conformist and ideological. Comte's positivism celebrates industrial society in its early capitalist form as the end of history: humanity must accept its place within the natural order of things and adapt to the necessary equilibrium between parts and wholes.

The anti-democratic nature of Comte's sociological positivism was a theme taken up later in the nineteenth century by Durkheim, while the analysis of the division of labour in the process of social development and the relation of civil society to economic production and political forms formed part of Marx's contribution to social science. Comte failed to develop the notion of society as an empirical and historical totality, conceiving it in organismic terms as a system dominated by external natural laws that reduced the efficacy of human action. The separation of dynamics from statics was artificial and theoretically misleading and in the discussion of the division of labour the dynamic aspect virtually disappeared in favour of static moralising.

Nevertheless, Comte had laid the foundations of a sociological positivism which was to remain the dominant paradigm during the course of the nineteenth century. But the positivism which developed after Comte increasingly abandoned his speculative philosophy of history and his theory of social evolution as the evolution of consciousness and mind through definite stages of social development.

Evolutionism and sociological positivism: Mill and Spencer

Comte's positivism conceived the concept of the social as a distinct sphere clearly separated from economics, politics and history; society was an autonomous object of scientific study, conceptualised as a system evolving in the direction of industrialisation. The development of sociological positivism after Comte took two forms: first, the widely accepted view that the methods of the social sciences were no different from those of the natural sciences involving the establishing of laws, the employment of experiment and observation and the elimination of the subjective element in social analysis – society was defined in terms of an organism evolving through the workings of specific natural laws. And secondly, the increasing awareness of empirical method and the value of statistics in the framing of hypotheses and modes of validation. Both forms of sociological positivism emphasised the necessity of eliminating philosophical concepts such as free will, intention and individual motives from social science and establishing sociology as an objective science. Two of the most important sociologists working within this broad positivist framework were J.S. Mill and Herbert Spencer, although both were critical of Comte's philosophy of history and, in the case of Spencer, sought to distance his sociological theories from positivism.

Mill's most significant contribution to sociology was his *System of Logic* (1843). Mill (1807–73) claimed that he was laying down the foundations of a science of society, a science based on 'general laws', experiment and observation. Unlike Comte and Spencer, he never developed an all-encompassing system of sociology, one embracing society, history and nature. Nevertheless, he accepted Comte's basic sociological principles, the theory of stages, the distinction between dynamics and statics, the historical method of analysis, and the concept of consensus. Comte's main conclusions, he wrote, were in all essentials 'irrefragable'. He agreed also with Comte's scientism arguing that there was no fundamental difference between the methods of the natural and the social sciences: science depended on its ability to predict, and comparing the social sciences with the physical sciences of meteorology, tidology (the science of tides) and astronomy, Mill concluded that while these sciences established the underlying laws governing the weather, the tides and planetary movements, with the exception of astronomy they failed to generate precise modes of prediction. Prediction necessitated knowledge of all the antecedent elements within a particular context and only in the case of astronomy was this possible. Mill thus concluded that social science was quite capable of achieving a comparable degree of prediction and thus of scientific status.

The context examined by the social sciences consisted of human beings: unlike Comte, Mill believed in the importance of psychology and to this end he advanced the claims of ethology as the science of the laws of human nature. Psychology was not part of Comte's hierarchy of the sciences; he believed that Gall's 'cerebral physiology' explained the source of thought and mind in terms of its physical location in the brain. But Mill argued that all social phenomena were structured in the laws governing the drives and motives of human nature. Describing his approach as the 'inverted-deductive' method, Mill argued that social science consisted of the empirical laws of sociology, demonstrated in statistical studies and surveys, the laws of psychology, derived less from empirical studies than philosophical reflection, and finally, linking the sociology and the psychology, the laws of ethology, the fundamental laws governing human nature:

> The laws of the phenomena of society are, and can be, nothing but the laws of actions and passions of human beings united together in the social state . . . obedient to the laws of individual human nature. Men are not, when brought together, converted into another kind of substance with different properties as hydrogen and oxygen are different from water (Mill, 1976).

Human nature is thus fixed: the socio-historical context constantly changes so that the task of positivist social science lay in explaining empirical observations and sociological laws by deductions from the universal law of human nature. In effect Mill proposed a reduction of the specifically social to the psychological:

> All phenomena of society are phenomena of human nature generated by the action of outward circumstances upon masses of human beings (Mill, 1976).

If human thought and action are dependent on fixed laws then clearly all social phenomena must conform to similar fixed laws. From this standpoint it is not surprising that Mill failed to develop either a systemic concept of society or an adequate sociological theory of social structure, social institutions and social change.

Mill's positivistic nominalism was ultimately less significant for the development of sociology than the positivist organicism of Herbert Spencer (1820–1903), who combined, within a broad evolutionary model of social development, a notion of society as system and as aggregate of individuals. Spencer's main focus was on the evolutionary growth of social structures and institutions and not mental states. Comte, he wrote, accounts for 'the progress of human conceptions . . . ideas' and seeks to interpret 'our knowledge of nature'; in contrast, 'my aim' is to account for 'the progress of the external world . . . of things' and to interpret 'the genesis of the phenomena which constitute nature'. Comte is subjective not objective. Nevertheless, as Comte sought to unify all knowledge in his hierarchy of the sciences, so Spencer aimed to unify all knowledge in his concept of evolution. The evolution of humanity was Spencer's theme in which society constituted a special instance of a universal law. 'There can be no complete acceptance of sociology as a science, so long as the belief in a social order not conforming to natural law, survives' (Spencer, 1961, Ch. XVI).

During the latter half of the nineteenth century Spencer's writings were enormously popular among the burgeoning middle-class reading public. His work attempted to synthesise a radical individualism based on *laissez-faire* political economy with a collectivist organicism derived from the natural sciences especially biology and physics. Spencer, in effect, offered a theory of progress built around the prestige of the natural sciences and the individualistic and competitive nature of nineteenth-century capitalism. Spencer had already formulated the basic constituents of his theory of evolution when

Darwin (1809–92) published his *Origin of Species* in 1859. Although he acknowledged the significance of Darwin's concept of 'natural selection' for the evolutionary process, Spencer tended to accept Lamarck's theory of the inheritance of acquired characteristics. He thus remained an evolutionary optimist arguing that through the transmission of both mental and physical innate elements humanity must necessarily develop to higher and higher levels of intellectual perfection.

Spencer's model of society was organismic. Societies were like living bodies which evolve out of a state of undifferentiated unity to highly complex, differentiated structures in which the individual parts, while becoming more autonomous and specialised, nevertheless come increasingly to depend on each other. This interdependence of parts implies integration for 'unlike parts' are 'so related as to make one another possible' and come to form an aggregate 'constituted on the same general principle as is an individual organism'. In simple societies the lack of differentiation means that the same individuals are both hunter and warriors. Society thus develops through progressive changes in the *structure* and *functions* of its basic institutions; social evolution does not depend on individual intentions and motives. Thus from a state of homogeneity human society *naturally* develops to a state of complex heterogeneity, a process which Spencer saw as characteristic of the inorganic world of matter, where evolution begins, the organic world of nature, and finally the living organisms in society, the last stage of evolution.

Spencer identified three laws of evolution: the law of 'the persistence of force' or the conservation of energy, from which is derived the law of the indestructability of matter and the law of the continuity of motion. The notion of the persistence of force forms the basis of Spencer's deductive system: the universe is characterised by a continual redistribution of matter and motion in terms of the processes of evolution and dissolution. Spencer noted four secondary propositions to these three laws: that laws are uniform in their workings; that force is transformed never lost; that everything moves along the line of least resistance or the greatest attraction; and finally, the principle of the rhythm, or alteration, of motion. All these laws and propositions are governed by the law of universal evolution which states that with the integration of matter, motion is dissipated and as matter becomes differentiated motion is absorbed: 'Evolution is an integration of matter and a concomitant dissipation of motion during which the matter passes from a relatively indefinite, incoherent homogeneity to a relatively coherent heterogeneity and during which the retained motion undergoes a parallel transformation.'

The evolution of society is defined by Spencer as the gradual socialisation of humanity, a process occurring independently of human practice. The actual origin of human society is located as the result of population pressure which compelled individuals to enter the social state and thus develop both social organisation and social feelings. But having identified the genesis of society Spencer analysed social formations in terms of the biological analogy. As with Comte the historical dimension of society disappears; the organismic analogy has the effect of emphasising synchronic rather than diachronic analysis.

Spencer's ahistorical and anti-humanist perspective is especially brought out in his frequent defence of the concept of the social organism which he sometimes defined as a useful analogy and at other times as a reality. Thus in *The Principles of Sociology* he writes that it is the character of both living and social bodies 'that while they increase in size they increase in structure', that as they acquire greater mass their parts multiply and differentiate. And in his article, 'The Social Organism' (1860), he defined society as a 'thing' which grows, evolving from small 'aggregations' so simple 'in structure as to be considered structureless' in which there is 'scarcely any mutual dependence of parts', to complex, differentiated structures in which the separate parts acquire mutual and functional dependence: society is a structure characterised by co-operation between parts and whole. Should anything 'disturb' this consensus, Spencer adds, the equilibrium of the whole system is endangered (i.e. if government artificially interferes with the workings of economic and social life). Although noting the differences between the biological organism and society – the parts are more dispersed and independent from the centre of society, individual members may die but the whole persists, in the biological organism the elements exist for the good of the

55

whole while in the social organism the whole exists for the good of its members – Spencer tended to equate the two:

> While comparison makes definite the obvious contrasts between organisms . . . and the social organism, it shows that even these contrasts are not so decided as was to be expected . . . Societies slowly augment in mass; they progress in complexity of structure; at the same time their parts become more mutually dependent . . . The *principles* of organisation are the same, and the differences are simply differences of application (Spencer, 1969a, p. 206).

Spencer distinguished 'militant' from 'industrial' societies in terms of this holistic approach. Militant societies were defined as lacking complex structural differentiation, dominated by a centralised state, rigid hierarchies of status and a tendency towards conformism; industrial societies, developing through the general law of evolution, were more complex and structurally differentiated and characterised by a multiplicity of beliefs, independent institutions, decentralisation and a tendency to individualisation. The organismic analogy, however, prevented Spencer from grasping the contradictions and conflicts of interest which industrial society actually engendered: unlike Ferguson, who rejected the organismic analogy, he failed to integrate the dialectical elements of social change into the holistic model, that evolution creates both differentiation of structure and differentiation of interest, that parts become independent through collective social organisation and the development of a common awareness by the members of different specialised organisations, and that their interests differ from the interests of others. Spencer had no conception of interest as a collective phenomenon, as class interest, group interest, etc. Rather, interests were conceived strictly in terms of Smithian individualism, that although society consisted of different, atomistic interests they nevertheless harmonised into a unity through the operation of a 'hidden hand' which synthesised private interests with the common good. Individuals seek private ends but because such actions take place within a complex society built on the interdependence of institutions, the human agent unconsciously and unintentionally serves the higher needs of society as a whole. In this way

Spencer attempted to reconcile his sociological individualism with his collective concept of the social organism.

One consequence of this argument was a rejection of social regulation as conceived by Comte and the forms of state intervention which Spencer saw increasingly dominating industrial society. For Spencer, society was regulated adequately if individuals were allowed to pursue their own interests free of collectivist intervention. Hence his hostility to state education, state medicine, the provision of free public libraries: institutions which 'artificially' preserve its 'feeblest members' lower the moral and intellectual standards of society as a whole. Spencer remained rigorously individualistic in his conception of human society. In *The Principles of Sociology* (1873), discussing the controversy between nominalists and realists, he argued that society was essentially 'a collective name for a number of individuals' and that there 'is no way of coming at a true theory of society but by inquiring into the nature of its component individuals' (Spencer, 1961, Ch. VI). In one important sense, therefore, Spencer's positivistic organicism and sociological individuals failed to develop much beyond Mill's psychological reductionism: on the one hand, society constituted the sum of individual actions and sociological analysis must focus on the biological and psychological characteristics of individuals; on the other hand, society was a system, a complex, highly differentiated structure consisting of phenomena that had evolved at the superorganic level. Spencer's sociology could not resolve this dualism, the conflict between a biological and evolutionary determinism and a profound belief in individual human action as the source of unity and social harmony. As Peel has observed, 'Spencer had no real sense of either the historical actor, or the sociologist, intervening or participating in the flow of events'. The pattern of evolution could not be changed by 'any "extra-evolutionary" action' (Peel, 1971, p. 164).

Spencer's sociological system, his concept of evolution as a cosmic process, his sociological individualism and organicist holism had no deep, lasting effects: some of his ideas crossed the Atlantic and found a congenial reception within early American sociology, but European sociology, in the general reaction against positivism at the close of the nineteenth-century, debated with Spencer's theories (especially Simmel and Durkheim), only to salvage such basic sociological concepts as structure, function, system, equilibrium, institution. Nevertheless, the anti-historical bias of Spencer's sociology influenced the later synchronically oriented sociologists and deflected attention away from those structural elements in societies which, through conflict and differential interests, promote social change. Spencer's organicist positivism, however, did succeed in grasping society as a structure, a system, and he was one of the first social theorists to identify industrialism with a new, decentred mode of social organisation. In this respect he differed sharply from the centralising notion of society developed by Comte. Indeed, Spencer's lasting contribution to sociological theory may well be his notion that an advanced society – industrial society – built around increasing differentiation of structure and differentiation of function and reciprocal relations between different institutions as well as between parts and whole, necessarily lacks a single, dominant centre. Comparing the social and the biological organism he noted that 'while in the individual organism there is but one centre of consciousness . . . there are, in the social organism, as many centres as there are individuals' (Spencer, 1969, p. 282). Spencer expressed the concept of decentred structure in atomistic terms but it is, nevertheless, an important insight. The implicit focus of Spencer's sociology is on civil society and its separation from the state. Of course, his synchronic, individualistic approach prevented a profound theorisation of the historical, systemic and contradictory nature of modern industrial society, that as industrialism expands the framework and frees the institutions of civil society it simultaneously generates centralising trends within the state itself. Spencer's concept of industrialism and social differentiation could be said to be deficient in one important respect: that it failed to grasp the historical specificity of industrialism as class structured, as a capitalist process.

3
Marxism: A Positive Science of Capitalist Development

Comte's theory of historical change had emphasised the concept of determinate laws, that history necessarily moved through a succession of stages culminating in the scientific epoch of positivism. For Comte, as with Montesquieu, Smith and Ferguson social change was not a random process dependent on purely subjective and accidental elements, but the result of an underlying structure of forces – material and moral – that generated both direction and meaning. As was argued in the previous chapter, many of Comte's fundamental ideas were derived from Saint-Simon, but in Comte's reworking of Saint-Simon's theories the concepts of industrialism, production, class formation and class conflict were stripped of their contradictory and negative aspects and integrated into an organismic, consensual model of society. But Saint-Simon's writings contain both positivistic and socialist elements. The development of socialism as both an intellectual current and socio-political movement owed much to the influence of Saint-Simon's followers. The Saint-Simonian school, in particular the writings of Enfantin and Bazard, argued that production must be socially organised, run by the producers themselves (not the parasitic 'idlers' and 'unproductive classes'), and society develop from rule by government and military organisation to administrative and industrial rule. During the 1830s this notion of the socialisation of production, and therefore of private property, became the corner-stone of socialist theory: employed for the first time by the Saint-Simonian, Pierre Leroux in 1832, socialism demanded the abolition of private property rights, the elimination of poverty, the assertion of equality and the organisation of production through the agency of the state.

Positivist sociology and socialist theory thus share a common source even though both socialism and sociology, as theories of social and political organisation, existed before they were named. But it was only during the crucial period between 1789 and 1830, in response to rapid political and economic changes, that the intellectual and institutional basis of sociology and socialism were laid as expressions of a developing opposition to the dominant ideas of political liberalism, individualism and the market economy.

Nineteenth-century socialism and sociology emerged after the intellectual consolidation of classical political economy largely in response to the doctrine of the immanent rationality of individual interests: sociologists and socialists both agreed that the private pursuit of interests must eventuate in the collapse of social and moral solidarity; the anarchy of the market place could not lead to social cohesion and stability. Comte's solution was authoritarian moral leadership; the Saint-Simonians demanded a socialised system of production. But socialist ideas made little impact on the nascent labour movement that had developed rapidly after the ending of the French revolutionary wars. In England working-class leaders worked closely with the bourgeoisie, advocating liberal rather than socialist ideas in opposition to the political domination of the aristocracy. The success of the 1832 Reform Act had the effect of separating the working-class movement from the bourgeoisie and instituting a distinct socialist alternative – Owenism and the Chartists in England, the Saint-Simonian school and Fourier in France. Both Robert Owen and Charles Fourier insisted on the necessity for co-operation not competition as the means of social organisation advocating the development of communities in which the worker would enjoy 'the fruits of his labour' to the full.

The early socialists tended to offer a moralising and Utopian critique of industrial capitalism, that as labour constituted the only source of value everyone, apart from the 'unproductive' workers, should work together and produce a society based on mutuality rather than private gain. The capitalist was effectively depriving the worker of that which was his own, an action clearly immoral and socially divisive. The solution was thus social transformation through moral criticism and action, a standpoint which led Engels to characterise Owen, Fourier and others as 'Utopian' not scientific socialists. In the sense that pre-Marxist socialism lacked both a theory of social change and a grasp of society in terms of the relations between economic organisation and the social and political system then it was utopian, basing the necessity for socialism on changes in human nature. And, of course, it was precisely the scientific grasp of social change that Engels admired in the work of Saint-Simon, especially the concept of historical laws, the necessary historical conflict between social classes – feudal and bourgeoisie, idlers and producers – and the central argument that changes within the political system depended, not on moral actions, but on economic institutions. Equally significant for the development of Marxist socialism was the assimilation of the Saint-Simonian doctrine that socialised production was possible only through the organisation of a centralised state. The emphasis on the ethical component of socialism, which plays such an important role in the work of Owen and Fourier, disappears in the socialism of Marx and Engels: the moral element is entirely dependent on the structure of the economy and polity.

The development of Marxism is thus organically bound up with a burgeoning labour movement – especially in England and France – the rapid growth of industry and the new social relations of capitalist production. Equally important was the critique of this new social order by 'dissident' intellectuals influenced by classical political economy, especially the labour theory of value, and the revolutionary trends associated with democratic republicanism. During the course of the 1840s and 1850s Marxism emerged as the first sociological theory which identified scientific analysis with the interests of a specific social class, the industrial proletariat; a theory of historical change grounded in the struggle between social classes and the priority of economic factors in the shaping of social and political structures. In effect the scientific study of historical development disclosed the necessity of socialism as the resolution of internal conflicts generated by capitalist production: Utopian socialism had disclosed no law-governed process in history, no historical necessity, and thus had ended with moral appeals in which socialism was defined as an ideal state realisable through education and co-operation.

The development of Marxism

Marx's first writings (1841–5) were largely philosophical, concerned with the problem of human alienation and freedom. It was only with *The German Ideology* (1846) that Marx 'settled his account' with his 'philosophic conscience' and developed the first outlines of what later would be called 'the materialist conception of history'. Co-written with Engels, *The German Ideology* advanced a sociological concept of society as a definite structure built around antagonistic social classes, division of labour and forms of private property. Ideas themselves are rooted in specific material contexts and have no independent existence apart from the social formation. Specific modes of production characterise historical development: society develops through different stages from slave and feudal, to capitalist. In the works which followed *The German Ideology* – *The Poverty of Philosophy* (1847), *The Communist Manifesto* (1848), *Wage Labour and Capital* (1849) – these themes were further developed within Marx's general historical theory, that social change occurs through conflict and struggle and more precisely through the contradictions existing between the productive forces of any society and its social relations. There is thus a pattern, a meaning to historical development located within the necessity for modes of production to develop towards higher social formations: socialism is thus given a scientific basis in necessary social change.

During the 1850s Marx produced a number of historical studies dealing with the problems of socialism and the working-class movement in Europe, especially France. But his most important work was the massive study of the economic foundations of modern capitalism, the *Grundrisse der Kritik politischen Okonomie* (*Outline of a Critique of Political Economy*), which remained unpublished during his lifetime becoming widely known only after its publication in East Germany in 1953. The importance of the *Grundrisse* in the development of Marxism lies in the continuity which it establishes between Marx's early writings on the alienation of labour and the concept of the active human subject, and the later, supposedly more scientific work, in which capitalism is defined as a social system governed by specific laws of motion and development. Nevertheless, while Marx employs the concept of alienation in the analysis of economic forms there are significant differences between the *Grundrisse* and the earlier works: the term labour-power replaces the concept of labour (labour power had been noted in *The Communist Manifesto* but only in a general sense); production is emphasised at the expense of exchange and the basis laid for the theory of surplus value, capital accumulation and economic crisis. These are the themes which dominate *Capital* (1867) of which only the first volume was published in Marx's lifetime. Yet the theory of alienation and dehumanisation are central issues in these later largely economic analyses and Marx remained faithful to the essential principles of Hegelian dialectics and humanism to the end of his life: capitalism was conceived as a system of production structured in contradictions, a social system which transformed human values into external things. In analysing Marx's sociology therefore, it is important to begin with Marx's own starting point.

Alienation of labour

In the *Economic and Philosophic Manuscripts* (1843–4) Marx defined labour as 'man's self-confirming essence', the activity which political economy had succeeded in transforming into an object, an external thing. For classical political economy the worker was 'an abstract activity and a belly . . . increasingly dependent upon all the fluctuations in market price, in the employment of capital, and in the caprices of the rich'. Human activity is thus defined in terms of the non-human.

But the concept of alienation was not part of political economy's conceptual structure or language and it was from

Hegel's dialectical philosophy that Marx derived the theory of alienation. In Hegel's *Phenomenology of Spirit* human culture was assimilated to the concept of 'Absolute Spirit' which progressively unfolds throughout history in a series of dialectical contradictions, eventuating in the expansion of human consciousness and increased self-knowledge; the ultimate stage is the assimilation of 'Spirit' to the 'ethical world'. History was thus defined as enclosing an immanent meaning in that it embodied a ceaseless activity and drive towards unlimited, total consciousness. 'Spirit' was, of course, humanity and the specific historical situations which constitute historical development are analysed by Hegel as 'moments' which, in their material form, embody the dialectical development of 'Absolute Spirit' from an unreflective unity to an organic and conscious unity with culture (the Renaissance, the Enlightenment, the French Revolution). But as 'spirit' unfolds dialectically it is confronted by each specific moment as part of itself, something its own activity has created; it thus experiences this activity as external and alien. 'Spirit' seeks to recover these alienated moments thus creating the movement which drives it towards total unity and thus a non-alienated consciousness.

Marx inverts Hegel's idealist account arguing that such speculative history ignores real individuals and real conditions; through his grasp of political economy Marx defined labour as the basis of human culture. Culture is no longer the expression of a supra-historical force but the product of human activity through labour. Alienation becomes a process in which humanity is progressively turned into a stranger in a world created by labour. This materialist inversion of Hegel was made possible by arguing that religion was merely humanity's essential nature refracted through ideas: religion, Ludwig Feuerbach (1804–72) wrote, 'is nothing other than the essence of man . . . the God of man is nothing other than the divinised essence of man'.

In the *Economic and Philosophic Manuscripts* Marx redefines religion and philosophy as constituting more than the embodiment of humanity's essence, the product of specific economic forces. Marx analyses alienation in terms of the division of labour arguing that it succeeds in creating vast accumulations of wealth at one pole of society, an increase in the value of things achieved only at the cost of a progressive devaluing of human life itself. Human labour becomes an object: 'This fact implies that the object produced by labour, its product, now stands opposed to it as an alien being, as a *power independent* of the producer. The product of labour is labour which has been embodied in an object and turned into a physical thing; this product is an objectification of labour'. Marx distinguishes objectification from alienation arguing, against Hegel, whose philosophy embraced both as synonymous terms, that objectification is a process through which humanity externalises itself in nature and society, producing tools for example, and thus necessarily entering into social relationships; alienation, however, occurs only when humanity, having externalised itself, encounters its own activity, its essence, operating as an external, alien and oppressive power. For Marx, objectification was unavoidable and as such not identical with alienation. By assimilating objectification to alienation, Hegel had concluded that humanity (the 'Absolute Spirit') must remain forever trapped in alienation as its essential and ultimately tragic condition. But by locating alienation with economic and material elements Marx defined it as an historical not universal state.

Marx identified four main characteristics of alienation: man's alienation from nature, from himself, from his 'species being' (a term taken from Feuerbach) and from others. Capitalism alienates humanity from its own activity, from the product of its labour ('alienation of things') thus turning labour's product into an alien object. The more the individual works the more he is dominated by the world of objects that labour has created: 'The worker puts his life into the object, and his life then belongs no longer to himself but to the object. The greater his activity . . . the less he possesses. What is embodied in the product of his labour is no longer his own. The greater this product is . . . the more he is diminished.' Man's 'self-confirming essence', his labour, turns increasingly against him under capitalist industry, becoming a 'forced activity', a denial of his being, serving to stunt his faculties, induce misery, exhaustion and mental despair. Work is wholly instrumental; a form of activity which is specifically human, becomes an oppressive necessity, an alien, external activity in which the individual feels free only outside work in leisure or with his family. Man feels free as an individual and is thus alienated as a species being, for unlike the animals man, through his activity, produces not simply for himself but for the whole of nature. He has, too, an awareness of this activity and continually reproduces himself in both consciousness and in real life. But alienated labour turns the product of labour from an activity of the species into an activity of the individual dominated by purely biological needs. Capitalism effectively defines the worker as possessing a saleable object, labour, which is thus purchased by 'another' so that his activity is no longer his own.

Marx's early writings thus propound two basic themes: first, that while humanity creates the social world through its own activity, the world is experienced as alien and hostile; and secondly, that both idealist philosophy and classical political economy, the theories which first disclosed this trend towards alienation, depict human relationships not as relations between persons but rather as relations between things. This process of reification is especially marked in political economy.

> It is self-evident that political economy treats the proletarian . . . [as] a *worker*. It can, therefore, propound the thesis that he, like a horse, must receive just as much as will enable him to work. Political economy does not deal with him in his free time, as a human being . . . but . . . conceives the worker only as a draught animal, as a beast whose needs are strictly limited to bodily needs (Marx, 1963, p. 132).

As the most alienated social class in capitalist society the proletariat exist on the basis of private property, itself the source of alienated labour. It is for this reason that Marx identifies the working class as a universal class 'for all human servitude is involved in the relation of the worker to production and all types of servitude are only modifications or consequences of this relation'. It thus follows that the whole of society is alienated, from capitalists whose life is dominated externally by the demands of profit, to writers and artists who sell their creative talents to the highest bidder. A total revolution is thus called for and the spearhead is the modern industrial proletariat, a class which constitutes the 'effective dissolution' of capitalism, for its demand that private property be abolished is only 'a *principle for society* what society has already made a principle *for the proletariat* and what the latter already involuntarily embodies as the negative result of society'. The dehumanised relation of capital to labour saturates the entire social structure; 'an inhuman power' rules everything.

Political economy could probe no further into the structure of alienated labour and explain the contradiction generated by an alienated social world and increasing material affluence. Political economy ended by celebrating bourgeois society and bourgeois thought as the close of history and as universal activity. The contradictions, the negative elements generated by this process, were simply eliminated: 'Political economy conceals the alienation in the nature of labour in so far as it does not examine the direct relationship between the worker ('work') and production.' Alienation is thus a denial of creative human potentiality, the dehumanisation of the subject and an obstacle to the building of a truly human community.

In Marx's early writings alienation is conceived both in socio-historical and philosophically abstract terms as, for example, the 'fragmentation' of labour and the 'fragmentation' of the human essence. It is important to note that Marx develops a concept of the *whole man* whose human stature is diminished by the external power of capital; man thus needs to be returned to a non-alienated state, reunited with nature, other men and society. As late as 1846, in *The German Ideology*, Marx could describe Communism in terms of these Utopian elements arguing that the division of labour would not function merely to allocate individuals to specific occupational roles but allow them 'to hunt in the morning, fish in the afternoon, rear cattle in the evening, criticise after dinner . . . without ever becoming a hunter, fisherman, shepherd or critic'. (Marx and Engels, 1964, Part 1.) Nevertheless, there is, within this particular text and those which followed, a shift of emphasis and the argument that the concept of alienation in the *Grundrisse* and *Capital* is identical with that of the *Economic and Philosophic Manuscripts* suggests the untenable view that, while Marx's theory of society and social change underwent extensive revision and development in the post-1845 works, the theory of alienation remained at the conceptual and empirical level of the earlier texts. By the 1850s Marx's economic theory, together with his political outlook, had changed considerably. Thus from a purely logical standpoint those concepts retained in the later writings clearly imply radically different meanings from their earlier usage. The present appeal of the *Economic and Philosophic Manuscripts* undoubtedly lies in their depiction of humanity as the ultimate arbiter of the social world and man as an active subject duplicating himself and his powers through his actions. Yet the picture which emerges from these writings does not suggest the voluntaristic theory which has often been claimed for them, for if alienation dominates the social world to the extent of wholly debilitating humanity's creative and natural powers, transforming the individual from an active subject into a passive object, then how is it possible for change to occur. *How is praxis possible?* Marx's concept of alienation suggests the impossibility of radical human action, for consciously planned change. It is this contradiction between the notions of *active* subject and *total* alienation which leads Marx to posit Communism as an ethical ideal which humanity ought to strive for, and the proletariat as the universal class which negates capitalist alienation. Marx's humanist concept of alienation, although based on the keenly felt empirical structure of classical political economy, is ultimately deterministic, philosophical and speculative lacking the sociological and economic framework of the later *Grundrisse* and *Capital*.

Between writing the *Economic and Philosophic Manuscripts* and *Capital* Marx decisively rejected Feuerbach's humanist philosophy as the starting point for social theory. His main criticism related to Feuerbach's essentialist concept of man: humanity constitutes the totality of social relations and thus research must investigate not man in general but man in society and society as a system structured around laws of change and development. But Marx did not abandon humanism. In *Capital* the concept of alienation is sparingly employed but the related notions of the 'fetishism of commodities' and reification are frequently discussed and form an important part of Marx's analysis of capitalist economic structure. In the *Grundrisse*, for example, the emphasis shifts to production; labour is defined as labour-power, a unique commodity found only within the capitalist mode of production. In the early writings Marx had followed Smith and Ricardo in defining labour as 'abstract general and social labour', an approach which succeeded in mystifying the precise relation between the creation of value (expressed in money, for example) and human activity (expressed in labour). Labour-power constitutes a commodity; labour in general does not. The creation of wealth is possible only through the exploitation of labour power, the transformation of labour from an affirmation to a denial of human values. Thus in *Capital* Marx argues that commodity production entails the separation of two specific kinds of value, exchange and use value, values which either command a price or satisfy a human and social need. All commodities embody both values but it is only capitalism as a system of commodity production which aims at the expansion of exchange value.

Human activity increasingly becomes subordinated to the external compulsions of exchange value. Money becomes the objective bond of society, the real community in a system dominated by exchange values. When in the first volume of *Capital* Marx refers to 'commodity fetishism' he describes a process in which human subjects no longer control the objects of labour as their own. The worker exists only to satisfy the demands of the economic system; material wealth does not exist to satisfy the needs of the worker's development. The social process of production effectively negates the need for community, co-operation becomes alienated and replaced by compulsion. Human relations become 'atomised' assuming a material character independent of human control and conscious activity. This process is especially expressed by the fact that products take the form of commodities (Marx, 1958, Vol. 1, Ch. XXVI).

In a society dominated by exchange value, the real social foundations of the unequal relation of capital to labour is hidden. In a famous passage Marx writes of the commodity as 'a mysterious thing' which disguises the social character of labour presenting the relations between the producers and the totality of their labour 'as a social relation, existing not between themselves, but between the products of their labour'. Social relations within capitalism are wholly inverted, 'every element, even the simplest, the commodity for example . . . causes relations between people to appear as attributes of things'. The social world of modern capitalism is a perverted world, the products of labour generating an apparent independence, in which objects begin 'to rule the producers instead of being ruled by them', while those engaged in production 'live in a bewitched world', their own relationships appearing to them 'as properties of things, as properties of the material elements of production'. Humanity becomes dominated by a world of things, by processes its own activity has created but which, through the workings of the capitalist economic system, turn against them, as objective independent processes (Marx, 1958, pp. 72–3). In the *Grundrisse* Marx writes that 'social wealth confronts labour in more powerful portions as an alien and dominant power . . . a monstrous objective power which, created through social labour belongs not to the worker, but . . . to capital'. The emphasis, Marx notes, is 'not on the state of being *objectified*, but . . . of being *alienated*, dispossessed, sold' (Marx, 1973, pp. 831–2). And, in almost identical language, he writes in *Capital*:

> We have seen that the growing accumulation of capital implies its growing concentration. Thus grows the power of capital, the alienation of the conditions of social production personified in the capitalist from the real producers. Capital . . . as a social power . . . no longer stands in any possible relation to that which the labour of a single individual can create. It becomes an alienated, independent social power, which stands opposed to society as an object, and as an object that is the capitalist's source of power (Marx, 1962, p. 259).

The extraction of surplus-value, the control over labour-power invested in the individual capitalist and capital, results in the development of a social world which progressively devalues human values and exalts the world of objects and things. In the *Economic and Philosophic Manuscripts* Marx had analysed this tendency: 'The worker becomes an ever cheaper commodity the more goods he creates. The devaluation of the human world increases in direct relation with the increase in value of the world of things.' The relation between the early and later writings is thus clearly stated; in a world dominated by commodity production and exploitation the worker's labour-power is quantified, measured as precisely as possible, treated entirely as an external thing. The analysis of capitalism as a system in the *Grundrisse* and *Capital* is based on similar concepts employed by Marx in his humanist critique of capitalism of the early writings. But in both the early and later writings reification is depicted as a process which so penetrates human and social relations that individuals comprehend the products of their labour as autonomous, objective forces unconnected with human activity.

This process of reification manifests itself most sharply in consciousness: those who comprehend the social world through reified categories emphasise the externality and inexorable *natural* determinism of a world apparently governed by blind laws beyond the control of human beings, a world in which things constitute the only active elements. In pre-industrial society, where use value was not dominated by exchange value, social relations were clear and unequivocal based on personalised ties and obligations, unequal relationships grounded in custom and tradition. The social structure of capitalism, however, is built around impersonal relationships based on the dominion of exchange value. In societies where exchange value has replaced direct use value a formal equality masks class relations; the world of capitalist commodity production appears as a world of equals bound by freely negotiated contracts. The exchange between capital and labour bears the illusion of a free exchange of equivalents (labour for wages) and it is at this point that the mystification of social relations occurs: the worker acts as if labour-power is not exploited, that in return for 'a fair day's work' there will be just reward. Capitalist inequality is thus defined as natural and therefore essential for the adequate functioning of society. The worker fails to understand that he has become part of capital itself and is but a special mode of its existence:

> Hence the productive power developed by the labourer when working in co-operation is the productive power of capital. This power is developed gratuitously, whenever the workmen are placed under given conditions, and it is capital that places them under such conditions. Because this power cost capital nothing, and because, on the other hand, the labourer himself does not develop it before his labour belongs to capital, it appears as a power with

which capital is endowed by Nature – a productive power that is immanent in capital (Marx, 1958, p. 333).

Marx's theory of alienation has thus become more empirical, historically specific and sociologically grounded in economic structures. In his early writings Marx had written of the 'inhuman power' dominating social life, frustrating humanity's essential powers and transforming him/her into an object. In *Capital* the concept of alienated subject is retained but within a theoretical framework which defines capitalism as an objective system and alienation in terms of the inner and contradictory movement of capitalist production, an alienation embodied in the transformation of labour power into a commodity. One result of this trend is the increasing importance of ideology for the development and maintenance of capitalist society.

The concept of ideology

Although the term ideology originated at the end of the eighteenth century in the work of the French philosopher Destutt de Tracy, Marxism is often credited with defining its relation to determine social, political and economic conditions and elucidating the process whereby the material 'base' of society (its economic infrastructure) necessarily generates a 'superstructure' (specific forms of thought). Society is explained not through ideas but rather ideas through society: ideas have no history other than as elements of society and history. In *The German Ideology* Marx and Engels postulated a strict, causal and mechanical relation between thought and the social world defining ideas as expressions of class interests. This theory of ideology therefore assumes a relation of correspondence between social structure and thought systems; ideas are merely the passive reflections of an external economic order. Knowledge is epiphenomenal, the product of objective social interests and thus incapable of exercising an active role in society and social change.

The concept of ideology as distorted thought, as a false consciousness which mystifies real relations in defence of class interests, is developed in great detail in *The German Ideology*.

Ideological thought conceives reality 'upside down', an inversion of the objectively real, as with religion which defines human life as an extension of God in opposition to the materialist doctrine of religion as a social product. In this first formulation ideology is equivalent to consciousness, the transposition of 'interests' into mere 'reflexes and echoes' of the 'life process':

> The phantoms formed in the human brain are . . . sublimates of . . . material life-processes, which is empirically verifiable and bound to material premises. Morality, religion, metaphysics, all the rest of ideology and their corresponding forms of consciousness, thus no longer retain their semblance of independence. They have no history, no development; but men, developing their material production and their material intercourse, alter, along with this real existence, their thinking and the products of their thinking. Life is not determined by consciousness but consciousness by life (Marx and Engels, 1964, pp. 37–8).

This thesis of a strict causal relation of economic base and ideological superstructure reappears in Marx's 1859 text, *A Contribution to a Critique of Political Economy*, in which it is argued that the forces of production 'constitute the economic structure of society, the real foundation on which arises a legal and political superstructure and to which correspond definite forms of social consciousness. The mode of production of material life conditions the general process of social, political and intellectual life' (Marx, 1971, pp. 20–1). In many of Engels's discussions of ideology it is this deterministic concept which predominates:

> Ideology is a process accomplished by the so-called thinker consciously indeed, but with a false consciousness. The real motives impelling him remain unknown to him, otherwise it would not be an ideological process at all (Marx and Engels, 1962, Vol. 2, p. 497).

On this basis all thought must qualify as ideology including Marxism itself. Engels's argument suggests a thoroughgoing relativism, a position not sustained consistently in his work for he clearly believed in the non-ideological advances made in nineteenth-century natural science. Engels insists that although ideology enjoys no independent existence apart from society, no separate history as an autonomous reality, there is, nevertheless, a degree of partial autonomy and although an inversion of the real world, and thus 'false', ideology is not wholly an epiphenomenal and passive reproduction of the socio-economic structure. Engels thus emphasises the *reciprocal* not mechanical nexus of ideas and society:

> The economic situation is the basis, but the various elements of the superstructure, political forms of the class struggle . . . juristic, philosophical theories, religious view . . . also exercise their influence upon the course of the historical struggles and in many cases preponderate their form (Marx and Engels, 1962, Vol. 2, pp. 488–9).

Mutual interaction between all elements exists but in the final resort 'the economic movement . . . asserts itself as necessary'.

Engels's formulation is full of ambiguity. To argue that the economic factor is one among many influences, yet the ultimate arbiter of ideology and all forms of knowledge, does not in itself suggest any criteria for judging truth from error or the means of validating one social theory over another. For example, are some social interests less likely to produce ideological distortion than others; and if this is so how is the economic factor ultimately decisive? In effect, Engels reverts to pre-Marxist concepts of multiple causation and context-bound explanations which fail to specify the exact relation of ideas to society, the structure of determinations and thus of autonomy. Writing of philosophy, for example, he argues:

> . . . through the operation of economic influences (which again generally act only under political etc. disguises) upon the existing philosophic material handed down by predecessors. Here economy creates nothing new, but it determines the way in which the thought material found in existence is altered and further developed, and that too for the most part indirectly, for it is the political, legal and moral reflexes which exercise the greatest influence upon philosophy (Marx and Engels, 1962, Vol. 2, pp. 495–6).

74

Engels's standpoint is that of eighteenth-century materialism, Montesquieu and Ferguson, mutual interaction of different elements within a given situation; the notion of partial autonomy in this context is merely another way of saying that complex situations are characterised by complex modes of interaction.

A second, more dialectical theory of ideology, one grounded in the category of mediation is, however, implicit in Engels's distinction between what he calls the 'higher' and the 'lower' ideologies ('pure' thought as opposed to concrete, economic thought). The closer that thought approaches abstract ideology the more it will be determined 'by accidental elements in its evolution . . . its curve will trace a zig-zag'. The interconnections 'between concepts and their material conditions of existence becomes more and more complicated, more and more obscured by intermediate links' (Marx and Engels, 1962, Vol. 2, p. 397). This is crudely expressed but it does suggest that the history of ideas is a dialectical and not a mechanically evolutionary process. In the *Grundrisse* Marx had posed the question of the relationship between economy and culture, art and social structure arguing that 'certain periods of the highest development of art stand in no direct connection with the general development of society, nor with the material basis and the skeleton structure of its organisation' (Marx, 1971, pp. 215–17). Ancient Greek art surpassed its economically undeveloped economic system while the developments in eighteenth-century French and German philosophy cannot be assimilated easily to the pre-industrial, semi-feudal structure of French and German society.

Marx's most important contribution to the theory of ideology, however, is his extensive critique of eighteenth and nineteenth-century political economy. Here Marx clearly distinguished science from ideology and the complex relation of class interests with thought. In the 'Afterword' to the second edition of *Capital* (1873) he argues that classical political economy (Smith and Ricardo) 'belongs to the period in which the class struggle was as yet undeveloped', a period characterised by rapid advances in economic science. But with the sharpening of class conflict at the beginning of the nineteenth-century and the eventual conquest of political power by the

French and English bourgeoisie 'the class struggle, practically as well as theoretically, took on a more and more outspoken and threatening form. It sounded the knell of scientific bourgeois economy . . . In place of disinterested inquiries there were hired prize-fighters; in place of genuine scientific research the bad conscience and the evil intent of apologetic'. From the moment when the bourgeoisie assumed the mantle of a dominant class then the class struggle between bourgeoisie and aristocracy became a conflict between bourgeoisie allied with the aristocracy against the burgeoning industrial proletariat (Marx, 1958, p. 15). Political economy now becomes entwined with the claims of ideological legitimation. In the *Theories of Surplus Value* Marx established two crucial elements of ideology:

1. All social thought adopts necessarily a position towards it object of study which is directly related to the practical interests and activity of its leading intellectuals: thus Smith and Ricardo expressed the interests of 'a revolutionary bourgeoisie' in conflict with the landowners.
2. Ideological knowledge will subvert scientific knowledge if the standpoint is that of an economically declining social group, what Marx describes as 'transition classes', such as the aristocracy and landowners.

Thus in his analysis of Smith and Ricardo, Marx frequently describes their work as 'honest inquiry' emphasising their commitment to a rigorous and objective scientific approach. Smith, in his discussion of labour, adopts the standpoint of capitalist production and approaches 'the very heart of the matter, hit(s) the nail on the head' by distinguishing unproductive from productive labour (unproductive exchanging for revenue such as wages and profits, productive producing capital). Smith's distinction was never made from the standpoint of the worker, rather from that of the capitalist. In contrast, Ricardo describes the necessary conflict engendered by the economically unequal relation between capitalist and worker and Marx comments that Ricardo 'wants production for the sake of production' irrespective of its social effects, 'a ruthlessness . . . not only scientifically honest but also . . . a scientific necessity from his point of view'. Ricardo's political economy thus expresses the historic triumph of the industrial bourgeoisie over society as a whole and in this sense his work is, in Marx's terms, genuinely scientific although, as with Smith, penetrated by ideological elements:

> Ricardo's conception is . . . in the interests of the industrial bourgeoisie, only because, and in so far as, their interests coincide with that of production or the productive development of human labour (Marx, 1964–72, Vol. 3, pp. 118–19).

Marx distinguishes, then, between ideological and scientific knowledge: 'The rough cynical character of classical economy' – its honesty – is in effect 'a critique of existing conditions', and he cites Smith's description of the clergy as 'unproductive labourers . . . maintained by a part of the annual produce of the industry of other people' bracketing them with 'lawyers, physicians and men of letters'. Marx writes:

> This is the language of the still revolutionary bourgeoisie which has not yet subjected to itself the whole of society, the State etc. All these illustrious and time-honoured occupations . . . are from an economic standpoint on the same level as the swarm of their own lackeys and jesters maintained by the bourgeoisie and by idle wealth (Marx, 1964–72, vol. 1, pp. 290–2).

As an intellectual expression of a 'rising class' classical political economy penetrated more deeply into the social and economic order than previous economic theory, its concepts organically bound up with its practice as an historically 'progressive' class whose worldly activity, in business and industry, linked it, not with past societies, but with the capitalist and industrial future. The work of Smith and Ricardo thus reflects the practice of a social class which had yet to establish its hegemony within the burgeoning capitalist order. Ricardo's economic theories justify capitalist development and the historic claims of the bourgeois class but this in itself does not make them ideological. Both Ricardo and Smith produced work which did not mystify the social world and conceal contradictions but rather illuminated the very nature of capitalist economic and social relations. Ricardo's contemporary, Malthus, in contrast produced economic analysis which justified the 'rents, sinecures, squandering, heartlessness' of the landed aristocracy, admiring and praising those groups within the state which Smith had criticised as unproductive labourers. To legitimise a 'transition' class clearly leads to ideology:

> But when a man seeks to accommodate science to a viewpoint which is derived not from science itself (however erroneous it may be) but from outside, external interests, then I call him 'base'. . . It is not a base action when Ricardo puts the proletariat on the same level as machinery or beasts of burden because (from his point of view) their being purely machinery or beasts of burden is conducive to 'production'. *This is stoic, objective, scientific* (Marx, 1964–72, Vol. 2, pp. 114–19).

From these texts it is possible to define more precisely Marx's concept of ideology. The relation of knowledge to society is conceived dialectically, characterised by contradictions, uneven in its development; knowledge is not a direct reproduction of class and economic interests. These formulations are clearly anchored in Marx's dictum that social existence, the 'ensemble of social relations', determines consciousness through the 'sensuous activity' of the human subject. Yet it might be argued that all Marx has demonstrated is that between 1760 and 1830 the English bourgeoisie 'needed' a specific mode of knowledge consonant with its historic role, and that political economy emerged as an historically necessary intellectual response to the burgeoning capitalist economic order. In other words, a functional not dialectical relation subsists between forms of knowledge and forms of society. But the fact that specific forms of knowledge are associated with specific material interests does not imply that the degree of determination automatically classifies all the knowledge-products as ideological. Marx makes the important distinction between the 'ideological component parts of the ruling class' and 'the free spiritual production of this particular social formation', arguing against a mechanical reduction of ideas to economic interests: economic structure develops unevenly and does not constitute a homogeneous unified whole which presents a coherent set of interests. Marx's arguments point to a concept of knowledge as objective and scientific, a reality independent of economic and social forces although necessarily linked to these elements for its social existence.

In contrast, ideology is epiphenomenal tied directly to economic and class interests, its function one of concealing contradictions, mystifying social relations and fetishising the world of appearances. Ideological knowledge, as distinct from scientific knowledge, begins from the alienated nature of human relations and is incapable of grasping the socio-historical foundation of alienation and its influence of social relations. Marx's theory of ideology is thus inseparable from the concept of alienation developed in his early writings: ideology cannot develop an adequate methodological stand-point to the study of society as an historical and sociological reality. Classical political economy combined both ideological analysis and objective scientific study of capitalism and thus produced from within its theoretical framework an empirical methodology which stressed the objective nature of economic facts and processes, while failing to comprehend the contradictions its own analysis yielded.

This complex relation of science to ideology, methodology to ideology is brought out with great clarity in Marx's analysis of the famous 'trinity' formula of 'vulgar' economics which asserted that production flowed from three factors of capital, land and labour, each constituting a separate source of value. In this formulation, writes Marx, the mystification and reification of social relations is accomplished by separating the historically specific forms of social production from the labour process, parts isolated from the whole, 'the enchanted, perverted, topsy-turvey world in which Monsieur le Capital and Madame de Terre do their ghost-walking as social characters and at the same time directly as mere things'. But as with many such formulations of classical political economy, the 'trinity formula' contains elements of truth: the producers *are* separated from the means of production, the revenue forms the income of three great classes of capitalism. 'These are relations or forms of distribution for they express the relations under which the newly produced total value is distributed among the owners of the various productive agencies'. The trinity formula, however, is more ideological than scientific based as it is on an acceptance of the surface pattern of economic relations rather than the 'inner, basic but hidden essential structure, and the conception corresponding to it'. If appearance and reality always coincided, Marx notes, all science would be superfluous: the task of social science lies precisely in discovering and analysing the underlying forms, the structures of society that lead to the 'law of appearances'. Thus the critical importance in Marx's thought of *method* (Marx, 1958, pp. 500, 877, 205).

Marx's method: materialism and dialectics

Marx's early writings, produced within a culture dominated by the idealist philosophy of Hegel, although employing Hegelian categories such as alienation, had rejected the metaphysical abstractions and methodology of the larger philosophy. But by 1858 Marx's view of Hegel had changed and he now described Hegel's *Logic* as rendering in an accessible form 'what is rational in the method which Hegel discovered but at the same time enveloped in mysticism'. This is the distinction Engels made later between Hegel's *method* and his *system*, the necessity to extract 'the rational kernel within the mystical shell' and develop a materialist dialectic. To achieve this Marx adopted the category of totality, not as a speculative, philosophical principle, but as a methodological instrument which grasps the relations of the simple to the complex, the part to the whole.

Thus Marx begins *Capital* with the simple form of value, the exchange of one commodity for another, arguing that the commodity contains the basic contradictions of capitalism. But the commodity is also a *part* which must be related to a *whole*, a totality, capitalism as an economic, political and social system. Marx's method, therefore, opposed the atomistic approach of methodological individualism (e.g. Utilitarianism, Rationalism) as well as those philosophies which defined the concept of whole as the simple sum of its parts: for Marx, totality is structured in the interconnectedness of phenomena, facts are not isolated and external datums but internally related elements existing in a necessary relation to the whole although enjoying independence from it. 'The relations of production of every society', Marx wrote, 'form a whole' and can be understood and analysed only in this sense.

Society is thus constantly developing through internal contradictions and disturbances; a totality is never static but in a state of tension between the parts and the whole. Marx's concept of totality includes social, political and economic institutions together with all forms of social consciousness, knowledge and ideology. Totality also includes the role of practice in social change. But totality has another meaning as a purely methodological precept lying at the heart of dialectical analysis. Marx's method consists in constantly moving from part to whole, and from whole to part, so that a fact is never a given datum to be isolated from other facts but related to the meaning-endowing structure of a larger whole:

> . . . a dress becomes really a dress only by being worn, a house which is unhabited is indeed not really a house; in other words a product as distinct from a simple natural object manifests itself as a product, *becomes* a product, only in consumption . . . which, by destroying the product, gives it the finishing touch, for the product is a product, not because it is materialised activity but only in so far as it is an object for an active subject (Marx, 1971, p. 196).

Facts are meaningful only through a process of *mediation*, in their intrinsic and extrinsic relationships with wholes; facts exist only within the totality of social relations and institutions. Marx is thus opposed to positivistic objectivism: all facts are saturated with meaning since they are mediated through human consciousness and practice. Science must assimilate this important relation of subject–object, whole and part into its analysis of society.

But does this argument suggest that objectivity is actually impossible? Much of the confusion which has surrounded Marx's sociology is linked to a misunderstanding of his methodology which actively seeks to unify the subjective and objective nature of social reality and social analysis. In the 'Preface' to *Capital* he writes that 'in the analysis of economic forms neither microscopes nor chemical reagents are of use. The force of abstraction must replace both', and in the *Grundrisse* he argues that while the correct scientific approach superficially begins from 'real and concrete elements', actual preconditions such as population or the world market, such a procedure is wrong for the apparently concrete is in reality abstract:

> Population is an abstraction if, for instance, one disregards the classes of which it is composed. These classes in turn remain empty terms if one does not know the factors on which they depend e.g. wage, labour, capital and so on. These presuppose exchange, division of labour, prices, etc. For example, capital is nothing without wages, labour, . . . value, money, price, etc. If one were to take population as the point of departure, it would be a very vague notion of a complex whole and through closer definition one would arrive analytically at increasingly simple concepts; from imaginary concrete terms one would move to more and more tenuous abstractions until one reached the most simple definitions. From here it would be necessary to make the journey again in the opposite direction until one arrived once more at the concept of population which is this time not a vague notion of a whole, but a totality comprising many determinations and relations (Marx, 1971, pp. 205–6).

Scientific method in the study of society is therefore the opposite of factual observation which always begins from the concrete and works towards the abstract; scientific inquiry does not adopt the standpoint of the raw material itself but seeks the 'inner structure' of the object by beginning from the general categories. Thus classical political economy was correct to start with population but wrong to define it as a concrete fact rather than as an abstract whole, which necessarily approximates to an ideal, general form emptied of complex and chaotic empirical material. To advance 'from the abstract to the concrete is simply the way in which thinking assimilates the concrete and reproduces it as a concrete mental category'. Thus the study of capitalism as a system must begin, not from particular capitals, competition and other elements which constitute its historic reality, but from 'capital as such', 'capital in general'. 'The introduction of many capitals must not interfere with the investigation here. The relation of the many is better explained after we have studied what they have in common, the quality of being capital . . . Capital in general as distinct from particular capitals does indeed appear (1) only as an abstraction; not an arbitrary abstraction, but one which grasps the specific differences which distinguish capital from other forms of wealth . . . (2) however, capital in general, as distinct from particular real capitals, is itself a real existence' (Marx, 1973, pp. 517, 449).

Capitalism is thus studied as an abstraction, a pure form, leaving out all the complex, historically specific complicating features, the 'appearance' as opposed to its 'inner essence or structure'. Marx's holistic methodology therefore assumes an ideal capitalism, one which is never actually present in reality, a model which is employed throughout his analysis of social change, class formation and social structure. The analysis of production, for example, is usually thought of in terms of specific persons or historical periods, but all stages of production share common features: '*Production in general* is an abstraction, but a sensible abstraction in so far as it actually emphasises and defines the common aspects and thus avoids repetition.' Marx argues that some features are found in 'the most modern as well as the most ancient epochs', but the 'so-called *general conditions* of all and every production . . . are nothing but the abstract conceptions which do not define any of the actual historical stages of production' (Marx, 1971, pp. 189–93). The relation between production, distribution, exchange and consumption can be established only by isolating the inner nature of production, the determinations common to all its forms and grasping the ways in which the historically specific elements depart from the general since in this lies the secret of their development.

Marx's method is thus to begin from a pre-given whole, such as population, production, the state, etc., and to abstract further the elements comprising the whole; then, through a process of successive approximations, relate these elements organically to the whole itself. When he writes that 'the subject, society, must always be envisaged . . . as the pre-condition of comprehension', Marx implies that no category, by itself, can constitute an adequate starting point for scientific social analysis. Both explanation and comprehension, the historical and genetic determinations of an object, together with a grasp of its inner structure and relations with the whole – the diachronic and synchronic – are unified within Marx's dialectical methodological framework. Thus, in the first two volumes of *Capital*, Marx abstracts and simplifies capitalist society to one basic relation, of capital to labour, its inner structure, arguing that if this constitutes the dominant relation then it becomes possible to determine the existence of laws, trends and the possibility of prediction. It is for this reason that any account of Marx's sociology of class, conflict and social change must relate to his discussion of methodology.

Class formation and class consciousness

In the *Philosophy of History* Hegel had argued that scientific understanding presupposed the ability of science to distinguish the essential from the inessential. For Marx, the 'leading thread' of his socio-historical-economic studies during the 1850s, led him to identify and isolate the mode of production as the basic determinant of social structure, class formation, class conflict and ideology. Marx's earlier writings had not accorded production a central role in the analysis of class formation and, in general, a simplified two-class model is postulated which derives its force, not from the concept of surplus value, but from a speculative, philosophical view of social development. In *The Communist Manifesto* the logic of capitalist economic development is described in terms of a sharp polarisation of class forces: 'Our epoch, the epoch of the bourgeoisie, possesses . . . this distinctive feature; it has simplified the class antagonism. Society as a whole is splitting up into two great hostile camps, into two great classes directly facing each other: Bourgeoisie and Proletariat' (Marx and Engels, 1962, Vol. 1, pp. 34–5).

In his polemical writings Marx frequently advanced this oversimplified model of capitalist stratification; in his more scientific and historical studies, however, this simplistic, dichotomic structure is repudiated. In his *The Eighteenth Brumaire of Louis Bonaparte* (1852), for example, Marx distinguished between the financial, industrial and petty-

84

bourgeoisie, proletariat, landlords and free farmers, while in other studies of France and Germany he noted the existence of bourgeoisie, farmers, peasants, agricultural workers, lumpen-proletariat (the 'dangerous classes') and feudal lords. Marx describes some of these categories as 'transition classes' their existence contradicted by the necessary historical development of capitalism, a standpoint which comes close to asserting that only bourgeoisie and proletariat constitute the essential structure of capitalist social formations. But, in general, Marx never articulated a simple two-class model as an *historical* fact emphasising rather the *complexity* of class formation and structure within capitalism.

Marx's second theory of class develops the concept of plurality of structure in which the category of middle class is especially important. The middle classes are defined as variegated groups comprising small producers, petty-bourgeoisie (employers of small fractions of labour), those engaged in the 'circulation of commodities' (marketing, buying, selling), the middle men (wholesalers, shopkeepers, speculators), those who 'command in the name of capital' (managers, etc.) and their assistants, supervisors, book-keepers, clerks, and finally 'ideological classes' embracing lawyers, journalists, clergy, state officials such as the military and police. In his historical studies the simplified model of the earlier philosophical writings disappears and Marx argues that the basic tendency of capitalism is not necessarily towards class polarisation but towards augmenting the middle classes especially those performing important 'social functions' such as professional groups, since they exercise significant roles in the maintenance of bourgeois society. As capitalism develops its productive forces, this class increases in size and influence and Marx suggests that 'the constantly growing number of the middle classes which, situated between the workers on the one side and the capitalists and landlords on the other side, [living] mainly and directly on revenue . . . press like a heavy burden on the labouring class, enlargening the social security and power of the upper ten thousand' (Marx, 1964–72, Vol. 2, p. 573).

These statements clearly contradict the view that Marx's theory of class is dichotomic for he accepts Thomas Malthus's statement, in his work on political economy (1836), that the growth of the middle classes and a constant decrease in the working proletariat is in effect 'the course of bourgeois society'. But to understand these statements it is essential to relate them to Marx's methodology. The analysis of capitalism was based initially on a 'pure' model purged of all complicating historical factors such as foreign trade, monopoly, colonialism, trade unions, the role of the state, a model dominated by the capital–labour relation. In the course of analysis, throughout the three volumes of *Capital* more and more empirically specific and complicating features are reintroduced so that the model increasingly approximates to a complex, rich, concrete historically specific capitalism.

In *Capital* Marx was mainly concerned with English capitalism as the most highly developed form in the nineteenth century and his comments on class are particularly significant. He identifies three broad social classes, the owners of labour-power, capital and land, their sources consisting of revenue, wages, profit and ground rent, arguing that they constitute the 'three big classes of modern society based on the capitalist mode of production'. In England, Marx adds, although the economic structure is highly developed, 'the stratification of classes does not appear in its pure form. *Middle and intermediate strata* even here obliterate lines of demarcation'. The tendency of capitalism in its pure form is to concentrate property in fewer hands, force the middle classes downwards into the proletariat and transform all labour into wage labour. But in reality capitalist development produces a complex structure of classes and class relations. Class is never a single homogeneous unity but rather a cluster of groups, or fractions, sharing a similar work function, values, aspirations and interests. This complex structure leads to frequent conflicts within the class itself, between the differentiated interests, as in the case of revenue derived from ground rent which is common both to landowners, mine-owners as well as property owners. Thus the dominant class is never a simple homogeneous whole but consists of fractions representing different economic and political interests, such as industrial and financial bourgeoisie, officials of the state apparatus and the leading 'ideological classes' within civil society, the law, politics, journalism. Similarly, the working class is differentiated through the various branches of industry, different skills and pay, and the weight of traditions. But Marx was insistent that a class is a class only when it is conscious of its interests and organised for pursuing those interests through its own institutions. This is the meaning of his remarks on the French peasantry:

> Their mode of production isolates them from one another instead of bringing them into mutual intercourse . . . In so far as millions of families live under economic conditions of existence that separate their mode of life, their interests and their culture from those of other classes and place them in opposition to them, *they constitute a class*. In so far as there is only a local connection between the small-holding peasants, and the identity of their interests *begets no community, and no political organisation*, they do not constitute a class (Marx and Engels, 1962, Vol. 1, p. 334).

The working class is thus only a class when organised for class action: 'There is one element of success the workers possess: its great numbers. But numbers will weigh in the balance only when united by organisation and guided by knowledge.' But in many ways the actual historical evolution of nineteenth-century capitalism suggested that revolutionary class consciousness would be sapped by 'complicating' elements such as Engels noted with the reformist policies pursued by trade unions. Marx's abstract, pure model of capitalism excluded any possibility of social mobility which would clearly function as a stabilising process in a context of class inequality. In volume three of *Capital*, as the analysis of capitalism approximates more closely to historical reality, Marx noted the possibility that numbers of propertyless individuals, by their own efforts and through their ability, accede to the capitalist class: 'Although this circumstance continually brings an unwelcome number of new soldiers of fortune into the field and into competition with the already existing capitalists, it also reinforces the supremacy of capital itself, expands its base and enables it to recruit ever new forces for itself out of the substratum of society . . . the more a ruling class is able to assimilate the foremost minds of the ruled class, the more stable and dangerous becomes its rule' (Marx, 1958, p. 587).

How then is change possible? The simple class conflict model postulated an inherent conflict of interests between bourgeoisie and proletariat leading inevitably to a heightening of class consciousness and the possibility of revolutionary practice. But if the course of capitalist development negates the development of a polarised class structure does this suggest that revolutionary consciousness is impossible, or at least extremely unlikely? To answer these questions it is necessary to examine Marx's theory of class in terms of his larger analysis of capitalism as a system dominated by objective laws of development.

Laws of development: the problem of historical determinism

Marx defined capitalist society as a system, a structured whole dominated by the mode of production and the contradictions generated between privately owned economic forces and collective, social relations of production. This law, which attributes social development to internal contradictions within the 'base' 'superstructure' model, is expressed in terms of the dichotomic structure of class forces in *The Communist Manifesto*, and capitalist society is characterised as splitting into two 'hostile camps' with irreconcilable interests. In *Capital* Marx discusses class at the end of the third volume and only then in fragmentary, unfinished form. His comments here will appear strange if his methodology is misunderstood, for, as I have argued, Marx is seeking the 'essential structure', the 'secret' of capitalist development, in the first two volumes of *Capital*. Marx's two-class model, 'the working class, disposing only of its labour-power, and the capitalist class, which has a monopoly of the social means of production', assumes that the 'laws of capitalist production operate in their pure form' and therefore:

1. With the labour–capital relation as the dominant element which structures the development and form of the capitalist social formation the analysis of change eliminates any active influence of the 'superstructure'.
2. The capital–labour relation is reduced to its simplest

form, capitalists and workers defined as standard types 'the personifications of economic categories, embodiments of particular class relations and class interests'. The capitalist is thus portrayed as 'fanatically bent on making value expand itself' and 'ruthlessly' forcing humanity to produce for the sake of production and the development of the productive powers of society.

The first volume of *Capital* operates at a high level of abstraction, the analysis of 'capital in general' with its assumption of society consisting solely of capitalists and workers; volume two deepens the analysis as Marx discusses the accumulation of capital, its reproduction and circulation, while in volume three 'capital in general' becomes 'many capitals', their relationships and thus capitalism as an historical–empirical reality. The abstractions underlying the first volume – commodities exchanging according to the cost of production in standard man-hours, the absence of monopoly, the appropriation of the entire economic surplus by the capitalist class (the state taking nothing), the two-class model, etc. – produce laws which must not be taken as concrete predictions about the future since they may be 'modified' by 'other circumstances' that comprise the specifically historical.

Marx's model of capitalism is a complex totality in which the 'superstructural' elements exercise an increasing role in modifying the generalisations of the first volume. This is particularly the case with Marx's concept of capitalist crisis which has frequently been interpreted as the historically inevitable consequence of economic laws working with 'iron necessity' towards intensified class conflict and social breakdown. It is true that in *Capital*, volume one, there are many passages which support this historicist interpretation, but when the concept of crisis is integrated within the context of totality a radically different view emerges:

From time to time the conflict of antagonistic tendencies finds vent in crises ... momentary and forcible solutions of the existing contradictions ... violent eruptions which for a time restore the disturbed equilibrium. The contradiction ... consists in that the capitalist mode of production involves a tendency towards the absolute development of the productive forces regardless of the value and the surplus-value it contains, and regardless of the social conditions under which capitalist production takes place; while on the other hand, its aim is to preserve the value of the existing capital and promote its self-expansion to the highest limit (Marx, 1958, pp. 243–4).

The law of the falling rate of profit can thus co-exist with the expansion of total profit and clearly Marx does not postulate a simple breakdown theory. Indeed, his emphasis on the active role of ideology and consciousness point emphatically towards practice if a transition from capitalism to socialism is to be possible. Marx emphasises that social change is not a mechanical process which casts humanity as passive onlooker; humanity is not simply a medium through which external historical laws operate.

Yet this was Engels's interpretation in his definition of historical materialism as historical explanation which seeks the 'ultimate cause' of the economic development of society in changes within the modes of production and exchange, division of labour and differentiation of society into antagonistic social classes. Engels defined Marxism as economic determinism, the ineluctable workings of the infrastructure of society, and the abolition of the creative human subject. This is clearly an inadequate interpretation in terms both of Marx's methodological standpoint in *Capital* and his insistence on the active role of the superstructure, and thus of ideas, on the course of social change. Social development is not inevitably mapped out by the workings of economic laws since historical laws exist only through individuals, through collective human action. Of course, socio-historical laws can be analysed as objective results of extra-human forces; but this process of mystification and reification is foreign to Marx's thought. The role of the active human subject in social development constitutes the most important element in the continuity that characterises the early and the later writings of Marx. Marx's concept of diachronic historical laws is not positivist for while the positivist trend in nineteenth-century natural science exerted a powerful influence on socialist thought it was Engels, not Marx, whose formulations approximated to scientism.

In *Anti-Duhring* (1877), for example, Engels argued that 'modern materialism is essentially dialectical, and no longer needs any philosophy standing above the other sciences. As soon as each individual science is bound to make clear its position in the great totality of things, a special science dealing with this totality is superfluous. That which survives independently of all earlier philosophy is the science of thought and its laws – formal logic and dialectics. Everything else is subsumed in the positive science of nature and history'. Engels thus dismisses philosophy in favour of a 'positive knowledge of the world', a 'positive science' which effectively eliminates the active role of the subject as is evidenced in his conceptions of base and superstructure and economic determination in the last instance. Other Marxists have followed Engels's positivist interpretation of Marxism restricting it to a method and mode of investigation, a heuristic device which facilitates analysis of the relations between discrete social and historical elements.

But Marx's theory of social change cannot be assimilated to this positivist reading: the active and creative role of the subject remains at the centre of the theories of class formation, conflict and consciousness. Unlike Comte, Marx did not summarily reject philosophy and when, in the writings of the early 1840s, he discussed the necessary abolition of philosophy he implied not its total repudiation but a transition to a self-conscious practice which would realise its immanent values socially and thus free it from abstract, speculative and alienated forms. In his eighth thesis on Feuerbach he postulated the dialectical union of human cognition and practical activity, a theoretical position he maintained throughout his life's work:

> Social life is essentially practical. All mysteries which mislead theory into mysticism find their rational solution in human practice and in the comprehension of this practice (Marx and Engels, 1964, pp. 645–7).

Practice negates passive contemplation as the basic structure of philosophical and thus worldly understanding; the significance of Marx's activist epistemology for his sociology cannot be exaggerated. Unlike Comte's sociological positivism, Marx depicts humanity as the active producer of the social world which transforms the external world as it transforms itself, not as isolated individuals, or individual wills, but as members of social groups and classes.

Nevertheless, Marx's sociological analysis of capitalism tends to conflict with his libertarian epistemology. He describes the underlying tendency of capitalism *as a system* to transform active individuals into passive objects, and produce a social world experienced and understood as an external, constraining datum eliminating all sense of creative autonomy. For the mature Marx humanity was conceived precisely in its relations with this social world, and although he argues that the course of social development hinges on the objective application of science and technology to production, it is humanity which ultimately changes the world. In the *Grundrisse* he writes:

> Nature builds no machines, no locomotives, railways . . . These are the products of human industry; natural material transformed into organs of the human will over nature, or of human participation in nature. They are organs of the human brain, created by human hand; the power of knowledge objectified (Marx, 1973, p. 706).

In the same humanist spirit he describes the development of west European agriculture:

> Not only do the objective conditions change in the act of reproduction, e.g. the village becomes a town, the wilderness a cleared field, etc. but the producers change too in that they bring out new qualities in themselves, develop themselves in production, transform themselves, develop new powers and ideas, new modes of intercourse, new needs and new language (Marx, 1973, p. 494).

It is impossible to understand the relation of Marx's 'iron laws' of capitalism – the concept of capitalism as a system existing independently of the individuals who comprise it – to his emphasis on the creative, individual subject – a collective subject organised in groups – unless these contradictory formulations are analysed in terms of his theory of civil society. Marx describes capitalism as effectively liberating civil society from the domination of the state and fostering the creation of a separate and independent spheres in which the new industrial classes, the bourgeoisie and the proletariat, develop their own distinctive institutions, political organisations and modes of activity. Capitalism as a mode of production made possible an enlargement of human practice and the reality of an active subject. Although initially 'the development of the capacity of the human species takes place at the cost of the majority of human individuals and even classes, at the end it breaks through this contradiction and coincides with the development of the individual; the higher development of individuality is thus only achieved by an historical process' (Marx, 1964–72, pp. 117–18).

The fundamental contradiction in Marx's social theory lies between the centralising trends of capitalist economic forces his work outlined, and the real expansion of human freedom and autonomy engendered by these same processes which find their expression in the form of social and cultural institutions. Capitalism, as a highly centralised system of economic production, comes into conflict with its potentially democratic culture. Marx's sociology of capitalism is structured around this contradiction: as with Comte, Marx defines society as a system in which objective laws operate independently of, and frequently against, the will of individuals; yet, as Marx emphasised, capitalism makes possible human practice, control and planning, the active intervention of the human subject in historical development. Marx's concept of laws, of course, differs sharply from Comte's: laws are man-made and not natural and thus open to drastic change through human intervention. But there is a limit to effective human intervention: capitalism *as a whole* eludes conscious control and Marx, following Smith, Ferguson and Hegel suggests again and again that social development emerges from the unintended effects of economic forces and human action. Marx's sociological model, therefore, is one which incorporates human action and practice into a systemic structure of collectivist and historically necessary forces.

This is the contradiction which lies at the heart of Marx's dialectical social theory illuminating the problems of the democratic strands in the theory of civil society – that change evolves through the collective, democratic actions of ordinary individuals seeking to develop their own social, political and cultural institutions – and the strongly collectivist elements of the capitalist social and economic order which suggest the eclipse of individuality and representative institutions. Marx failed to resolve the contradictions in his thought between the historicist notion of economic necessity and his humanist sociology.

PART II
CLASSICAL SOCIOLOGY

4
Critique of Positivism: I Durkheim

Durkheim and the development of sociology

Emile Durkheim (1858–1917) has the distinction of being the first professional, academic French sociologist to be appointed to a Chair in Sociology (Paris, 1913). For Durkheim, sociology was a vocation. Almost single-handed he forced the academic community to accept sociology as a rigorous and scientific discipline. In his teaching and in his research Durkheim laid down the standards whereby sociology was to be judged. In 1895 he published the first major methodology study of sociology in which he observed that none of the nineteenth-century sociologists – Comte, Mill, Spencer – 'hardly went beyond generalities concerning the nature of societies, the relationships between the social and the biological realms' and were largely 'content . . . to make a cursory inquiry into the most general resources that sociological research has at its command' (Durkheim, 1982, p. 48.) Durkheim set himself the task of defining the object of sociology and the methods appropriate to it. His contributions to the study of industrialisation, suicide, religion, morality and the methodology of social science aroused enormous controversy, but their influence on the development of sociology as well as other areas of social science, especially anthropology, have been far-reaching.

Durkheim began his career in sociology at a time when the French educational system was being expanded and modernised. This was the period which followed the national humiliation of defeat in the Franco-Prussian war (1870–1) and

97

the German annexation of Alsace-Lorraine. The intense nationalism of the third French Republic formed the ideological context for the secular reforms carried out by the state throughout the higher educational system. Durkheim's sociology has been described as contributing to the formation of a new civic ethic, a modern republican ideology which rejected both traditional French Catholicism and a deeply entrenched social conservatism. Thus the educational reforms of the 1880s and 1890s were mainly designed to free the French university system from the grip of traditional ideological influences especially those associated with residual, pre-bourgeois social groups.

In 1887 Durkheim took up a teaching appointment at the University of Bordeaux, which was the first French university to provide organised courses in the field of the social sciences especially sociology. The teaching of social science had a practical basis in supporting the modernising ideals of educational reform. Durkheim's first courses, for example, were specifically addressed to teachers and covered an impressive range of topics from ethics, social change, suicide, the family and education to socialism and the history of sociology itself. Durkheim was particularly concerned to clarify the scientific status of sociology and clearly differentiate it from socialism. In late nineteenth-century France sociology was often regarded as synonymous with socialism and therefore hostile to bourgeois culture and values, to religion and the family and peaceful social change.

In the years between 1887 and 1902, when he became Professor of Education at the Sorbonne, Durkheim produced a series of studies which defined the nature of a scientific sociology. *The Division of Labour* (1893), *The Rules of Sociological Method* (1895), *Suicide* (1897) together with *The Elementary Forms of the Religious Life* (1912) are works in which Durkheim set out his conception of sociology as 'the science of institutions, their genesis and their functioning' (Durkheim, 1982, p. 45) in opposition to the eclectic, individualistic and often crudely journalistic approaches of other contemporary social scientists. In particular Durkheim sought to distinguish sociology, as the science which studies the objective reality of 'social facts', from psychology which he defined as the study of individual consciousness. Sociological explanation dealt with collective, not individual forces. The concept of social fact became one of Durkheim's 'fundamental principles' referring to all objects of knowledge which have to be built up, not through mental activity, but from observation and experiment. Social phenomena were external things reflecting a reality very different from the reality conceived by an individual. In the genesis of a social fact, Durkheim argued, individuals exercise a role but 'in order for a social fact to exist several individuals . . . must have interacted together' (Durkheim, 1982, p. 45).

Durkheim's definition of the field of sociology – the study of external social facts – does not necessarily imply a thoroughgoing positivism. Social facts were not simple objects, or things, existing independently of human consciousness and action and therefore objectively 'visible' to the observer. A social fact was a collective entity – family, religion, professional organisation – characterised by an underlying order, or structure, hidden from ordinary perception. Durkheim's sociology was an attempt to establish the pattern which lay behind all observable phenomena. Thus Spencer's 'individualism' contrasts sharply with Durkheim's 'methodological collectivism'. Social facts were thus defined by Durkheim as structures which, through their manifest forms, constrain and regulate human actions. External to the individual, social facts are 'invested with coercive power' which enable them to 'impose' their influence on individuals even against their will: 'We can no more choose the design of our houses than the cut of our clothes – at least, the one is as much obligatory as the other' (Durkheim, 1982, p. 58). Thus language is a social fact in Durkheim's sense, a system of rules which determine the nature of individual utterances although the speaker will have no knowledge of the rules that govern ordinary speech performance.

Social facts thus become internalised and rule individuals 'from within' becoming 'an integral part' of the self. In this way society enters the individual as a moral force. Sociology was therefore not the study of external facts but rather the ways in which social facts are saturated with moral elements. In *The Division of Labour* Durkheim described morality as the 'least indispensable, the strictly necessary, the daily bread without which societies cannot exist'. Sociology was concerned essentially with social cohesion and social order, the ways whereby individuals are integrated into a functioning social whole.

Thus although committed to the ideals of objective, empirical science Durkheim's work, especially in *The Division of Labour*, falls firmly within the Grand Theory Tradition of nineteenth-century social thought. His theory of the development of society from a 'mechanical' to an 'organic' type is similar to the philosophy of history which underpins the sociology of Comte and Spencer. Beginning from philosophy Durkheim was frequently brought back to its central issues in his later work; he remained extremely sensitive to the relation of sociology to philosophy, his many discussions and analyses of concepts such as anomie, social change and the division of labour are saturated with philosophical implications. The concept of social crisis, for example, is defined largely in moral terms and clearly indebted to Saint-Simon and Comte, a point emphasised in the 'Preface' to the first edition of *The Division of Labour*. It was not a question of extracting ethics from science, he argued, but rather of establishing 'the science of ethics', treating the facts of moral life according to the methods of the positive sciences. Although the study of reality does not necessarily imply any reforming commitment 'we should judge our researches to have no worth at all if they were to have only a speculative interest'. Social science must study the 'state of moral health' in relation to changes in the environment. The result, Durkehim argued, is not intellectual indifference but 'extreme prudence'; social science governs practice in that science provides 'the rules of action for the future', and by establishing the laws of society distinguishes the 'normal' and 'healthy' forms of social organisation from the 'pathological' and 'abnormal' (Lukes, 1973, pp. 87–8).

In many important respects, therefore, Durkheim remained a faithful disciple of Comte's positivism. He rejected Comte's theory of the unity of the sciences and the law of three stages as metaphysical speculation, but accepted Comte's notion of consensus and the sociologism and scientism that underpinned the fatalistic concept of the human subject. Durkheim defined society as the sum total of social facts, objective, thing-like elements, moulds 'into which we are forced to cast our actions' which resist all attempts to change and modify them by individual volition. Humanity is thus determined by things which stand outside itself for 'even when we succeed in triumphing, the opposition we have encountered suffices to alert us that we are faced with something independent of ourselves' (Durkheim, 1982, p. 70). But in what sense do social facts control human actions? As we have seen, Durkheim argued that the individual experiences objective reality subjectively acting in conformity to its constraining nature. But this formulation assumes a passive relation of subject to object, a position which Durkheim does not sustain in all his sociological studies notably *Suicide*, where he comes close to accepting that action which follows the constraining influence of social facts does so because the individual, the subject, has interpreted the external facts in specific ways. Nevertheless, there is a strong, mechanical element in Durkheim's sociology as, for example, when he argues that 'states of consciousness can and ought to be considered from without and not from the point of view of the consciousness experiencing it', a standpoint reiterated in his brief discussion of Marxist methodology:

> We consider as fruitful this idea that social life must be explained, not by the conception of it held by those who participate in it, but by the profound causes which escape consciousness; and we also think that these causes must be sought chiefly in the way in which the associated individuals are grouped. We even think that it is on this condition, and on this condition alone, that history can become a science and sociology in consequence exist (Lukes, 1973, p. 231).

Durkheim's sympathy towards mechanical materialism was clearly related to his attempt to rid sociology of the atomism inherent in other contemporary social theorists such as Tarde, but the result was a conception of society less the product of collective human labour than as a constraining abstraction. Durkheim's epistemology has the effect of splitting society into two separate structures, 'social milieu as the determining factor of social evolution' enabling the sociologist to establish causal relations, and the subjective state defined as a passive process of socialisation.

In Durkheim's writings the concept of milieu plays a crucial role. The term itself characterised virtually all forms of nineteenth-century positivism (Taine, for example) but was never adequately theorised. Durkheim's usage derived also from the natural scientist, Claude Bernard, who employed milieu as the key to analysing the internal system of living organisms, the blood system, its various fluids, their functional relations in the maintenance of a constant body temperature and thus equilibrium. It is not surprising that Durkheim's sociology enjoins the methodological principle of externality with the concept of society as an inherently equilibrating organism.

But Durkheim did not hold to a rigidly mechanical conception of society. For Durkheim society was a moral reality. Thus he was especially critical of Spencer's contractual notion of social relations in which the moral element played no part: 'The division of labour does not present individuals to one another', he wrote in opposition to Spencer's exchange theory of the division of work, 'but social functions'. Social solidarity could never flow from an atomistic concept of individuals freely pursuing their own private interests: social reality could not be defined in terms of individuals who exchange goods and services and thus contribute to social cohesion.

Durkheim firmly rejected utilitarian atomism as an adequate perspective for social science. Society was a moral fact and science must recognise this. Thus he was equally opposed to the influential work produced by the German sociologist Ferdinand Tönnies (1855–1936), *Gemeinschaft und Gesellschaft* (1887) (translated as *Community and Association*), which advanced the view that modern industrial capitalism, a society increasingly dominated by purely economic forces, was losing the authentic naturalism of earlier, pre-industrial social formations. Tönnies's depiction of modern society was one in which the cash nexus penetrated all spheres of social life determining the basic forms of social relationships. For Durkheim, Tönnies's concept of society, which largely derived from the writings of Marx and the German socialist, Lassalle, represented everything in their darkest colours, a simple dichotomy being established between the assumed spontaneous social solidarity of pre-industrial village life and the atomised, egoistic individualism of modern urban culture (Tönnies, 1973, pp. 245–7). Tönnies's analysis suggested that social cohesion and social regulation were possible only through the intervention of an external institution, namely the state.

Durkheim's early sociological writings, while defining society externally, posed the problem of social cohesion in terms which suggest that as social solidarity is moral it can never flow from above, that is, be imposed on civil society itself. Durkheim agreed with Tönnies in rejecting Spencer's notion of an immanent harmony of individual interests that by themselves promote a spontaneous cohesion, but they disagreed on the role which centralised authority must play in a modern industrial society. In this sense Durkheim's sociology was opposed both to Comte's authoritarian Positivist Church as the means of promoting social solidarity, as well as Marxist socialism with its central tenet of a centralised state functioning as the prime agency for social reorganisation and development of human communities.

It is this latter emphasis which has led some critics to argue that Durkheim's sociology was merely an attempt to combat 'the positions of the class conscious socialist movement' which had developed during the latter half of the nineteenth century (Therborn, 1976, p. 269). During the 1890s many of Marx's important writings appeared in Franch translation and a distinctive Marxist intellectual and political culture emerged. French university students formed reading groups explicitly to study *Capital*, while many of the leading academic journals discussed Marxist ideas, reviewed books on Marxism and posed the whole question of the scientific status of Marxist theory. Durkheim criticised Marxism for the class bias of its theory noting, in 1899, that the 'malaise' within modern society was not something centred on a particular class 'but is general throughout the whole of society', affecting both employers and employees although taking different forms in each case, 'an anxious and painful restlessness in the case of the capitalist, discontent and irritation in that of the worker'. State socialism was not the solution, for the crisis of modern society was not one of conflicting material interests but essentially a matter of 'remaking the moral constitution of society' (Lukes, 1973, p. 323).

Durkheim rejected, therefore, the political assumptions and theory of revolutionary socialism insisting that class conflict derived less from any basic structure within capitalism than from the necessary transition from traditional to industrial society, involving the disintegration of one set of values without their replacement by other cogent values: property ownership was secondary to this problem as was the forms of class tension. Both Marx's theoretical and revolutionary socialist conceptions, although widely discussed in French intellectual circles especially through the work of Georges Sorel (1847–1922) who at one time sought to synthesise the work of Marx and Durkheim, exerted little influence on the development of Durkheim's sociology. Nevertheless, Durkheim was acquainted with Marx's writings and followed the debate between Marxists and other social scientists with great interest although inclining to the view that the value of *Capital* lay in its 'suggestive philosophical perspectives' rather than its 'scientific' conclusions. Durkheim's understanding of Marxism, however, relied almost entirely on secondary sources and these tended to be mechanistic and positivist. The Marxist and socialist movement which developed both in France and in Germany during the latter part of the nineteenth century has been described as intellectually shallow, simplifying and vulgarising Marx's theories into a crude economic determinism. Contemporary Marxism in fact made no lasting contribution to the development of sociology being largely defined as a mistaken, although useful doctrine against which the genuinely scientific claims of sociology could be tested.

Durkheim's main thrust against Marxism was its emphasis on centralised authority as the only viable foundation of social order and therefore the assimilation of the social and the political to the economic. By 1902, in the second edition of *The Division of Labour*, Durkheim was advocating occupational associations centred within civil society as the most effective means of regulating the anomic state of modern industry, arguing that with 'the establishment of an occupational ethic and law in the different economic occupations, the corporations, instead of remaining a confused aggregate, without unity, would have to become again a defined, organised group . . . a public institution'. It was only through such collective institutions that the individualistic and particular interests of modern society might be subordinated harmoniously to the general interest: 'A group is not only a moral authority which dominates the life of its members; it is also a source of life *sui generis*. From it comes a warmth which animates its members, making them intensely human, destroying their egotisms.' The relation of state and corporations, state and individuals is 'intercalated', mediated by 'a whole series of secondary groups' close to the individual and thus able to integrate him/her into 'the general torrent of social life'. It is the 'density' of these occupational groups that enables them to exercise a regulative moral role and fill the void, for without such a system of organs 'the normal functioning of the common life is found wanting' (Durkheim, 1964, pp. 26–9).

Durkheim's concept of modern society, then, separated the state from civil society, identifying the sources of social solidarity within the civil institutions. The implication of Durkheim's formulations is that without a living, vibrant and independent civic culture society as a whole must disintegrate into anarchy and anomie. There is, therefore, a contradiction between the views expressed in *The Division of Labour* that the individual is basically passive, the product of society (the standpoint of nineteenth-century positivist sociology) demanding an external mode of social regulation, and Durkheim's later views which emphasise the concept of society as constructed through the mediations of autonomous institutions which, by their very nature, are organically bound up with the individuals they effectively regulate. This subtle shift of emphasis in Durkheim's sociology is related to the whole problematic of positivism.

Positivism and morality

Durkheim's sociology was initially conceived within the evolutionary theoretical framework of Comte and Spencer. Society constituted an organic whole in which the various elements functioned to maintain equilibrium. Durkheim rejected Spencer's version of methodological individualism and its utilitarian postulates, as well as the prevailing atomism of contemporary French social scientists such as Gabriel Tarde. Sociological explanation, he argued, must be independent of psychology and subjective consciousness. Writing in the 'Preface' of the second volume of *L'Année Sociologique* he advocated techniques of social investigation that would establish types of laws and the interconnectedness of facts:

> The principle underlying this method is . . . that religion, juridicial, moral and economic facts must all be treated in conformance with their nature as social facts. Whether describing or explaining them, one must relate them to a particular social milieu, to a definite type of society (Wolff, 1964, p. 348).

Wholes cannot be analysed sociologically in terms of individuals: the unit of analysis is 'milieu', the collective forces and facts which thus constitute the object of social science. For Durkheim, the social was irreducible, a *sui generis*, and thus the psychological element was irrelevant. Durkheim's social realism was clearly opposed to those social scientists who adopted a voluntaristic, subjective and psychological standpoint. In his debate with Durkheim, Tarde wrote: 'I am a nominalist. There can only be individual actions and interactions. The rest is nothing but a metaphysical entity, and mysticism' (Lukes, 1973, p. 313). In *Suicide* Durkheim explicitly took issue with Tarde's sociological atomism arguing that social facts were objective datums, things which exist independently of individuals, of individual psychology and human interactions: social facts can never be reduced to another order. Much of Durkheim's analysis in *Suicide* is aimed precisely at the reductionist implications in Tarde's formulation. The suicide rate is thus defined as embodying more than the sum total of individual acts of suicide; the suicide rate is a social fact, *sui generis*, characterised by its own unity, individuality and specific nature. The genuine sociological question is not *who* will commit suicide but the ways in which the suicide rate as an external social fact determines the propensity of individuals to kill themselves.

One of the fundamental problems of positivist sociology was the question of mediations: generally the individual subject was defined in terms of a simple, mechanical, one-to-one relationship with society, a relation in which consciousness, social action and social institutions constituted the products of a determinate external process of causation. The social and historical world was defined as a constraining, external datum, as a milieu with its own specific laws. Thus Comte's law of human progress, the theory that all societies necessarily pass through three stages of evolution from the theological to the positive becomes an external natural law that relegates the most outstanding individuals to the status of mere 'instruments' or 'organs of a predestined movement'. Durkheim accepted these Comtist formulations arguing that in 'affirming the specificity of social facts' he was following the Comtist sociological tradition: 'No further progress could be made until it was established that the laws of society are no different from those governing the rest of nature and that the method by which they are discovered is identical with that of the other sciences. This was Auguste Comte's contribution.' The social constitutes the true object of sociology and must be rigorously distinguished from other levels of human existence: the social is 'a reality *sui generis* in society, which exists by itself and by virtue of specific and necessary causes, and which, consequently, confound themselves with man's own nature' (Lukes, 1973, p. 68).

Durkheim's sociological positivism, however, differed sharply from Comte's in its solution to the problem of social cohesion: the key element in social solidarity is the autonomy of moral action. Durkheim's sociology is permeated by rationalist principles that lead away from his dogmatic positivism. In *The Division of Labour*, for example, he argues that 'a mechanistic conception of society does not preclude ideals', for demonstrating that 'things happen in accordance with laws, it does not follow that we have nothing to do'. Durkheim never satisfactorily solved this dualism of the autonomy of the moral act and the determinism of social facts and his later sociological work revolves around this problem of human action and a constraining milieu. Comte had remained insensitive to the human dimension of social evolution, Vico's injunction that the social world was the work of man; Durkheim's positivism grapples precisely with this problem.

Both Comte and Durkheim argued that the social system necessitated social regulation and as early as 1886 Durkheim wrote that society must be bound together by strong social bonds that were moral in nature. The point here is that although society is an organism it does not spontaneously produce equilibrium. Its normal, healthy state is one of harmony between its various elements, but Durkheim emphasised that in the absence of a strong moral centre society must inevitably collapse into anarchy and destruction. Sociological positivism defines society as a system, a structure of social facts in which unity develops only through moral action. It is in this sense, therefore, that Durkheim's sociology is rationalistic in that social cohesion is less the product of the workings of social milieu than the moral dimensions of social facts themselves. Pessimistic about humanity's possible sociability, with its insatiable appetites and egoism, Durkheim argued that there was nothing 'within an individual which constrains . . . appetites'; they can be constrained effectively only by external forces. If these are absent from the system then the result is general 'morbidity'

> What is needed if social order is to reign is that the mass of men be content with their lot. But what is needed for them to be content, is not that they have more or less but they be convinced they have no right to more. And for this, it is absolutely essential that there be an authority whose superiority they acknowledge and which tells them what is right (Durkheim, 1958, p. 200).

Social solidarity is not spontaneously produced by the internal workings of the social system. Durkheim's solution was a sociology which sought to integrate the subjective factor within his general positivist methodology. In effect, Durkheim argued that humanity, out of its own nature, creates a mode of voluntary social regulation that carries the force of moral obligation. It is important to grasp the shift in emphasis which occurs within Durkheim's work. In the essays written during 1897–9 the concept of 'collective representations' is further developed, and although closely related to the notion of social fact as collective phenomenon it is nevertheless a modification of the positivistic formulations of *The Division of Labour* and *The Rules of Sociological Method*. Already in the 'Preface' to *The Division of Labour* Durkheim had noted that modern society was increasingly losing the collective authority that flowed from 'traditional discipline' (Durkheim, 1964). Durkheim's solution was to argue that social solidarity rested in the collective representations of a universal system of thought.

In his essay, 'The Determination of Moral Facts' (1906) he identified morality with the universality of religious belief, arguing that social life itself can never 'shed all the characteristics that it holds in common with religion' (Durkheim, 1953, p. 48). Morality and religion are inextricably interwoven: there has always been 'morality in religion, and elements of the religious in morality'. It thus seemed to follow that moral life, and thus social life, possesses a 'sacred character' which inspires respect, awe and obedience. 'In the beginning, all is religious', wrote Durkheim, in opposition to the Marxist thesis that social and cultural life constituted mere derivatives of economic forces, and social change the automatic product of material conditions. Social life is more than this, a moral structure consisting of universal precepts built around religious values and ideas.

Many of these ideas can be traced to the influence of Kant whose rationalist philosophy exerted a powerful impact on Durkheim's intellectual contemporaries. Kantian philosophy offered an alternative to the scepticism and relativism implicit in nineteenth-century empiricism and positivism. Kant's rationalism postulated a universal concept of morality. Moral actions were defined in terms of the 'autonomy of the will' and the 'categorical imperative' and not as the product of external situation or experience. For Kant, morality was bound up with a voluntaristic subject rationally acting on the basis of universal axioms which were binding on everyone. The universality of morals demanded that subjects acted from duty to the ethical principles. Duty and willing were thus the basis of Kant's moral philosophy. And it was these elements which find their expression – not on an individual but communal level – in Durkheim's theory of collective representations and the constraining power of moral norms.

Comte's positivism had ended with a relativisation of all values: 'There is nothing good and bad absolutely speaking', he had written, 'everything is relative. This is the only absolute statement'. On this basis the moral anarchy which Durkheim identified as characterising nineteenth-century European society could be solved by many solutions including Comte's authoritarianism, Spencerian *laissez-faire* and even revolutionary socialism since all were equally relative and thus equally valid. Durkheim rejected Comte's positivist relativism by transforming sociological positivism into a science of moral activity in which social facts were related to a subjective, human element: there is, within Durkheim's sociology, especially the post-1895 writings, an implicit acceptance that humanity itself creates the social institutions that constrain and demand moral obligation, that it is humanity which develops out of its own nature the basis of social cohesion.

In the latter part of *Suicide* Durkheim argued that social life was made up of what he called 'collective representations', collective symbols through which society becomes 'conscious of itself'. Society can be constituted only by the creation of ideals which 'are simply the ideas' through which society sees itself. A mechanistic, purely external concept of society he now argued tended to eliminate its 'soul which is the composition of collective ideals' (Durkheim, 1952, pp. 312–16). Social facts are objective entities, Durkheim emphasised, but they also contain a significant subjective element which, combining within the individual's consciousness, forms representations of the social world. Collective life – social life – is thus reflected in these representations which effectively 'become autonomous realities independent of individuals' (Durkheim, 1953, pp. 23–6). Durkheim emphasised that collective representations differ from individual representations: for example, the conception of religion is more than individual feelings, rather a system which unifies states of mind, 'a characteristic way of thinking of collective existence'. In his essay on 'Pragmatism and Sociology' (1913) Durkheim noted democracy and the class struggle as further examples of collective representations, authority which imposes itself on the different members of the social group. Collective representations thus constitute the source of all human action for humanity is never motivated entirely by purely physical needs and desires but rather by residues from the past, 'habits', 'prejudices' all of which exercise an active role in social life.

Durkheim's sociological positivism thus redefined consciousness and ideology as more than epiphenomenal elements of material existence, 'but specifically mental phenomenon' which brings to light from time to time the collective representations of social life. Collective representations are 'expressly obligatory', proof of a higher source than the individual: collective representations flow from society itself. The subjective factor is thus embodied in the very nature of the social.

Durkheim defined authority, then, not in strict religious terms but in broad societal categories, for 'in the world of experience . . . only one being . . . possesses a richer and more complex reality than our own, and that is the collective being'. Only the collectivity – family, church, corporation – enjoys the essential attribute of 'sacredness' which Durkheim saw as necessary for moral authority. Duty and obligation are the stuff of morality commanding compliance because they 'direct our actions to ends that transcend us while at the same time appearing desirable'. Society transcends the individual, absorbs him; and society 'commands us because it is exterior and superior to us' and 'the moral distance between it and us makes it an authority before which our will defers'. Society is 'within us', it 'is us' and the 'collective sentiments' constitute 'the echo within us of the great voice of the collective' (Durkheim, 1953, p. 58).

Durkheim's critique of sociological positivism, however, raises serious problems: the reifed concept of social fact in *The Rules of Sociological Method* has been transformed into a collective and objective structure which functions in similar ways to facts as things. The notion of the great voice of the collective, for example, suggests a category of mediation missing from Durkheim's early work but it nevertheless remains committed to the central postulate of regulation. Humanity must be regulated although not by a purely external force. In one of his last writings Durkheim returned to this problem by defining human nature as dualistic, comprising both of sensory egoistic appetites and, since man is 'a thinking being', the faculty of conceptual thought and moral activity. Defining an egoist as one who pursues selfish ends, Durkheim argued that egoism was largely biological while morality was pre-eminently social. He concluded that humanity therefore 'cannot pursue moral ends without causing a split within ourselves' and yet at the same time 'we cannot live without representing to ourselves the world around us'. And arguing from his earlier standpoint which linked religion with morality he concluded that:

> ... even to the secular mind, duty, the moral imperative, is something august and sacred; and reason, the indispensable ally of moral activity, naturally inspires similar feelings. The duality of our nature is thus only a particular case of that division of things into the sacred and the profane that is the foundation of all religion (Wolff, 1964, pp. 325–39).

Two states of consciousness thus express on an individual level man's organic nature (egoism), while on a social and collective level they connect him with something that 'surpasses' him turning him towards the pursuit of other ends 'that we hold in common with other men; it is through them and them alone that we can communicate with others' (Wolff, 1964).

Durkheim's sociological positivism is therefore not as mechanistic as some of his early formulations might suggest. Consciousness is not the sum of determinate external influences. Rather, Durkheim attempts to show how society, necessarily forced to repress appetites, does so through an authority whose norms embody and express the other, moral/ conceptual and rational side of man's being. The division of 'normal' and 'pathological' flows precisely from this standpoint; the normal are those forces promoting social health, social integration with the collectivity, while the pathological reflect the breakdown of social solidarity. Durkheim's concept of sociology as a science of morals, his concern with social regulation and the possibility of community is central to his studies of the division of labour and suicide.

Division of labour, social cohesion and conflict

The Division of Labour develops a theory of historical evolution in which societies pass from a state of mechanical to organic solidarity, a process necessarily determined by the structure of the division of labour. In the 'Preface' to the first edition

Durkheim noted that the origins of the division of labour were bound up with the relation of the individual to social solidarity: 'Why does the individual, while becoming more autonomous, depend more upon society? How can he be at once more individual and more solidarity? Certainly these two movements, contradictory as they appear, develop in parallel fashion . . . what resolves this apparent antinomy is a transformation of social solidarity due to the steadily growing development of the division of labour'. The relation of the division of labour to social solidarity is conceived in moral terms, for although fulfilling specific material needs, its existence is bound up with relations of friendship and community: Dukheim writes that the 'true' function of the division of labour is 'to create in two or more persons a feeling of solidarity'. Mechanical forms of social solidarity are defined as essentially pre-industrial; social organisation is highly undifferentiated, characterised by similarity of functions, resemblances and a common consciousness. Its morphological structure is segmental consisting of different organs co-ordinated and subordinated to a central authority, a low level of interdependence and weak social bonds, a low volume of population and material and moral density. Collective sentiments and beliefs predominate and the individual consciousness is scarcely identifiable; the social and religious are unified so that religious ideas saturate the whole society. Law is repressive, expiatory and diffuse, functioning not through specialised institutions but the whole society: 'In primitive societies . . . law is wholly penal, it is the assembly of the people which renders justice' (Durkheim, 1964, pp. 37–8, 56, 76). The essence of Durkheim's concept of mechanical solidarity is well summed up in a passage employing the collective pronoun to good effect: 'When *we* desire the repression of crime, it is not *we* that *we* desire to avenge personally, but to avenge something sacred which *we* feel more or less confusedly outside and above *us*' (Durkheim, 1964, p. 100).

Mechanical solidarity is defined as a structure of resemblances linking the individual directly and harmoniously with society so much so that individual action is always spontaneous, unreflective and collective. In contrast, the basis of organic solidarity is the division of labour and social differentiation; the social structure is characterised by a high level of interdependence, industrial development and a high volume of population and moral and material density. Solidarity through social likeness is replaced by solidarity through difference and a strengthening of social bonds. The individual is no longer wholly enveloped by the collective conscience but develops greater individuality and personality. In this situation it is necessary that 'the collective leave open a part of the individual conscience in order that special functions may be established there, functions which it cannot regulate. The more this region is extended, the stronger is the cohesion which results from this solidarity . . . each one depends as much more strictly on society as labour is more divided; and, on the other, the activity of each is as much more personal as it is more specialised'.

Initiative and individuality create a society 'capable of collective movement', one in which 'each of its elements has more freedom of movement'. Durkheim compares this form of solidarity with that of the 'higher animals' in which each organ 'has its special physiognomy, its autonomy . . . the unity of the organism is as great as the individuation of the parts is more marked' (Durkheim, 1964, p. 131). Thus the term organic solidarity refers to a system of differentiated and specialised functions unified by the relations between its various parts; the individual depends on society through a dependence on the parts which comprise it. Law is restitutive and co-operative; social norms create the legal rules which permeate civil law, commercial law, administrative and constitutional law, all of which operate through specialised organs such as administrative tribunals and an autonomous magistracy. While repressive law 'corresponds to the heart, the centre of the common conscience', restitutive law is less central and more diffuse (Durkheim, 1964, p. 112).

Durkheim's main focus in *The Division of Labour* was on the social problems engendered by the transition from one social order to another, and the problematic nature of the social bonds which united individuals with each other and with society as a whole. He praised Comte for recognising that the division of labour was more than an economic institution but was sociological and moral in its necessary relation with social solidarity, even though its practical workings had the effect of creating social disintegration and moral deregulation. Durkheim was particularly critical of Herbert Spencer's individualistic concept of the division of labour and his argument that if left to itself the mechanism of specialisation would lead to the unity of the whole. Durkheim rejected Spencer's contractual theory of society since its atomistic individualism failed to grasp that every contractual relationship involved both third parties and antecedent social norms which regulated the relationship. For Durkheim, the advance of science and industry, in the absence of universalising moral norms, must eventuate in anomie, a moral vacuum. The evolution of societies from mechanical to organic forms of solidarity would not result in the harmonious social differentiation envisaged by Spencer, but rather 'extreme moral disorder' and 'egoism' if the process remained unregulated by a consensus of moral beliefs.

Durkheim argued, against Comte, that this 'moral vacuum' was not the result of the inherent nature of the division of labour but rather the absence of a moral consensus regulating the division of labour: normally the division of work produces social solidarity, social reciprocity and shared moral values which then regulate the various branches of industry and social life generally. It is only through what Durkheim called its 'abnormal forms' with its dispersion of interests that organic solidarity is undermined. Durkheim's concept of the abnormal refers essentially to modern industry, capitalist forms of the division of labour exemplified in economic crisis and class conflict. Durkheim identified social inequality as the major source of the abnormal form arguing that 'external inequality' has the effect of threatening organic solidarity by no longer enabling natural ability to correspond with social status. For Durkheim, a normal mode of production was one in which the work of each employee of an organisation was functionally co-ordinated and unity achieved. The point here is Durkheim's assumption that given 'normal' circumstances organic solidarity is self-regulating; but if abnormal forms predominate social order is clearly threatened.

There is, however, more than structural instability within the system: although agreeing with Saint-Simon that the social crisis was essentially moral in nature, Durkheim accepted Comte's one-sided view of human nature, that humanity is basically in need of control because of 'insatiable appetites'. In

The Division of Labour and *Suicide* Durkheim couched his theory of anomie, 'normlessness', in Hobbesian terms although with one crucial difference. In the course of the eighteenth and nineteenth centuries the function of egoism in social theory changes from its polemical standpoint in Hobbes, as a criticism of residual feudal elements and ideology in favour of capitalist enterprise and values, to a moral–evaluative and negative standpoint in Comte and Durkheim. The glorification of capitalist values embodied in the concept of egoism demanded a one-sided characterisation of human nature which, in the writings of late eighteenth-century thinkers, became increasingly problematical. Adam Smith, for example, conceived egoism and altruism as two distinct components of human nature which he treated separately, egoism in *The Wealth of Nations*, altruism or sympathy in the *Theory of Moral Sentiments* (1759), a division which prompted the so-called 'Adam Smith problem' in academic scholarship based on the failure to integrate these polarities into a unified whole.

But egoism as a conservative and universal precept develops only at the end of the eighteenth and beginning of the nineteenth century in the work of Burke and Comte in which it is identified as the source of the disintegration of social bonds. Durkheim's description of modern society in terms of a 'malady of infinite aspirations', 'a thirst [for] novelties, unfamiliar pleasures, nameless sensations' and an absence of 'a healthy discipline' is moral–evaluative and not scientific, a philosophical and conservative analysis which identifies egoism with conflict and normlessness. The problem of reconciling a biological concept of human nature with a sociological concept of regulation persists throughout Durkheim's work and is particularly acute in his studies of class conflict and suicide.

In *The Division of Labour* the anomic and normless condition of modern society is linked with trade and industry, a sphere of life in which deregulation is most pronounced. Yet to describe nineteenth-century industry as 'normless' seems hardly credible: the evidence adduced by Durkheim, that an anomic division of labour was responsible for class conflict and industrial crises replacing organic solidarity, can easily be interpreted as evidence of working-class solidarity and cohesion mediated through specific working-class institutions (trade unions) expressing opposition to capitalist regimentation and inequality. A strike of nineteenth-century industrial workers constituted a 'healthy' and normal rather than 'morbid' and 'abnormal' form of social activity. That Durkheim interprets industrialisation in these terms is somewhat surprising since the basic thrust of his argument of an increasing organic solidarity in modern society suggests that co-operation and mutuality are precisely the characteristic effects of the 'true' functioning of the division of labour. Indeed, he argues that the values of individualism ('the culture of the individual'), generated by the French Revolution and Enlightenment philosophy, constitute part of the movement towards organic solidarity: the progressive emancipation of the individual from a centralised authority and culture implied a strengthening, not a weakening, of the social bonds. Thus individualism progresses in proportion to the diversification of labour and is not necessarily to be identified as egoism since the breakdown of the social bond flows only from one form of individualism. The nineteenth-century labour movement clearly represented individualism in the form of wage-labour, labour which was free and dependent on market forces; it was necessarily combined with collectivism and mutuality and the strengthening of social bonds within the working-class communities.

Anomie

What, then, does Durkheim mean by anomie? Anomie is identified with the goals sought by the individual and their possible realisation; these goals, desires, are partly biological, partly social. In general Durkheim analysed nineteenth-century industrial society as one in which norms regulating the 'getting' were either weakly institutionalised or absent. It is this absence of norms which Durkheim analysed as anomie, a situation occurring when 'society is disturbed by some painful crisis or by . . . abrupt transitions . . . In the case of economic disasters, indeed, something like a declassification occurs which suddenly casts certain individuals into a lower state than their previous one'. For Durkheim, anomie is clearly centred in the economic structure: in the sphere of trade and industry social life is in 'a chronic state' since economic development has severed industrial relations 'from all regulation', from the discipline exerted by religion, and occupational associations. Appetites have thus been freed 'and from top to bottom of the ladder, greed is aroused', aspirations are no longer effectively contained, no one recognises 'the limits proper to them'. With the growth of industrialisation desires multiply and 'at the very moment when traditional rules have lost their authority, the richer prize offered these appetites stimulates them and makes them more exigent and impatient of control. The state of deregulation or anomie is thus further heightened by passions being less disciplined, precisely when they need more discipline' (Durkheim, 1952, pp. 252–4).

For individual passions can be checked only by an authority which everyone 'respects' and to which they yield spontaneously. Only society itself possesses the power 'to stipulate law and set the point beyond which the passions must not go . . . It alone can estimate the reward to be prospectively offered to every class of functionary, in the name of common interest'. In the 'moral consciousness' of society the limits are vaguely fixed and generally accepted: the worker usually knows his position and 'realises the extreme limit set by his ambitions and aspires to nothing beyond. At least if he *respects regulations* and is docile to collective authority, that is has a *wholesome social constitution* . . . Thus an end and a goal are set to the passions'. Not that these goals are rigidly defined for some improvement is always possible but the point remains 'to make men contented with their lot while stimulating them modestly to improve it' (Durkheim, 1952, pp. 249–58).

Durkheim's discussion of anomie, organic solidarity and individualism suggest a theory of compliance with the existing society in terms of its basic institutional structure. At the same time he was critical of the failure of industrial society to achieve a 'normal' division of labour which might adequately regulate human passions and establish a 'normal' relation between natural and social inequality. Durkheim's idealised concept of the division of labour has the effect of eliminating all relations of conflict from analysis and assimilating contradictions to an underlying unity. To conceptualise social development in terms of ahistorical abstractions – mechanical and organic solidarity – is to empty sociology of historical specificity and define society less as an empirical whole but as the expression of an inner essence – the 'normal' state from which modern industrial societies deviate in terms of their lack of regulation. Thus Durkheim's sociology of industrial society oscillates between two distinct poles: on the one hand it outlined theoretically the development of complex, multi-layered social structures in which the collective forces enabled individuals to become increasingly autonomous; and on the other it failed to grasp that this process of structural differentiation is effectively a democratisation of culture, an expansion of civil society and its institutions which enabled individuals, collectively organised into unions, political parties and professional associations, to articulate specific interests which bring them into conflict with other groups, classes and the state itself. Structural differentiation in effect allows for greater participation, democratisation and activity within the institutions of civil society: anomie is thus an expression of the increasing autonomy of the human subject struggling against social forces which seek to control and repudiate his/her interests.

Durkheim had no adequate theory of the subject. He conceived evolution from one type of society to another largely as the product of impersonal natural laws; equally, he failed to understand that structural differentiation itself flows from human action, the pressures exerted continuously from 'below' the major, 'official' institutions of society, from within the culture of the broad masses. But like Comte, Saint-Simon, Marx and his contemporaries, Pareto, Michels, Weber and Mosca, Durkheim mistrusted popular democracy and feared the consequences of that process of democratisation which industrialism and the division of labour had set in motion, and which his own analysis had disclosed.

Suicide and social solidarity

Durkheim never analysed social stratification in ways which would have filled out or modified his general social theory. Instead the concept of anomie is illustrated, statistically, through his study of suicide. He intended this analysis not simply as a closely argued monograph on a specific sociological problem but as a general contribution to the analysis of the culture of industrial society.

Suicide, one of the most private and personal acts, was studied by Durkheim because although superficially a phenomenon more suited to psychological, not sociological explanation, the act itself clearly related to the problem of social cohesion and the social bonds holding society together. There was, too, the practical issue of a falling birth rate and the possibility that the family might decline in significance. 'A high suicide rate', Durkheim wrote in 1888, could · indicate a regression of 'domestic solidarity' in which the 'cold wind of egoism freezes . . . hearts and weakens . . . spirits' (Lukes, 1973, p. 195). Suicide had been widely studied in France, Belgium and Germany, first as a moral and then as a social problem with correlations established between the suicide rate and numerous social factors which included rapid social change, economic depression, socio-economic status, and urbanism. But the originality of Durkheim's discussion, as Anthony Giddens has pointed out, was to develop a systematic and coherent sociological theory of differential suicide rates within a sociological framework that assimilated the existing empirical findings (Giddens, 1977, p. 324). The language which Durkheim employed in his study reflects this sociological concern: the causes of suicide are linked to the state of society, currents of opinion, excessive individualism, and pessimistic currents within the culture – an emphasis on notions such as 'forces' and 'currents' which tend to disguise his concern with the socio-psychological conditions for social health. This aggressive sociological language, Steven Lukes has suggested 'was altogether less suited to what he wished to say than the language of "social bonds", attaching individuals to social goals and regulating their desires' (Lukes, 1973, p. 216).

Durkheim identified four types of suicide – egoistic, anomic, altruistic and fatalistic (this latter type is not discussed in any detail and is noted simply as resulting from 'an excess of regulations'). The types are closely bound up with Durkheim's theory of morality and social solidarity, that the degree of cohesion present in a society will generate a tendency to certain forms of suicide. Suicide is social and collective; suicide proneness exists only in relation to specific social conditions. Thus the suicide current is defined externally, a social fact related to certain types of social structure. Egoistic and anomic suicide, for example, are mainly found in modern industrial societies, in social structures characterised by an absence of strong regulative norms and lack of integration. It is the currents which determine the suicide rate and in this sense Durkheim's sociological explanation was not designed to account for individual suicides. This has led many critics to point out that both the rate of suicide and the specific individual act must flow from the same cause and therefore Durkheim's account is, and must be, both an explanation of the collective as well as individual acts of suicide. Yet he insisted that the causes of suicide must be determined 'without concerning ourselves with the forms they can assume in particular individuals'. It is psychology which studies the question, *who* commits suicide; sociology studies the broad social concomitants, the social currents that determine suicide as a collective force. Durkheim was surely right to argue that to explain suicide as a social phenomena, as a unified structure with permanent and variable features, analysis could not begin from the individual suicide since such a procedure would never account for the specific statistical distribution of suicide as a whole. The individual only exists as an individual within the framework of a social whole: 'We start from the exterior because it alone is immediately given, but only to reach the interior' (Durkheim, 1952, p. 315). But while establishing suicide as an external structure, *Suicide* is, in effect, a complex and subtle study of the relation between individuals and the social whole and the mediations involved in this process, of the institutions which function to integrate individuals by attaching them to certain social ends and values, thus moderating their biological desires and appetites through social and moral regulation.

In *Suicide* Durkheim established a number of correlations between the suicide rate and specific socio-cultural elements and values. Catholic countries enjoy a lower suicide rate than Protestant countries although both religions condemn the act itself. The suicide rate decreases during wartime and in periods of political turmoil (an example of what Durkheim termed, 'acute anomie'). Married women have a lower suicide rate than single women of the same age although married women without children are more likely to kill themselves than unmarried women (an example of 'chronic anomie'). A higher 'co-efficient of preservation' characterises married women with children than childless marriages. Thus the suicide rate varies inversely with the degree of religious, political and family density. Durkheim concluded that the suicide rate was closely connected with the presence of society within individuals: anomic forms of suicide result from the failure of social norms to restrain individual passions.

He argued, then, that 'suicide varies inversely with the degree of integration of the social groups to which the individual forms a part', and that Protestants have a much higher suicide rate than Catholics for the following reasons:

1. Catholic communities possess the stronger traditions and shared beliefs conducive to an integrated 'state of society' and 'a collective life' which restrains the suicidal tendencies endemic in industrial society.
2. The causes of suicide lie in the weakening of the power of 'collective representations' through the collapse of 'traditional beliefs' and cohesive communities in the face of industrial development and social fragmentation.

Durkheim established a positive statistical relationship between the suicide rate and educational and religious institutions. The influence of education is particularly important because the more educated a social group the more it is prone to question tradition and authority. Durkheim also provided an explanation of differential suicide rates in terms of the consciousness of those committing suicide, that is, by reference to 'collective representations'.

Superficially his argument is simple: the state of society produces either strong or weak suicidal currents and the extent to which a particular individual is affected depends entirely on the nature of the social bonds and degree of his/her integration in the social group. Discussing egoistic suicide, for example, Durkheim cited evidence showing that education and suicide were closely connected in that the more educated Protestants kill themselves more frequently than the less educated Catholics. Education fosters a spirit of free inquiry and develops a critical attitude towards traditional authorities. But Jews, who are more educated than Catholics, have a markedly lower suicide rate. Now this could mean that those Jews with a higher education kill themselves more frequently than those with a poor education. Durkheim, however, did not differentiate the different layers within a social group. By so doing he might have preserved the correlation between education and the suicide rate: but this would have meant cutting across his main argument that it is the lack of integration within a religious group which constitutes the fundamental cause of suicide, and more particularly, the break with tradition engendered by education and individualism.

Durkheim argued that 'free inquiry' – 'the relentless spirit of criticism' – is especially marked among Protestants but this in itself is not the cause of suicide. The need for 'free inquiry', he suggested, has a cause of its own – 'the overthrow of traditional beliefs', the questioning and criticism of established authority:

> . . . for ideas shared by an entire society draw from this consensus an authority which makes them sacrosanct and raises them above dispute (Durkheim, 1952, Ch. 2).

High suicide rates flow from a weak social morality. And morality, for Durkheim, was closely bound up with religion. With this in mind his account of the low suicide rate among English Protestants is particularly illuminating for the statistics clearly threatened the whole thrust of Durkheim's analysis of suicide. As with the example of Jewish suicide statistics, Protestant English statistics are simply assimilated to another explanatory structure and interpreted as buttressing, not invalidating, Durkheim's argument. For the statistics are not what they seem: in England there exist laws sanctioning 'religious requirements', the power of Sunday observance and the prohibition of religious representation on the stage, respect for tradition is 'general and powerful' so much so that 'religious society . . . is much more strongly constituted and to this extent resembles the Catholic Church' (Durkheim, 1952, p. 161).

Durkheim offers no evidence for this assertion, but the significance of his remarks lies in the shift of emphasis from the concept of the suicide rate as a social fact, a *sui generis*, correlated closely with specific forms of social structure to a view of society that depends for its validity on the interpretation by the subject. For to argue that in England society is cohesive and regulated, that social bonds are strong notwithstanding the pervasive influence of Protestant ideology, is to postulate that this is how individuals actually perceive the social structure.

Similar problems confronted Durkheim in his analysis of Jewish suicide statistics, for having claimed an external link between the decline of traditional authority and education (the Protestants in France) he was forced to analyse these as an exception. Religious minorities, Durkheim suggested, suffering from continuous persecution, use knowledge 'not . . . to replace [their] collective prejudices by reflective thought, but merely to be better armed for the struggle'. In other words, education has a different meaning for Jews than it has for Protestants, and therefore Durkheim concluded that a high degree of education does not necessarily imply a weakening of traditional authority among the Jews. In effect, Durkheim has imported meanings into his sociological analysis to explain away statistics which cannot be adequately analysed in terms of external social facts and social forces.

The construction of meaning on the part of the acting subject is as significant for the analysis of suicide as the external determinations. Durkheim claimed, on the one hand, that suicide was a collective phenomenon characterised by a definite external structure and laws; and, on the other hand, he stressed the internal nature of such facts thus implying some notion of meaning. As was argued above, Durkheim never solved satisfactorily the dualism of internal consciousness and meaning and external socio-moral determinations. Thus in *Suicide* he failed to discuss attempted suicide which is far more common than successful suicide: attempted suicide, as a 'cry for help' constitutes a communicative act involving the construction of meaning on the part of the actor and its assumed effects on those for whom the act is intended. But Durkheim was less concerned with the subject as creator of meaning than the reactions of subjects to collective social forces; *Suicide* was a paradigmatic study of the dislocations within modern society, the implications for the human community of the collapse of social bonds. There is a strong ideological thrust to Durkheim's theory of suicide exemplified in his uncritical acceptance of official statistics, his reliance on coroners reports and their commonsense definition of suicide. The collection of suicide statistics is itself highly problematical: many social groups, for religious and social reasons, tend to under-report suicide. The statistics on which Durkheim relied were inherently biased by official definitions and method of classification, but nevertheless unproblematically integrated into his general theory.

Functionalism, holism and political theory

Although Durkheim rejected Comte's philosophy of history he accepted his attempted synthesis of science and reform. Comte's sociological positivism was based on the natural laws of social evolution governing human society and the strict application of natural science to the study of social institutions. Durkheim defined society as a social fact but also as a moral reality. As a moral structure society dominated the individual, its various parts functioning in relation, not to the individual, but to the whole. Durkheim's debt to Comte is thus clear: the holistic concept of society suggests that the basic tendency of its institutions – its parts – is the promotion of social 'health', social solidarity, stability, equilibrium. As with Comte, Durkheim defined the normal state of society as one of social harmony in which social forces work to produce conformity to the dominant norms.

By defining society as an organic whole Durkheim analysed social processes and institutions in terms of their relevant functions for the needs of the system. To explain a social phenomenon, he argued in *The Rules of Sociological Method* (Ch. 5), it is necessary to separate the 'efficient cause' which produces it from the 'functions it fulfils'. Thus in *The Elementary Forms of the Religious Life* Durkheim analysed religion in terms of its functions for strengthening social bonds and integrating the individual into society. Religious beliefs express the collective nature of society through representations, while religious rites organise and regulate its functioning. Religion expresses universal values, a role which is indispensable for the adequate functioning of all human societies. Similarly, the division of labour normally contributes to the promotion of social solidarity while both the 'forced' (specialisation being no longer based on the natural talents of individuals) and the anomic forms are abnormal in that they fail to contribute to the development of social co-operation and cohesion. Durkheim's central argument, in his studies of the division of labour, suicide and religion, was the necessity for a moral order that adequately regulated social institutions thus facilitating the promotion of social solidarity. Functions are thus explicated in terms of the 'needs' of the social system.

One result of Durkheim's holistic functionalism was a somewhat paradoxical argument of the social function of 'deviant' behaviour such as crime and suicide. Crime, for example, was 'normal' in those societies not dominated by a *conscience collective*, in which individualism has developed a sense of moral responsibility, and where some individuals will diverge from the collective norms; only in this way was moral change itself possible. Durkheim was opposed to the assimilation of the individual into the collectivity, advocating the development of personal autonomy and individual differences as the only viable basis of genuine individualism. The relation of the individual to the collectivity preoccupied his later writings as he sought to define the mediating institutions between the individual and the state. A social function cannot exist without moral discipline: economic functions, for example, are only a means to an end which is the harmonious community. Durkheim thus advocated occupational groups, or corporations, which would morally regulate economic activity and provide the basis of genuine social solidarity. In the 'Preface' to the second edition of *The Division of Labour* he described these secondary institutions as professional groupings consisting of lawyers, judges, soldiers and priests; the various industries would be governed by an elected administrative council exercising broadly similar functions to those of the old guilds such as labour relations, regulation of wages, conditions of work, promotion, etc. These groupings would also exercise a more general function, that of developing and encouraging intellectual and moral solidarity.

These proposals formed part of Durkheim's general theory that organic solidarity gradually dissolves coercive power in society so that a co-operative social order emerges regulated not by state institutions but increasingly by professional associations and their ethic of service to the community. In his *Professional Ethics and Civic Morals* (1957) he argued that these institutions were essential if the state was not to oppress the individual. The state must be subordinated to civil society although the institutions are closely related to it; state intervention is not abandoned but Durkheim's essential point was that the state could never constitute the source of moral unity for a modern complex society. It was for these reasons that he rejected Tönnies's form of state socialism, for while the intermediary institutions were largely autonomous they nevertheless were supervised by the state.

Durkheim's arguments are important because they focus on one of the central problems of sociology, that of maximising individual freedom and personal autonomy with the increasing collectivist trends of modern industrial society. A democratic society was one in which the source of moral obligation flowed out of the institutions of civil society, the source of social solidarity was immanent and not something imposed externally from above. Nevertheless, Durkheim remained within the positivist paradigm in that the mediating institutions were never defined in ways which maximised human activity and reflected popular democratic forms: Durkheim's professional associations are close to a bureaucratic structure whose function is the maintenance of social harmony; they are not institutions through which popular dissent and the conflict of interests can find expression, but the means of assimilating such elements to an underlying concern with social order. Their function is quasi-religious in the sense of expressing a system of collective beliefs and practices which command obedience, the symbols and sentiments which transform society into a community in which individual differences, while significant, are merged ultimately into a higher unity.

For Durkheim social cohesion remained the highest principle to such an extent that his notion of mediating institutions is itself collectivist, its bureaucratic implications clearly detracting from its democratic potential. There is a sense in which Durkheim's reifed concept of society finds its expression in a reifed notion of mediation. Durkheim's holistic functionalism defines society in static terms, minimising the historical basis of institutions as the products of human action in favour of institutions as things which regulate human action. Society was an organism and thus Durkheim writes of the 'pathological state' of modern society, its 'morbidity', 'pessimism' and 'abnormal', 'anomic' division of labour: the social organism has 'reached a degree of abnormal intensity'. Thus anarchists, mystics and socialist revolutionaries share a profound hatred of the present and 'disgust for the existing order' developing only 'a single craving to destroy and escape from reality'. Life is often harsh, Durkheim writes, 'treacherous or empty' and the task of sociology is to identify the means of establishing a collective authority which will regulate the degree of 'collective sadness' in society and prevent it from reaching 'morbid' heights' (Durkheim, 1952, pp. 360ff). Yet, as one of Durkheim's students, Maurice Halbwachs observed, if high suicide rates are found in all advanced societies in what sense can they be categorised as 'morbid?': 'Are all European societies unhealthy? Can a single society remain in a pathological state for three-quarters of a century?' (Lukes, 1973, p. 225).

5
Critique of Positivism: II Social Action

Understanding and the social sciences: Dilthey

The dominant methodological orientation of nineteenth-century sociology was positivism: society was defined in holistic, organicist terms as a system determined by the existence of specific laws which worked to promote change and cohesion through different stages of evolution. It was assumed that a fundamental continuity subsisted between the realms of nature and society. The methods appropriate to the study of the natural sciences were thus appropriate to the study of human society and culture.

In Germany the emergence of sociology as a distinctive discipline owed much to this positivist tradition, but in striving to define its own specific methodology and concept of society many of the central assumptions of positivist orthodoxy were abandoned. The major influences on the development of German sociology were philosophers – Wilhelm Dilthey (1833–1911), Heinrich Rickert (1863–1936) and Wilhelm Windelband (1848–1915) – concerned with epistemological issues and problems of methodology in the social and cultural sciences. Towards the end of the nineteenth century positivism had become an increasingly significant current of thought within German intellectual culture. For these philosophers, the Comtist notion of sociology as the queen of the sciences represented a serious threat to the study of human action and human culture. It was argued that positivism foundered first because human society constituted a realm of unique, not recurrent, law-like processes in which human autonomy and freedom were decisive elements; and secondly, because society itself did not exist in any meaningful sense apart from the individuals who comprised it together with their unique human actions. Thus the methods of the natural sciences were considered inappropriate for social and cultural study. Effectively, therefore, the possibility of sociology as a science was rendered extremely problematic.

One of the fundamental assumptions in this critique of positivism was that the socio-historical realm could be understood only because it had been created by humanity. 'Mind can only understand what it has created', wrote Dilthey. 'Nature, the subject-matter of the physical sciences, embraces the reality which has arisen independently of the activity of mind. Everything on which man has actively impressed his stamp forms the subject-matter of the human studies' (Dilthey, 1976, p. 192). Dilthey made an important distinction between explanation and understanding: to explain an event, or an institution, assumed an external, mechanical relation between the human subject and the world of reality; explanation was conceived in terms of mechanical causation which effectively eliminated the subjective aspects of human life from the analysis. But human culture consisted also of the category of understanding, the interpretation of reality by human subjects which saturates everyday life and without which society would be impossible. Because positivism treated human subjects externally, as objective datums, it failed to integrate this element of understanding into its methodological framework.

For Dilthey, understanding and interpreting constituted the true methods of the human sciences: 'All functions are united through them. They contain all the truths of the human studies. At every stage the understanding reveals a world.' The understanding of others develops through experience 'and on our understanding of it, and on the continuous interplay of experience and understanding'. The task of the cultural sciences, Dilthey argued, was to systematise this simple form of understanding, which exists at the everyday level, into a coherent, conceptual tool that embraces the higher, complex forms of understanding.

Dilthey's distinction between the simple and complex forms of understanding is not easy to grasp: he seems to suggest that as everyday life is shaped by momentary interests everyday understanding is so determined, while complex understanding seeks to link human activity with definite goals within a broad, historical and human context. Elementary understanding, he argues, contains 'no return to the life-complex as a whole'. The simple form of understanding is that through which the individual grasps the meaning of the actions of others, a pragmatic form of understanding that differs from hermeneutical or historical understanding which seeks to interpret the meaning of culture as a whole. Understanding in this latter sense reveals a whole, not simply the isolated individual act. For Dilthey, understanding relates to the historical context seeking to link together circumstances, ends and means with the 'life-structure'. The emphasis is therefore on both explanation *and* understanding, although explanation is not defined in positivist terms. To explain is to incorporate those subjective elements in human action which orientates the individual to ends and means.

Methodologically, understanding is not simply the re-experiencing of the actions of others, the re-enactment of an individual experience. Understanding is always connected with the concept of cultural whole:

> Life consists of parts, of experiences which are inwardly related to each other. Every particular experience refers to a self of which it is part . . . structurally interrelated to other parts: interconnectedness is, therefore, a category originating from life (Dilthey, 1976, p. 211).

The historical world, out of which understanding develops, is thus defined both in terms of its constituent parts, individual experiences and interactions that constitute the source of values and purposes, and as a 'comprehensive, structural whole'. Dilthey's holism is methodological in that a totality, or a cultural artefact, can be understood only through its individual elements and their relations with the whole itself; a complete understanding of each element necessarily presupposes an understanding of the whole. Meaning, therefore, is determined by the relations of parts to whole for every experience is significantly connected with a whole as words in a sentence. Individual events in the external world have a relation to something they signify.

From these arguments it is fairly clear that Dilthey's concept of understanding is historicist: the meaning of any human act flows from the task of inserting it into an objective world of culture and in so doing elucidating its inner structure. Dilthey opposed the reduction of understanding to psychological categories and the reliving of the experience of others. Hermeneutic understanding seeks to produce *historical knowledge* – not psychologial knowledge – of the part to whole. Understanding is, therefore, not a form of empathic penetration and reconstruction of individual action and consciousness, but an interpretation of cultural forms that have been created and experienced by individuals. In this sense humanity only becomes the subject-matter of the cultural sciences 'when we experience human states, give expressions to them and understand these expressions'. The natural sciences had defined humanity as a physical fact apprehended through the senses; the cultural sciences – the moral sciences, *Geisteswissenschaften* – mould their subject-matter by seeking to penetrate the subjectivity of humanity (Dilthey, 1976, p. 175). Dilthey includes history, economics, politics, literature, music, aesthetics in the category of the cultural sciences, but not, significantly, sociology. The study of contemporary society is subsumed under history: sociology is identified with the naturalistic positivism of Comte and Spencer, the reduction of historical reality and culture to mechanistic laws and materialist concepts which excluded the category of understanding. It must be emphasised that Dilthey was not opposed to empirical method and his critique of positivism was directed against its assimilation of complex human experience to deterministic external processes. It is impossible, he argued, to integrate the category of meaning into a methodology that emphasised the externality of the social and cultural world. Human actions and experiences were not external datums but idiosyncratically subjective and formed part of a humanly created historical whole.

Dilthey's separation of the natural from the cultural sciences was a distinction between what Windelband called the *nomo-*

thetic sciences, concerned with establishing general laws, and general phenomena, and the *idiographic* sciences which were concerned with unique and unrepeatable events. Rickert further developed this distinction by equating the scientific with the *nomothetic* methodology and the cultural with the *idiographic* methodology. The essential difference between the sciences was defined not so much in terms of subject-matter or content, but rather in terms of their distinctive method: as an individualising method, the cultural sciences were concerned with the analysis of reality in terms of values not laws. Rickert emphasised that the cultural sciences explored questions of meaning in relation to the concept of culture as something produced through human action and thereby saturated with human values. The methodology of the cultural sciences was individualising and related to values (what Rickert termed, 'value-relevance'). In contrast, the natural sciences investigated objects separated from values. The cultural sciences should, however, avoid value-judgements seeking merely to relate objects to values. It was this concept of value relevance – or value-relatedness – which played an important role in the development of Weber's interpretative sociology. Rickert did not imply the necessity to make *a priori* judgements on the value of cultural elements or actions, only that cultural forms can be analysed in terms of the values of the culture of which they form part.

In general Rickert was concerned with method. To interpret socio-cultural phenomena in terms of value and meaning did not mean abandoning causal analysis:

> History, too, with its individualising method and its orientation to values, has to investigate the causal relations subsisting among the unique and individual events with which it is concerned. These causal relations do not coincide with the universal *laws* of nature, no matter how far general concepts may be required as constructive *elements* of historical concepts in order to represent *individual causal relations*. The only thing that matters is that the methodological principle governing the selection of what is *essential* in history involves reference to values even in the inquiry into *cause* (Rickert, 1962, p. 93).

Rickert's opposition to universal laws of nature, and the teleology this implied, was shared by Dilthey. But Rickert differed sharply from Dilthey over the question of causality within the historical and social realm. Yet if understanding is to be linked with explanation, as Dilthey seems to suggest, then it clearly demands the kind of causal analysis that was to be proposed in the sociology of Weber.

Formal sociology: Simmel and sociation

Rickert had argued that the object of study in the cultural sciences must be constructed by the researcher through methodology; he rigorously opposed the 'naive realism' of historians by postulating a concept of reality as formless and chaotic unless ordered through theoretical categories. One result of this standpoint was to empty the concept of society of all substance other than unique individuals who comprised it. Society was no objective datum governed by laws of development, no whole exercising ontological priority over its parts. Society was defined in nominalist terms and in the sociology which emerged out of the methodological debate over the status of the cultural sciences the categories of understanding and the human subject lay at its centre.

Although important differences distinguish the sociology of Ferdinand Tönnies (1855–1936) and Georg Simmel (1858–1918), they shared a common humanist notion of sociology defining its subject-matter as forms of social interaction between active human subjects and arguing that the structure of such action always involves complex cultural meanings. It was not, therefore, a question of individuals as such, but of the ways in which individuals act socially: thus Simmel rejected the positivist argument that society constituted an objective system dominating its members; Simmel defined society as an intricate web of multiple interactions and relations between individuals which embody the principle of sociation. Society consisted of individuals connected by interaction; institutions such as the family, religion, economic organisations and bureaucracy constituted the forms taken by the social content of such interaction. The object of sociology was thus sociation.

Tönnies equally rejected the organismic holistic concept of society and sought to differentiate sociology from other disciplines especially biology and psychology. The sociological perspective, he argued, was concerned primarily with the facts of 'reciprocal affirmation', of social relations as mutual relationships in which each individual 'makes and asserts a claim to a certain – regular or occasional, more or less permanent – conduct of the other person or persons'. Tönnies argued that all apparent non-rational thought and action implied a meaning 'reducible to human volition'. The social, he concluded, flows from human action, from the intentions of human subjects to relate to one another. Social reality, therefore, exists only in the sense of being perceived, experienced, known and willed by individuals (Tönnies, 1971, p. 89).

Both Tönnies and Simmel attempted, on the basis of this humanist standpoint, to develop a 'pure' sociology in which concepts such as Tönnies' *Gemeinschaft* and *Gesellschaft* provided the necessary order to the variety and complexity of empirical reality. Tönnies' concepts clearly do not refer to existing societies; they do not describe objective facts, but constitute abstractions from 'real situations', from the facts of social interaction. All societies are characterised by elements from both *Gemeinschaft* and *Gesellschaft* but as concepts they are purely formal, ideal types essential for the sociological analysis of historical reality. This is one of the fundamental themes of Simmel's sociology through which he opposed the positivist assumption of laws of social development and thus concepts which reflected this necessary process.

Simmel's work covered an enormous range of topics and issues, including problems of methodology in the social sciences: *Problems of the Philosophy of History* (1892) which influenced Weber's work on methodology, 'The Problem of Sociology' (1894), 'How is society possible?' (1908) 'The Field of Sociology' (1917); contributions to cultural theory – *The Philosophy of Money* (1910), *Philosophical Culture* (1911); and essays and studies in philosophy, music, literature, fashion and general problems of aesthetics.

His first important sociological work, *On Social Differentiation*

(1890), was written under the influence of Spencer and positivism, although the central argument that society progresses from a state of undifferentiated group existence to a condition in which human autonomy and individualism are possible, because of differentiated social structures, remained a significant element in the later anti-positivist and anti-evolutionary sociology. Yet even in Simmel's early writings the influence of Dilthey was marked. Dilthey had defined society in terms of interactions and the individual as an element in the various systems of interaction. Simmel criticised Dilthey, however, for dismissing the claims of sociology on this basis, that society was merely individuals interacting with each other. Simmel sought to define this principle of interaction sociologically by conceptualising society in terms of forms. In the *Problems of the Philosophy of History* he defended the notion of man as the cognitive subject whose actions produce the historical world. Historical knowledge is possible, not as a simple reflection of an external reality, but as a form of human experience. The world itself becomes an object of knowledge through the analysis of forms (Simmel, 1977, pp. 16–18, 60–1). What Simmel meant by form was a category, or number of categories, through which the world of experience becomes transmuted into a taxonomy, a conceptual scheme with both epistemolSogcal and ontological status. Law, sexuality, society are thus forms in this sense. Forms provide coherence to the world of diverse and incoherent objects: Simmel suggests that the concept of form is immanent and can never be deduced from the context or from the artefact (Simmel, 1980, p. 6).

Thus for Simmel the problem of social reality was solved by recourse to Kantian philosophy. Kant had argued that knowledge was possible only through the immanent categories of the mind and not by reference to experience and context. Similarly, Simmel argued that social reality becomes meaningful only through the organising principles associated with specific, universal forms. It followed that science did not develop out of content, which was merely random, objective facts pertaining to experience; rather, science always implied interpretation and ordering according to concepts which remain *a priori* for the different sciences. In the elaboration of science, concepts have priority. There are no objective laws, no totality. Simmel rejects the hypostatised notion of society found in Comte and Spencer in favour of an active, ceaseless interaction of many elements that constitute a complex structure. Simmel was opposed to those modes of sociology which reifed society, defining it as a reality external to the individual and existing as if it had a life of its own separate from human action. The concept of form enabled Simmel to analyse institutions and social processes objectively while retaining the notion of the active human subject. Sociation did not imply isolated individuals who lack development and therefore interaction. Without forms there is no society; forms inhere in reality itself although reality in its empirical immediacy is structureless. It is only through what Simmel calls the 'great forms' that the complex reality of human society is rendered intelligible.

There is, therefore, a structure, or order, which expresses itself in sociation. Form is rigorously separated from content. Simmel writes:

> I designate as the *content*, as the *material*, as it were, of sociation. In themselves, these materials with which life is filled, the motivations by which it is propelled, are not social. Strictly speaking, neither hunger nor love, neither work nor religiosity . . . are social. They are factors in sociation only when they transform the mere aggregation of isolated individuals into specific forms . . . subsumed under the general concept of interaction. Sociation is the form . . . in which individuals grow together into units that satisfy their interests (Simmel, 1950, p. 41).

It is these reciprocal forms of sociation which constitute the object of sociology, not individual actions or isolated elements which Simmel identifies as the content or material of sociation. Through the forms of sociation individuals develop into a unity; love, purposes and inclinations become transposed from individual properties into the social through their realisation in forms. Forms of sociation include hierarchies, corporations, marriage, friendship; forms do not produce society, forms *are* society. If all interaction ceased then society itself would no longer exist. Simmel's distinction between form and content enables him to argue that although the content of institutions and actions may vary, the forms remain. Thus the form of sociation among a band of robbers may be the same as that characterising an industrial enterprise; economic interests may be realised in forms of competition as well as co-operation. Power becomes a sociological form through a structure of interaction which links the dominator and the dominated: absolute power, for example, always involves an interaction, an exchange between the action of the superordinate and the subordinate.

Perhaps the best known of Simmel's forms is the dyad which he defines as a relation of two individuals involved in immediate reciprocity. The dyadic form can comprise different contents such as teacher/student, doctor/patient, husband/wife, etc., but its essential character hinges on the dependence of the whole on each individual: the withdrawal of one destroys both the relation and the whole itself. But should another individual join the group creating a triad a qualitative change occurs in which there is no longer immediate reciprocity but mediation. The dyad is not experienced as a supra-individual element, a collectivity; in contrast the triad is experienced as a social structure standing outside and independent of the individual.

In these formulations Simmel opposed the reductionism of psychology which failed to grasp the sociological fact that a change in the forms of sociation, a change in numbers, necessarily engendered the development of new properties which cannot be derived from studying the individuals alone. Similarly, in his discussion of secrecy, which he describes as 'one of man's greatest achievements', Simmel analysed it as a form which enhances, not diminishes, human life in that it produces an intimate, private world alongside the public world, a world in which the exclusion of outsiders leads to a heightened sense of moral solidarity on the part of those who share the secret. But as secrecy is surrounded by the permanent possibility of detection it therefore generates tension between the individual's capacity to keep the secret or a weakness to reveal it: 'Out of the counterplay of these two interests, in concealing and revealing, spring nuances and fates of human interaction that permeate it in its entirety . . . every human relation is characterised, among other things, by the amount of secrecy that is in and around it' (Simmel, 1950, pp. 118–20, 330–4).

The task of sociology, as Simmel formulated it, was thus to identify the 'pure forms' of sociation and engage both with the uniqueness of historical phenomena and the underlying uniformities. Society is the product of human activity in the sense that society is sociation, and sociation itself exists at the level of ordinary everyday life as forms which bind individuals together. Forms have no separate reality apart from content in the same way as the individual has no separate reality from society. Individuals create society and forms; and simultaneously exist externally to both. The individual's relation with society is dualistic, both within and outside it, 'both social link and being for himself, both product of society and life from an autonomous centre' (Simmel, 1956, pp. 22–3). Without sociation the human subject could hardly exist; but the forms of sociation restrict his autonomy. Simmel's concept of society is one built around the dualisms of human existence: sociation entails conflict and harmony, attraction and repulsion, hate and love, independence and dependence. Clearly this is a different sociological standpoint from the nominalism of Tarde: society is not conceived in atomistic terms but is structured through forms that realise both the individuality and regularity of human action.

Nevertheless, Simmel emphasised that human existence is real only in individuals and that to confine sociology to the study of 'large social formations resembles the older science of anatomy with its limitation to the major, definitely circumscribed organs such as heart, liver, lungs, and stomach, and with its neglect of the innumerable . . . tissues'. The study of major social formations constitutes the traditional subject-matter of social science, and by accepting this approach 'the real life of society as we encounter it in our experience' would play no role in sociological analysis (Simmel, 1965, pp. 312–32). The object of sociology is interactions 'among the atoms of society', and in his essay, 'The Problem of Sociology', Simmel rejected the notion that sociology was defined by its contents. Sociology was neither a dumping pot for the other human sciences, history, psychology, jurisprudence, nor a summation of other disciplines. Sociology was defined as a distinctive method, an instrument of investigation: 'In so far as sociology is based on the facts that man must be understood as a social being and that society is the medium of the historical process, it contains no subject matter not already treated in one of the existing sciences.' The study of form clearly distinguishes sociology from the other sciences: thus sociation constitutes a form stripped of all psychological, biological and historical elements and although these latter disciplines are useful in the description of facts they always 'remain outside the purpose of sociological investigation'. As forms are not reducible to, or defined by, their content so sociology is conceived in terms of the categories of its analysis and perspective. Sociology abstracts from the complexity of social life that which is 'purely society', that is, sociation. The sociological approach is therefore its mode of abstraction, the means whereby the essential features of concrete phenomena are extracted from reality and exaggerated so that the underlying configurations and relations, which are not actually realised in reality itself, are clarified. In this way it becomes possible to compare social phenomena that have radically different contents but share a similarity of form (Simmel, 1965, pp. 312–32).

The purpose of these 'ideal types' is to facilitate the analysis of meaning. In his discussions of forms such as the dyad, secrecy and fashion, Simmel's main concern is always with the meanings of the actions that comprise the structure, understanding the modes of sociation from the standpoint of both the subject and the whole. Social interaction is always more than the sum of the actions, involving both the form or structure as well as the relations within the form itself. Society is not analysed from a holistic standpoint but from the perspective of social interaction conceived as a network of hidden relationships.

Simmel's sociological approach has been characterised as a form of sociological impressionism, the network of interrelationships constituting a labyrinth rather than system, his sociology dismissed for its failure to develop a constructive view of society as a whole. But the significance of Simmel's sociology lies precisely in the fact that it opposed the anti-humanist, scientistic approaches of positivism and vulgar Marxism and sought to recover the concept of society as the product of socially mediated human action. Thus forms explain the resilience of human society, its toughness, elasticity, colourfulness, 'so striking and yet so mysterious', the interactions that constitute sociation producing the social bonds which 'makes for the wonderful indissolubility of society, the fluctuations of its life, which constantly attains, loses and shifts the equilibrium of its elements' (Simmel, 1965, p. 328). The point is, of course, that Simmel *was* concerned with society as a whole, with large-scale social formations, but not as external structures stripped of their human determinations. Simmel's sociology rejected all modes of reifying social institutions and processes for while forms are external to individuals they only *appear* as autonomous entities. 'The deepest problems of modern life', he wrote, 'derive from the claim of the individual to preserve the autonomy and individuality of his existence in the face of overwhelming social forces, of historical heritage, of external culture, and of the technique of life' (1950, p. 409).

Simmel had developed a sociological perspective which exerted a great influence on subsequent German sociology especially that of Max Weber. Although Durkheim's *The Rules of Sociological Method* was translated into German and published in 1904, it had little impact and it was Simmel's notions of understanding, social action and methodology which triumphed. Durkheim's *positive* sociology contrasts sharply with Simmel's *ambiguous* sociology. In a review of Simmel's work written in 1900 Durkheim had drawn attention to what he considered an entirely arbitrary distinction between form and content: but Simmel constantly emphasised the impossibility of rigorously distinguishing form and content. It is 'impossible to avoid ambiguity', he wrote, 'the treatment of a particular problem will appear to belong now in one category, now in another'. Ambiguity even extended to methodology and Simmel argued that there existed no clear technique for the application of his fundamental sociological concept of sociation (Simmel, 1965, p. 324). It was the implication here of the arbitrary nature of sociological method, as well as the ambiguity over form and content, which clearly differentiated Simmel's humanist sociology from the nineteenth-century positivist tradition and it was these themes which were further developed in Weber's sociology.

Understanding and the problem of method: Weber

The sociology of Max Weber (1864–1920) sought to synthesise the positivist emphasis on causal analysis with the hermeneutic concept of understanding. Although Weber shared with Simmel a concern with integrating the human subject into the cultural sciences within a social action framework, he differed from Simmel in his emphasis on macrosociological studies of institutions and processes conceived from a broad historical perspective. Both were concerned with the fate of the individual within modern culture, but whereas Simmel focused his analysis on the atoms of society Weber dealt with such holistic categories as the Protestant ethic, pre-industrial social structures, bureaucracy and the nation state. The range of Weber's empirical and historical studies is truly encyclopaedic covering economic history, political economy, the comparative study of religions, and the methodology of the social sciences.

Originally trained in jurisprudence and the history of law, Weber's first studies examined the structure of East German agriculture and the recruitment of Polish workers; in 1896–7 he published studies of the decline of the ancient world and the stock exchange. At the outset of his intellectual career Weber was not a sociologist and rarely used the term in his first writings. At university he lectured on law and political economy and at the age of thirty-one became Professor of Political Economy at Freiburg before moving to Heidelberg in 1896. Weber thus came to sociology from economics and history; his early sociological writings reflect a concern with the methodological and epistemological issues raised by the positivist intrusions into German historical scholarship during the latter part of the nineteenth-century. German social science had been strongly influenced both by the evolutionary theory of society conceived by Comte and Spencer, as well as the burgeoning Marxist intellectual culture that emerged in the 1890s. Under the leadership of Karl Kautsky and Eduard Bernstein, the German Social Democrats became the single most important Marxist political party in Europe commanding widespread support from the German working class. The rise and institutionalisation of German sociology effectively coincided with the development of a political mass movement committed to Marxism and an intellectual culture which attempted to systematise Marxist materialism into a coherent science of society. Weber's sociology developed both as a response to evolutionary positivism on the one hand and to dogmatic Marxism on the other.

Weber defined Marxism as a form of economic determinism, a theory postulating a strict functional relation between modes of thought and economic interests: ideas, whether they were religious or political, were merely epiphenomena lacking any vestige of autonomy. For Weber, Marxism defined knowledge as ideology, as the reflection in consciousness of class and economic interests: concepts were scientific in so far as they reproduced this objective reality while pointing the way forward to the historical inevitability of socialism and communism. Society was thus a system dominated entirely by its mode of production and laws of development. Human subjects exercised no constituting role but were the passive objects of an historically evolving whole.

Weber's opposition to the concept of objective determining laws was based on the argument that such laws – whether Marxist or positivist – eliminated the active and conscious elements of a culture transforming all ideas to the status of automatic reflexes of external, material forces. Like Simmel, Weber adopted a nominalist standpoint arguing that holistic and collectivist concepts such as the state, corporation, and bureaucracy could be analysed only as the results and modes of organisation embodied in human action. Bureaucracies do not act. The burden of his early methodological essays is to demonstrate that the fundamental task of social science lies in analysing society as a structure of meaning-endowing actions centred on the human subject.

In his essay, 'Objectivity in Social Science' (1904), Weber outlined his approach in terms of understanding 'the characteristic uniqueness of the reality in which we move', a reality which consists in 'an infinite multiplicity of successively and co-existing emerging and disappearing events, both "within" and "outside" ourselves'. The study of so-called objective laws, or the relations between the various external elements that constitute a social system, does not, by itself, generate meaning. Weber insisted that the category of meaning is produced only through social action when the acting subject attaches a subjective meaning to behaviour. For Weber, history possessed no immanent meaning as historicists had suggested: history is simply the human context in which individuals and groups struggle to define and achieve certain values and goals. Weber followed Nietzsche's stoic refusal to accept the existence of universal values: there is no meaning apart from the concrete actions of human subjects (Weber, 1949, p. 72).

Weber defined society in terms of sociation, 'social relationships' which 'denote the behaviour of a plurality of actors in so far as, in its meaningful content, the action of each takes account of that of others and is oriented in these terms'. Social action is oriented towards human subjects not things, the acting individual saturating the social context with meanings. This concept of social action assumes intentional behaviour involving motives and feelings; sociology as a cultural science is thus concerned with meaningful action rather than with purely reactive or mechanical behaviour. Sociology is defined as a science 'which attempts the interpretative understanding of social action in order . . . to arrive at a causal explanation of its course and effects' (Weber, 1964, p. 118). Explanation is interpretative in the sense of seeking to understand the meanings of the actor through empathy, and causal in the sense of seeking to relate the action to means and ends. Weber did not define sociology as a subjective, intuitive mode of investigation: because human action is subjective it does not follow that it is unpredictable. Social action hinges on the subject selecting means to realise specific ends and it is this rational component which separates human action from natural processes. Action which is social is thus governed by norms relating to the means–ends continuum and it is this patterned aspect of social action that Weber identifies as the element enabling the sociologist to undertake causal analysis (Weber, 1964, p. 88).

Objective knowledge, then, is possible within the cultural sciences; the fact that the object of study is cultural values does not imply a subjectivist sociology. Weber distinguishes evaluation (*wertung*) from value-relatedness or value-relevance (*wertbeziehung*) to emphasise the point that social phenomena have significance only through their relation with a specific value system which will clearly influence the ways in which the scientist selects the object of study but not the analysis of it. Ethical neutrality forms an essential element of a valid social science, and Weber stresses that the social scientist must never impose his own values on the mode of investigation and interpretation of empirical material. Cultural science cannot evaluate ends only render explicit those ideas which underpin the ends themselves. 'It is self-evident that one of the most important tasks of every science of cultural life is to arrive at a rational understanding of these "ideas" for which men either really or allegedly struggle' (Weber, 1949, pp. 53–4). The task of social science is not to pass judgments but to isolate the structure of values within a given social context and demonstrate the relevance of these values for an objective understanding of social action. Interpretative understanding (*verstehen*) and causal explanation are essential modes of analysis for the attainment of scientific, objective knowledge. The subjective meaning of social action is grasped through empathy and reliving, but unlike Dilthey, Weber's interpretative understanding becomes scientific through its integration into objective, causal explanation. Thus Weber criticises Simmel for his failure to distinguish between subjectively intended and objectively 'valid' meanings which are often treated 'as belonging together' (Weber, 1964, p. 88).

Culture is the realm of values but 'empirical reality only becomes "culture" to us because and in so far as we relate it to value ideas'. Culture in this sense includes those elements which are significant because of their value relevance and it is impossible to discover 'what is meaningful to us by means of a "presuppositionless" investigation of empirical data'. Weber's argument is that not everything within culture is worth investigating for 'only a small portion of existing concrete reality is coloured by our value-conditioned interest and it alone is significant to us' (Weber, 1949, p. 76). The positivist separation of facts and values is here clearly articulated, the choice between values regarded as a matter of faith not of science. But to accept the existence of certain values which predispose the researcher to the selection of the essential from the non-essential segments of reality and on this basis develop a methodology is to ignore the problem of ideology. Weber's standpoint is agnostic positivism, the acceptance of differing and possibly antagonistic cultural values (although this aspect is never adequately discussed). Thus he argues that in order to make sense out of the flux which is reality, a concept must be 'highly selective' and valid only 'within the scope of its own postulates'. Weber writes:

> Life with its irrational reality and its store of possible meanings is inexhaustible. The *concrete* form in which value relevance occurs remains perceptually in flux, ever subject to change in the dimly seen future of human culture. The light which emanates from these highest evaluative ideas always falls on an ever changing finite segment of the vast chaotic stream of events, which flows away through time (Weber, 1949, p. 111).

Totality has been eliminated from social theory; there is no whole, no 'essence' to history and society, but a constantly fluctuating culture of meaning-endowing social actions; social relationships are conceived in inter-subjective terms as embodying purposive activity. Social structure is therefore the product of action and social collectivities such as bureaucracy, corporations, and states treated as results of subjectively understandable action. Weber thus rejects the methodology 'which proceeds from the whole to the parts' arguing that this can accomplish only a preliminary analysis of reality: as there is no external, objective social world determined in its structure by laws of development so there is no correspondence between scientific, sociological concepts and an objectively 'real' datum.

Sociological concepts are pure types which do not reflect reality but, through the processes of abstraction and selection governed by value-relevance and significance, embody the essential elements of different phenomena. Weber's ideal types are in effect Simmel's pure forms, analytical constructs enabling the researcher to make comparisons with many different phenomena which, although characterised by different content or material, belong to the same form. These forms are constituted through action. As there are no objective laws governing society so action must be defined in terms of 'probability' rather than 'necessity' and the structure of sociological concepts built around this probabilistic perspective.

Ideal types and social action

Weber's sociology sought to combine explanation with understanding; social action was both subjective and objective; but
subjective understanding was the specific characteristic of
sociological knowledge. Weber did not advocate intuitive
understanding, for human relationships enjoy regular and
consistent patterns so that causality can be defined but only in
terms of probability. Probability refers to the chances that in
specific contexts human subjects will orient their behaviour to
certain norms so that a given observable event will be followed,
or accompanied, by another event. Social action is always
probable rather than certain because the unique nature of
social relationships generates the possibility of deviation from
the expected course of action. The ideal type is the means of
analysing the probability that actors will follow one course of
action rather than another.

Ideal types are concerned with the subjective elements in
social life, those unique and unrepeatable elements of culture
disregarded by positivist social theory. Ideal types involve
selection,

> . . . the one-sided accentuation of one or more points of view and by
> the synthesis of a great many diffuse, discrete, more-or-less present
> and occasionally absent concrete individual phenomena which are
> arranged according to those one-sidedly emphasised viewpoints
> into a unified analytical construct (Weber, 1949, p. 90).

The ideal type is no description of reality but a mental
construction which incorporates the essential, not the average,
properties of a particular phenomenon. The term ideal type
implies no moral standpoint; it is a methodological concept
which facilitates the understanding and explanation of social
phenomena. It neither corresponds with an external objective
reality nor constitutes 'essence' in the manner of an Hegelian
'spirit'. Ideal types are pure forms; some of its features will
therefore be absent from its concrete forms. For Weber, ideal
types were tools of analysis, their value purely heuristic, a mode
of 'revealing concrete cultural phenomena in their interdependence, their causal conditions and their significance' (Weber,
1949, p. 92).

Weber's method is thus to construct unreal relations in order to analyse real historical relations; reality is known through concepts and abstractions. He identified three distinct ideal types: historical formations such as modern capitalism and the Protestant ethic characterised by their specificity; abstract ideal types such as bureaucracy and feudalism which characterise different historical and cultural periods; and finally, types of action. The level of abstraction varies with each of these ideal types although Weber argues, as we have seen above, that social formations and large-scale institutions always designate categories of human interaction and that the role of sociology is to reduce these concepts to understandable action, to the actions of participating individuals. He identifies four types of social action:

1. Rational action (*wertrational*) oriented to the attainment of an absolute value which may be aesthetic, religious, ethical; the goal is pursued for its own sake and not because of the possibility of success.
2. Rational goal-oriented action (*zweckrational*) in which goal and means are rationally chosen.
3. Affectual action determined by the emotional effects on the actor.
4. Traditional action which is guided by custom and habit.

These four types of social action are defined in terms of their distance from the borderline of meaningfully oriented action: thus *wertrational* and *zweckrational* action both involve some measure of conscious choice in ends and means while affectual and traditional action approaches the borderline of purely reactive behaviour. Weber was especially concerned with rational action, rationality being defined exclusively in terms of the means not the ends, the latter being outside the province of science.

For Weber, action governed by rational norms is always more predictable in its possible effects than so-called irrational action. The more a value is absolute so the action corresponding to its achievement becomes irrational for 'the more unconditionally the actor devotes himself to this value for its own sake, to pure sentiment or beauty ... the less is he influenced by considerations of the consequences of his actions'. The norm of rationality against which all social action is measured is the ends–means relationship, the goals defined by the acting subject as well as the choice of means necessary to attain them. Rational action is social action in so far as the subject must take account of others in his course of action. Rationality and irrationality – irrationality being deviations from the rational norm – are structured, therefore, in the concrete, existing situation, the world as it is, the world of human experience. Weber, here, approaches a positivistic standpoint. The ideal type, which does not exhaust all the possibilities of a particular phenomenon is the conceptually pure form to which actual action closely approximates, the classification being useful only in terms of its results (Weber, 1964, pp. 117–18).

Weber is arguing, then, that sociology seeks to formulate type concepts and generalisable uniformities: human behaviour, whether external or internal, displays relations and regularities which are understandable in terms of the cultural significance attached to them by the acting subject. Sociology is both interpretative understanding of the complex structures of meaning of typical social actions *and* causal explanation based on the probability that one event will be followed by another. Ideal types must therefore be constructed both in terms of their 'adequacy on the level of meaning' and causal adequacy.

The sociologist must interpret the meaning of social action as rigorously as those explanations which are offered in the natural sciences. Weber's distinction between the methods of the natural and the social sciences does not imply that the social sciences are less scientific, less objective and do not offer grounds for verifying hypotheses. Objective knowledge and certainty constitute the aims of sociology even though the nature of reality as defined by Weber makes it virtually impossible to achieve these ends. In analysing social action it is not necessary to invoke any mode of intuitive understanding or seek to grasp the whole of a person's experience: one does not have to be Caesar in order to understand Caesar. Weber's concept of understanding differentiates behaviour from action, the former lacking subjective meaning being simply habit or reactive behaviour, and he postulates two distinct modes of understanding: direct, observational understanding and explanatory or motivational understanding. By direct understanding Weber means explanation in terms of observable, objective properties within a given context and which are immediately understandable, such as the action of someone chopping wood, or the writing down of the formula $2 \times 2 = 4$; explanatory understanding, in contrast, involves knowledge of motives, the subjective meanings attributed to the action by the actor.

This distinction is not particularly helpful however. To take the example of the woodcutter: the action involved in cutting wood contains a referential meaning in that the act always assumes an end to which the product of the act – wood – is to be used, for making toys, for building, for fire; this meaning is built into every act of chopping wood even in those cases where the individual is merely engaged in physical exercise. Both direct and explanatory understanding imply a context of meaning and it is virtually impossible to differentiate them in Weber's terms. Weber's ambivalent attitude to positivism is evident here: the context of meaning and its norms are given datums. The ends of human action, too, are defined as falling outside the domain of science. But in criticising positivism Weber argues that before explaining why an individual followed a specific course of action it is essential to understand the meaning of the action itself. Sociological analysis must be adequate both in terms of meaning and causality. Ideal type categories of action, therefore, are constructions in which actors are related both to other actors, or subjects, and to the historical context; ideal type analysis is interpretative-causal linking meanings to ends.

For Weber, sociological positivism and Marxism lacked the categories of meaning and motivational understanding other than as derivations from external laws and inevitable historical development; the human subject was determined by the workings of laws to the extent that historical events automatically occurred irrespective of the subjective intentions of the actors. In contrast, Weber emphasised that meaning is inter-subjective and not, as with Marx, systemic, the social whole conferring historical meaning on individual actions. But one such whole, capitalism, is defined by Weber as a structure of social actions and seeking an explanation of its specific and unique historical development involves the sociologist in asking the question: what motivated individuals to save and invest rather than to spend and consume.

Religion and social action: capitalism and the Protestant ethic

Weber's first major sociological study was *The Protestant Ethic and the Spirit of Capitalism* (first published in article form, 1904–5) in which he raised the problem of the sociological analysis of a unique social formation, modern European capitalism and sought to explain its historical development through the method of the ideal type. By 1904 Weber was turning increasingly away from historical studies towards sociology, although he continued to employ the concept of culture rather than the concept of society in his writings. The influence of Rickert is clearly evident in Weber's concept of cultural significance which linked the uniqueness of the historical phenomenon with its interpretation in terms of specific cultural values. Ideal types bring out the cultural significance of that particular segment of reality defined as significant; and they function, too, as heuristic tools investigating questions of cultural values. Weber emphasised particularly the historical dimension of social phenomena arguing that cultural significance can be judged only on this basis. The study of the relation of Protestant theology and capitalism is both a study in historical sociology and a methodological exercise in systematic sociology through the application of typical constructs to complex empirical material.

For Weber, capitalism was the product of a unique historical phenomenon, ascetic Protestantism, and its cultural significance was bound up in these 'ideal' origins and resulting motivational structure which effectively predisposed certain individuals to a particular orientation to work and rational social action. The relation of religion to economic activity had been widely discussed by many scholars before Weber, although it was not until the turn of the century that detailed statistical analysis which linked religious affiliation with occupation became available. A negative correlation was established, for example, between Catholicism and successful business activity. Weber was particularly concerned to demonstrate that ideal elements, such as religious ideas, were not mechanically linked to the economic structure but actively shaped the ways in which individuals carried out their ordinary day-to-day activities.

Weber's study was initially intended as a preliminary analysis, although subsequent criticism has often assumed it as a final statement. During the years following the publication of the articles, Weber replied to his many German critics and in particular began work on a vast comparative study of world religions. In 1920 he published a new introduction to the Protestant ethic study and shortly after his death further important material was published in his *General Economic History*. In these writings Weber rejected the commonly held view that his study merely reversed the Marxist argument of the priority of economic forces in social change making religious ideas the causal factor in social development. In the 1920 introduction he emphasised that his analysis was treating 'only one side of the causal chain', while in the early articles he pointed out that he was not substituting for the 'one-sided' materialist approach of Marxism 'an equally one-sided spiritualistic causal interpretation of history and culture' (Weber, 1930, p. 183). His comparative studies of world religions sought to analyse the plurality of factors which influenced the course of economic development and explored in greater detail the broad cultural implications of religious ideas on the formation of capitalism as a system. Only if Marxism is defined as a one factor theory of social change can Weber's study be regarded as its opposite and its refutation.

The question Weber posed in his preliminary analysis of Protestantism, and in his later studies of Chinese, Indian and Palestinian religions, was why did capitalism, defined as a highly rationalised system, develop only in Western Europe. In India, Palestine and China the material infrastructure of capitalism also existed – markets, division of labour, money economy, trade routes – yet only in Western Europe did capitalism fully emerge out of such conditions. Weber notes, for example, that Indian geometry, natural sciences, medicine, political and historical thought, while all highly developed, lacked systematic concepts and methodology. In China science remained unorganised; there was no 'rational, systematic and specialised pursuit of science'. The existence of specific material conditions is insufficient to form a basis for capitalist development and in particular capitalist economic action 'which rests on the expectation of profit by the utilisation of opportunities for exchange, that is on [formally] peaceful chances of profit'. One of the most important points Weber makes is that if capitalism is defined loosely as a mode of money-making then it is characteristic of all civilised societies, China, India and Mediterranean antiquity:

> The impulse to acquisition, pursuit of gain, of money, of the greatest possible amount of money, has in itself nothing to do with capitalism. This impulse exists and has existed among waiters, physicians, coachmen, artists, prostitutes . . . gamblers and beggars . . . it has been common to all sorts and conditions of men at all times . . . whatever the objective possibility of it is or has been given . . . Unlimited greed for gain is not in the least identical with capitalism, and still less its spirit (Weber, 1930, p. 17).

By capitalism Weber meant a system characterised by a rational organisation of formally free labour, the separation of business from the household, the development of rational book-keeping and rational systems of law and administration. Weber was careful to distinguish his concept of capitalism from contemporary sociologists such as Simmel and Sombart: Simmel, in his *Philosophy of Money*, assimilated capitalism to the concept of 'money economy', while Sombart, in his *Modern Capitalism*, identified capitalism with economic 'adventurers' (entrepreneurs seeking to maximise their profits through courage and excessive risk taking) and high consumption particularly in luxury goods. Neither consumption nor the money economy was unique to the West: but a world view which abjures consumption and luxury demanding of those who accept its tenets that they work and invest, not to expiate sin as with Catholicism, but for the promise of salvation, is unique to

Western Europe. The unique, economic structure of Western capitalism is thus homologous with the unique Protestant theology, especially Calvinism, which developed during the sixteenth and seventeenth centuries. Weber adds that by the eighteenth century capitalism had become effectively independent of its religious foundations.

For Weber, then, sociological explanation of the capitalist social formation, while recognising the importance of purely economic factors, identifies the modes of rationalism which are unique to it with forms of social conduct and action. The fundamental issue between Marxism and Weber's sociology lies ultimately in Weber's rejection of the Marxist philosophy of history, the view that capitalism necessarily develops through the workings of objective, economic laws determined by material forces which effectively render the subjective component – human action – irrelevant. This interpretation of Marxism assimilates meaning to historicism: human actions have meaning only in terms of the developing whole and the ultimate end of the historical process, the reconciliation of contradictions in Communist society. For Weber, Marxism lacked a concept of motivation: change occurs through the workings of external, impersonal forces in which human action is reduced to the status of total passivity. But change is always change through the actions of human agents: human subjects are motivated to act in specific ways, to accept or reject the prevailing system of ideas, to reject luxury and immediate consumption, to postpone their worldly gratification and avoid 'all spontaneous enjoyment of life' in favour of a rigorous asceticism. It is the motivational structure of action which constitutes the spirit of capitalism, a spirit not found in India or China, but bound up with Protestant ideology.

The term, spirit, suggests some notion of essence outside history and society, a metaphysical concept rather than sociological category. Although there is ambiguity in Weber's formulation the weight of his argument nevertheless suggests that spirit is the active element of a world view which, in its everyday forms, structures human action. In his 1905 essay he defines spirit as 'a complex of elements associated in historical reality which we unite into a conceptual whole from the standpoint of their cultural significance'. The spirit of capitalism is thus a methodological concept, an abstraction 'put together out of the individual parts which are taken from historical reality . . . a conceptual formulation . . . that is the best from the point of view which interests us'. As such the spirit of capitalism is expressed in a rationalising attitude to life, in such maxims of conduct as be prudent, diligent, punctilious in repayment of debts and loans, avoid idleness since time is money, be frugal in consumption and so on. The spirit of capitalism is a social ethic, a structure of attitudes and behaviour closely identified with ascetic Protestantism and its associated religious sects such as the Puritans and the Calvinists (Weber, 1930, pp. 47–53).

Although Puritanism, Pietism, Methodism and the Anabaptist sects exemplified the capitalist spirit, Weber particularly emphasised the significance of Calvinism. For Weber, Calvinism constituted a form of inner worldly asceticism built around the notion of worldly vocation or calling. It was Luther, however, who originally emphasised that the fulfilment of worldly duties 'is under all circumstances the only way to live acceptably to God . . . it alone is the will of God, and hence every legitimate calling has exactly the same worth in the sight of God'. But Luther's attitude to capitalism, argued Weber, was broadly traditional identifying 'absolute obedience to God's will with absolute acceptance of things as they were'. The individual was encouraged to remain in the station and calling which God had determined and 'restrain his worldly activity within the limits imposed by his established station in life'. Thus Lutheranism could never establish any new connection between worldly activity and religious principles (Weber, 1930, pp. 81–5).

Of all the Protestant sects it was the Calvinists who successfully combined the notion of calling with values appropriate to capitalist development. Calvinism advocated the concept of predestination which superficially suggests a fatalistic rather than positive approach to the world on the part of the believer. Weber's argument is that it was precisely because the Calvinists had to prove their election through good works that their religious beliefs acted as a dynamic and not passive element in social change: the Calvinist, he writes, 'creates his own salvation, or, as would be more correct, the conviction of it'. Hard work and the moral pursuit of a calling, while not constituting infallible evidence of salvation, nevertheless functions to assuage the fear of damnation. The Calvinists effectively required some sign, some criteria 'by which membership of the *electi* could be known'. It was not a question of accumulating good works, as with Catholicism 'but rather (of) systematic self-control' in relation to material pleasures and 'the constructive use of time'. Idleness, gambling, excessive sleep are proof only of imperfect grace. The faithful must attend not simply to their ordinary spiritual obligations, such as prayer, but strive hard in their worldly callings. Weber stresses that there was nothing especially original in the maxims of Protestantism: many religions had condemned idleness and hedonism but the Calvinists went much further in demanding adherence to their maxims of everyday conduct, not as proof of salvation, but as evidence that one may not be among the damned. Religious grace 'could not be guaranteed by any magical sacraments, by relief in the confession' but the individual must methodically supervise 'his own state of grace in his own conduct, and thus to penetrate it with asceticism . . . a rational planning of the whole of one's life in accordance with God's will . . . something which could be required of everyone who would be certain of salvation' (Weber, 1930, p. 153).

Weber concludes by arguing that only as long as the psychological sanctions which develop from the notion of predestination and the concept of proof remain efficacious 'does such an ethic gain an independent influence on the conduct of life and thus on the economic order'. It is not, therefore, Weber's argument that the ideas of specific theologians exercised a decisive role in the genesis of capitalism, but of the influence 'of those psychological sanctions which, originating in religious belief . . . gave a direction to practical conduct and held the individual to it' (Weber, 1930, p. 197). Religious leaders did not set out consciously to produce an ethic for capitalism; the unintended consequences of social action effectively led to that situation. The human subject, non-consciously but actively, transforms humanity, ideas and society.

Weber has, therefore, linked action with the social system and social development, although his stated methodological approach rejects collective concepts in favour of methodological individualism. The 'elective affinity' between the norms of ascetic Protestantism and the psychological–motivational structure of capitalist values eliminates any notion of a deterministic relation of economic 'base' and cultural 'superstructure'. It must be emphasised that Weber is not arguing that the existence of ascetic Protestant values automatically led to capitalist development – the most frequent criticism of Weber's thesis is to identify different countries, and different areas within a country, where Protestant asceticism existed but capitalism failed to develop, such as Calvin's own homeland of Switzerland and seventeenth-century Scotland – rather that the social ethic constitutes one of many elements which, through a process of mutual interaction, leads to social change.

This is not to suggest that there are no problems with Weber's formulation of a necessary link between religious ideas and economic forms. The evidence which he selects to defend his thesis is largely derived from writers who lived after Calvin such as Richard Baxter (1615–91), John Wesley (1703–91) and particularly, Benjamin Franklin (1706–90) and his analysis assumes a direct relation between the ideas expressed in their literary works and social action. He offers no independent evidence that prominent Protestant businessmen subscribed significantly to ascetic Protestant ideas, or that Protestant business communities adhered to the theological maxims regulating everyday conduct. What is more striking is Weber's failure to elucidate the precise ways in which businessmen interpreted Protestant maxims, to grasp the meanings of theological concepts for the subject. Meanings are in effect *imputed* to the subject on the basis of an interpretation of texts by the sociologist. As many critics have pointed out, Weber offers no other evidence in support of his thesis. Finally it has been suggested that Weber's exemplary figure of Franklin, far from embodying ascetic norms of conduct, enjoyed a private life dominated by hedonistic principles, engaging in extra-marital affairs, cultivating a taste for good food and wine, theatre and sports. Franklin was a far more complex figure than the single-minded Puritan portrayed by Weber (Kolko, 1960).

In a similar way, critics have emphasised that many Protestant businessmen were involved in 'traditional' economic activity such as war-profiteering, colonial expeditions, land and currency speculation. But no evidence is advanced which relates to such individuals and groups. Weber's thesis is at its weakest here: the evidence offered in support of his thesis is largely derived from the social teaching of the Protestant sects (itself culled from Ernst Troeltsch's work on the Christian Churches and their social values) and never from the actors themselves (Marshall, 1982, pp. 116–19).

Weber's basic argument is, however, clearly against reductionist, mono-causal explanation. There is scope within Weber's general approach to account for the ways in which capitalism itself affects Protestant values:

> For those to whom no causal explanation is adequate without an economic (or materialistic as it is still unfortunately called) interpretation, it may be remarked that I consider the influence of economic development on the fate of religious ideas to be very important . . . religious ideas themselves simply cannot be deduced from economic circumstances. They are in themselves . . . the most powerful plastic elements of national character, and contain a law of development and a compelling force entirely their own (Weber, 1930, pp. 277–8).

In rejecting one-factor theories of social development Weber approaches an agnostic, pluralistic perspective: the causal chain, he argues, can run from the technical to the economic, at other times from the political to the religious. It is impossible to bring this process of pluralistic causation to a single resting-point. Yet as he shows in the study of the Protestant ethic, there exists immanent properties within certain religious ideologies which successfully effect a transformation of the culture: thus although rejecting evolutionary theory, Weber seems to adopt a similar standpoint with his argument on rationalisation. The rationalising process is immanent within the Protestant religion, and as the major characteristic of Western culture rationalisation constitutes a law of development. Yet Weber's study of religion stresses the active role of the subject: social development is not inevitable, the fate of humanity has not been decided in advance. Weber's sociology thus moves ambiguously between the poles of certitude and agnosticism, between the subject as active agent and society as external determining process.

Capitalism and culture: Sombart and Simmel

The sociology of culture, as it developed in the work of Weber, Tönnies, Simmel and Sombart identified culture as a unique realm of values which expressed an immanent historical process. As we have seen with Weber's study of Protestantism, culture exercised an active role in social action and the development of social formations: it could not be reduced to a reflection of economic forces. Comparing the specific and unique development of Western rationalised capitalism with the failure of capitalism to emerge as a system in India, China and the Near East, Weber argued that it was the absence of a cultural orientation to the world, a motivational structure built around rational values, which accounted for the difference. The whole of Western architecture, mathematics, science and music, he suggested, could be identified as products and as active elements of a rationalising culture. In his unfinished study of music – *The Social and Rational Foundations of Music*, written in 1912 but not published until 1921 as an appendix to *Economy and Society* – Weber attempted to show how Western music, once it became an autonomous art-form based on tonality, polyphony and the study of counterpoint, and modern musical notation which facilitated structural composition leaving little scope for improvisation, became highly rationalised: sonatas, symphonies, operas, together with instruments such as the organ, piano and violin were unknown in non-Western cultures. Thus although polyphonic music was known in other cultures the absence of rational harmony was the decisive element (Weber, 1958b).

Weber's theme of the rationalisation of culture informs much of Simmel's work notably his *Philosophy of Money* (1900) which, in many ways, constitutes a pioneering study of the cultural foundations and crisis of the modern capitalist economic system. Before discussing Simmel's work, however, it is instructive to analyse the contribution of one other contemporary German sociologist, Werner Sombart (1863–1938) who, like Weber, investigated in massive detail the cultural foundations of modern capitalism. As with Weber, Sombart argued that capitalism constituted a unique social formation. Although influenced by Marxism, Sombert rejected the view that capitalism must inevitably decline as the new socialist society develops within the womb of the old society; such an historicist argument presupposed a rigidly deterministic relation of culture to economic forms. Culture, Sombart argued, generated its own values: it was not a mere prelude to the 'higher' social order of socialism. In a series of works, *The Jews and Modern Capitalism*, *Modern Capitalism*, *Luxury and Capitalism* Sombart outlined the cultural prerequisites of capitalist economic development.

In *Luxury and Capitalism* (1913) Sombart argued that during the period 1200–1800 a highly secularised culture developed in Italy, France, Germany and England based almost entirely on the principles of ostentatious consumption: the rising, urban bourgeoisie, in order to achieve social esteem, followed the consumption patterns of the nobility so that 'luxury expenditures' assumed 'gigantic proportions almost overnight' as 'the great need for luxuries on the part of the nouveaux riches . . . initiated a craving for enjoyment and a striving for pleasure and vain ostentation which swept Europe like a plague'. Lavish displays and extraordinary expenditure on finery, furniture, food, buildings, the support of expensive art-forms such as opera combined with drastic changes in sexual mores to produce a city-based hedonistic culture. Sombart particularly emphasised the important role women played in this process: the courtesan emerges as a significant figure in the extraordinary splendour of court life, her role the result of a new hedonistic conception of love freed from the taboos of feudal ideology. This secularisation of love and sexuality gradually saturated other social strata with the result a domestication of luxury itself: 'Anything that charms the eye, the ear, the nose, the palate, or the touch, tends to find an ever more perfect expression in objects of daily use. And it is precisely the outlay for such objects that constitutes luxury. In the last analysis, it is our sexual life that lies at the root of the desire to refine and multiply the means of stimulating our senses, for sensuous . . . and erotic pleasure are essentially the same.' The growth of luxury springs from the sex impulse: the accumulation of wealth develops only in those societies in which human sexuality can find free expression.

Capitalism is thus the product of a combination of factors but especially the process of the secularisation of sexuality and the status-striving of rising social groups. Large-scale industry originated initially in luxury trades, especially in the manufacture of silk, lace, porcelain, glass and, with changes in culinary habits, sugar refining. Luxury was therefore a signifying system of social action whether located in the courts, with their large retinue of servants and extravagant expenditures, or in its domesticated form, the accumulation of objects within the home. Sombart concluded by correlating the rise of rococo art and decline of baroque art at the beginning of the eighteenth century with 'the final and complete triumph of the female who deliberately uses her sex to secure a dominant role'. The essentially feminine nature of rococo art, he adds, dominates all domains of culture: art comes to reflect and glorify the 'triumphant female'. Thus Sombart concludes that luxury, 'itself a legitimate child of illicit love . . . gave birth to capitalism' (Sombart, 1967, pp. 61–96, 171).

Sombart's thesis contrasts sharply with Weber's argument on the creative role of ascetic culture in the genesis of capitalism. And whereas Weber developed a distinctive method of analysis Sombart exhibits a cavalier attitude towards empirical evidence with an overreliance on literary sources and a too-generalising approach to different societies and time-scales. Sombart's work on culture lacks the rigour of Weber and Durkheim. Yet it is a bold thesis identifying culture as an autonomous realm of human activity and linking capitalism, as a system, with the everyday world of objective and domesticated culture, fashion, food and art. Many of Sombart's major themes, the social significance of innate sexuality for example, although exaggerated and reducing the complexity of capitalist culture to a psychological universal, illuminate the active element in everyday sociation.

Unlike Sombart, Simmel was not concerned with investigating the historical genesis of large-scale social formations; Simmel's concept of sociation predisposed him to the study of the small-scale, the molecular processes involved in such significant social relationships as the dyad and secret society. His range of interests was far greater than any other contemporary sociologist: he wrote extensively on aesthetic problems, on art and literature (essays and reviews of Rembrandt, Dante, Michelangelo, Stefan George, Rodin, Goethe), architecture, the structure of the human face, the cultural significance of fashion, the relation of thought to urban life (in his 1903 essay 'The Metropolis and Mental life'). But his major contribution to the sociology of culture was *The Philosophy of Money*, a work which influenced the later studies of reification and culture carried out by Lukács and the Frankfurt School.

On one level *The Philosophy of Money* is an abstract, non-historical, non-genetic, 'phenomenological' analysis of the social and cultural significance of money in modern industrial society. Simmel knew Marx's work and clearly regarded his own contribution as supplementing *Capital*, constructing 'a new story beneath historical materialism such that the explanatory value of the incorporation of economic life into the causes of intellectual culture is preserved, while these economic forms themselves are recognised as the result of more profound valuations and currents of psychological, even metaphysical preconditions' (Simmel, 1978, p. 56). Clearly, cultural analysis required the methods of the cultural sciences. Like Sombart, Simmel regarded culture as irreducible to the economic structure but went beyond Sombart's broad historical analysis to define culture as a 'form' in which purposive social action finds expression. Simmel's sociology assumes the world as a structureless mass unless organised into forms, for while experience constitutes the content of the form, ultimately the world is apprehended through what Simmel calls the 'great forms'. Forms shape the raw, unmediated reality into a coherent order. The world is thus a totality of forms – art, science, religion – which bring together diversity and unity: without forms there would be only 'an indifferent simultaneous juxtaposition of contents'. In his essay, 'The Aesthetic Significance of the Face', Simmel argued that unity has significance and meaning only to the extent that it contrasts with the multiplicity of those elements, the different shapes and surfaces which merge into a whole. Simmel's concept of society is aesthetic: the 'spirit' of society lies in the content of its diverse interactions, but the unity, of which the spirit is an expression, goes beyond the sum of interactions. Form, Simmel insists, must embrace its parts fusing them into an 'absolute unity of meaning' (Simmel, 1959, pp. 279–93).

The Philosophy of Money examines the ways in which the money economy transforms cultural forms into external objects and breaks up the unity of individual and society. For Simmel, culture is a specifically human and meaning-endowing activity of the subject, for 'by cultivating objects, that is, by increasing their value beyond the performance of their natural constitution, we cultivate ourselves . . . In refining objects, man creates them in his own image'. Culture, as 'the supra-natural growth of the energies of things, is . . . the embodiment of the identical growth of *our* energies'. What Simmel terms the 'tragedy of modern culture' is the simultaneous development of science, technology and art, the availability of knowledge, and the decline of individual culture. 'Every day and from all sides', he writes, 'the wealth of objective culture increases, but the individual mind can enrich the forms and contents of its own development only by distancing itself still further from that culture . . .' The result is the domination of objective culture over subjective culture (Simmel, 1978, pp. 446–8).

Thus culture, the realm of human purposes and meanings, becomes externalised. In his essay on urbanism he noted the 'frightful disproportion' between the immense culture embodied in material things and the subject's understanding and knowledge of this process. Like Ferguson and Smith, Simmel identified the division of labour as the factor responsible for reducing the individual to a 'negligible quantity' able to cope less and less with the growth of objective culture, becoming a 'mere cog in an enormous organisation of things and powers which tear from his hands all progress, spirituality, and value in order to transform them from their subjective form into the form of purely objective life' (Simmel, 1950, p. 422). Thus, although the culture of modern society enables the individual to participate in more groups and circles than the culture of pre-industrial society – the individual is no longer immersed wholly in kinship groups or guilds to the detriment of individuality – this shift from cultural homogeneity to cultural differentiation is wrought at great cost. Simmel develops a dialectical concept of social development structured around the notion of sociation as dualistic, the simultaneous embodiment of harmony and conflict, attraction and repulsion, love and hatred.

On one level, therefore, Simmel advanced the view that social development leads to a decentred culture in which there is no dominant structure which wholly absorbs the individual: modern culture is essentially characterised by multiple participation in a complex of social circles which, for Simmel constituted the most important criterion of human development. But as modern society becomes institutionally decentred, culture becomes increasingly rationalised and money, with its 'colourless and indifference' the common denominator of all values: the modern mind is calculating, quantitative values replace qualitative values, the world is fixed by mathematical formulas, dehumanised by 'stable and impersonal' time schedules; punctuality, calculability and exactness pervade all spheres of culture. The tension between objective culture and subjective culture becomes increasingly marked with the development of the division of labour and a money economy. In *The Philosophy of Money* Simmel depicts this fragmentation and alienation as the result of a specific historical process which transforms cultural objects, created by human subjects for human subjects, into autonomous *things* which have the appearance of 'autonomous mobility'. Modern man, he writes, 'is so surrounded by nothing but impersonal objects that he becomes more and more conditioned into accepting the idea of anti-individualistic social order (i.e. socialist ideas) . . . cultural objects increasingly evolve into an interconnected enclosed world that has increasingly fewer points at which the subjective soul can interpose its will and feelings'. The real tragedy of culture is thus the tendency to turn the creative subject into an object, to reify the products of human culture and effectively eliminate purposive human action (Simmel, 1978, pp. 296–7, 448–61).

For Simmel cultural development necessarily entails both the objectification of social relationships brought about by the money economy (social relationships in modern urban society are mediated by pecuniary considerations which have the effect of creating a functional distance between different individuals), and the increasing separation of individuals from the products of their labour (the relation of the subject with the object is mediated through money, and thus commodity values, leading to an increasing mental distancing from the objects themselves). Simmel's concept of 'distance' is important for his general theory of culture for it is only by standing back from the cultural objects that the human subject can grasp reality at all. A money economy, especially advanced capitalist forms, develops this sense of distance (for example, credit transactions which effectively reduce the personal and therefore the psychological immediacy of monetary exchange). For Simmel, the whole concept of the aesthetic and its role in social life hinges on distance and perspective. It is precisely this process of objectification which ensures that cultural objects possess aesthetic value. Thus cultural development is structured around irreconcilable contradictions: the source of Simmel's cultural pessimism lay in his awareness that the realisation of human potential depends in part on the expansion of objective culture, that the growth of subjective culture with its rich inner life flows from the reification of culture itself.

In Simmel's later writings, especially the essay, 'The Concept and Tragedy of Culture' which formed part of his *Philosophical Culture* (1911), the contradictions between objective and subjective culture are increasingly analysed not in terms of social formations, historical processes or social structures, but rather as the necessary fate of humanity which is merely the agent, not the active subject, of the immanent logic of culture. This is a different standpoint from the sociological perspective of *The Philosophy of Money* which, while defining the sphere of culture in terms of autonomous forms, analysed their necessary, active relations with economic and social structures.

Social action and social system: Pareto

Weber and Simmel rediscovered the active human subject through their critique of the holistic, systemic approaches of positivism and determinism of sociological evolutionism. As we have seen, both thinkers were concerned with the sociology of everyday activity, with sociation and the meaning–structures of culture. Although Simmel's sociology can be criticised for its tendency to adopt an excessively abstract and atomistic concept of social structure, Weber was more rigorously historical in his approach to the relation of subject to society. Weber's theory of social action is not, strictly speaking, separable from a theory of social system. In his study of Protestantism the role of the subject is conceived in terms of its relation with capitalism as an economic system, an objective structure both historical and sociological. The social action and social system perspectives co-exist within Weber's sociology in a state of fruitful tension. Sociological positivism had conceptualised the social system, often in organicist terms, as an external constraining datum built around an inherent need for order and equilibrium: social action theory, more optimistic through its concept of human agency, strove to integrate the meaning–endowing role of the subject with the larger, external socio-cultural whole. The sociology of Weber and Simmel is therefore opposed to the holistic determinism which was later developed by American Functionalists who absorbed the notion of system at the expense of action.

Although the concept of system is implicit in much of the empirical and historical work of the founding fathers of modern sociology – Tönnies, Simmel, Durkheim, Weber – it was the Italian sociologist, Vilfredo Pareto (1848–1923) who, in the course of criticising nineteenth-century positivism, evolutionism, Social Darwinism and especially Marxism, defined society explicitly as a social system. Pareto's sociology constitutes a complex mixture of voluntarism and determinism, a rejection of the humanist tradition in social theory (especially Vico) in favour of a pessimistic and fatalistic notion of a fixed human nature, while simultaneously advancing the concept of society as the product of *non-logical* social action.

A controversial figure in the history of sociology (Mussolini offered him a seat in the Italian Senate which he refused), Pareto began his intellectual career in engineering, mathematics and the natural sciences, gravitating towards economics and sociology later in life. His early work reflected the influences of positivism and Social Darwinism elements of which can be found in his later writings. Like Durkheim he was concerned with *facts* not metaphysical theories or speculative doctrines which mixed fact with values. *Les Systemes Socialistes* (1902) is a sustained and hostile critique of Marxism which praised Marx's sociological theory of class and class conflict, while rejecting his claim to have established a scientific socialism and scientific theory of society as a whole. In 1916 Pareto published his monumental study, *A Treatise on General Sociology*, which, in striking contrast to the contemporary sociology of Durkheim and Weber, is less concerned with the specific historical development of industrial society than with the history of human society and culture from the earliest times. For Pareto, history was to be ransacked to provide examples and proofs for broad, general theorems. Throughout the *Treatise* Pareto exhibits a cavalier disdain for the 'rules of sociological method', with arbitrary illustration, wrenched from its historical context, employed as the basis of verification. The *Treatise* is characterised by a poverty of empirical research, absence of specific socio-historical data carefully collected and systematically ordered, combined with a withering contempt for previous sociology. Pareto rejected nineteenth-century theories of progress, condemned Enlightenment philosophical rationalism, debunked humanitarian philosophy and modern mass democracy. Political theories such as Marxism and Liberalism were of interest only because they were popular and therefore required psychological explanation. Pareto's hostility towards humanism and collectivist democracy flowed from his belief that historical development was the work of 'active minorities' invested with attributes enabling them to dominate the passive masses.

Pareto's sociology is built around two fundamental principles: first, the concept of science as logico-experimental employing the method of induction and based on experience and observation. The purpose of sociology, he wrote, was 'to discover theories that picture facts of experience and observation' (Pareto, 1963, p. 1511). Thus although one of the first social scientists to discuss the sociological phenomenon of social mobility, Pareto presented, as evidence for his arguments on the rise and fall of social groups and societies, largely anecdotal evidence drawn from speculative observations (the *Treatise* examines, among other things, the decline of Rome, the development of the Reformation, thirteenth-century Venice and nineteenth-century Germany, the 1789 French Revolution and the English suffragette movement). In this respect Pareto is closer to Comte than to either Weber or Durkheim.

It should be noted that although critical of positivism, Pareto differed from Weber in accepting natural science as a basis of sociology: the emphasis on an objective world of experience as the basic datum of sociological study eliminated the problem of interpretation and meaning from sociological analysis. The social sciences, in Pareto's view, have not yet achieved the precision of the logico-experimental method of the natural sciences. Pareto's second principle is the concept of society as a system: he emphasised continually the necessity to analyse human society as whole not, however, in terms of objective social structures and institutions, but rather as the synthesis of a plurality of non-logical action: there is nothing in the *Treatise* that approaches the empirical–historical analysis of cultural institutions and their relation with economic structures which characterises Weber's sociology; nor is Pareto interested in identifying the specific processes of change which occur between different elements of the social whole. Perhaps Pareto's most extraordinary achievement is to define society as a system in abstract, ahistorical and ultimately non-sociological terms. For Pareto, society is a unity, never perfectly integrated 'because the requirement of uniformity is very strong in some individuals, moderately strong in others, very feeble in still others, and almost entirely absent in a few'. Society, in other words, is the product of psychological forces, the result of the workings out of human nature (Pareto, 1963, p. 1727).

Pareto defined sociology as the study of non-logical action, a category he believed had been largely neglected by sociologists. Non-logical action refers to the realm of values, beliefs, sentiments. In his analysis of the social system Pareto was especially concerned with these elements, or parts, which determine the nature of society. Individuals or actors were the molecules of the system, their actions influenced by non-human forces within the environment, but more significantly by the immanent properties of the system itself, by interest, knowledge, 'residues' and 'derivations'. Pareto's *Treatise* is largely concerned with the latter two categories. The social system achieves a state of equilibrium according to the distribution of residues and derivations within the population as a whole.

What does Pareto mean by these terms? Residues, he argues, 'correspond to certain instincts in human beings' although they must not be confused with them: residues are manifestations of sentiments and instincts which work to maintain society; derivations, much more variable, approximate to subjective explanation of events, the rationalisations employed by individuals to explain their conduct and beliefs. Pareto defined six classes of residues: the instinct for combinations; group persistences or persistences of aggregates; the manifestation of sentiments through external acts such as religious ecstasies; residues of sociality such as social ranking, self-sacrifice, asceticism; the residue of personal integrity that produces action which seeks to restore lost integrity; and finally, a sixth class, the sex residue. The six classes are further subdivided into other elements but the essential point is that Pareto's classification is both arbitrary and intellectually sterile. For example, no explanation is offered for the choice of six groups as opposed to twelve or more. Nor does Pareto attempt to validate his concepts through detailed empirical and factual analysis: discussing Class IV residues, for example, he observes:

> Sentiments of ranking on the part of inferiors as well as superiors are observable in animals. They are very widespread in human societies . . . no human society at all complex could survive without them. Relationships of superiority and inferiority are changed in forms, but none the less kept, in societies that ostensibly proclaim equality for all individuals. A sort of temporary feudalism is the rule in such societies, with a progressive descent in rankings from the politicians at the top to the politicians at the bottom. Anyone doubting this need only try to obtain something, in Italy and France . . . without the support of the local 'boss' . . . the 'powers that be' in art, science and public service (Pareto, 1963, p. 686).

Pareto's *Treatise* is full of such commonplaces: propositions stating the distribution of residues within a particular society, or social class, are illustrated from journalistic, literary and classical sources. Although residues are observable they are never analysed historically: Pareto assumes that residues are fixed and that historical change is one of endless repetition. Rejecting evolutionary theory Pareto advocated a theory of historical cycles pessimistically concluding that while historical and social forms change the inner forces remain the same. These latter are the residues. The distribution of Class I residues of combination and Class II residues of the persistence of aggregates within a population effectively determines the nature of the social equilibrium. For Pareto, class circulation depends on the proportion of Class I and Class II residues within the élite especially its 'governing class' (those involved in some branch of government).

History is thus 'the graveyard of aristocracies' since all élites necessarily decay, not only in numbers, but also in 'quality in the sense that they lose their vigour' by the decline 'in the proportions of the residues which enabled them to win their power and hold it'. Elites become incompetent through the concentration of inherited wealth and power, processes which prevent the free circulation of ability. The governing class is restored through the rise from below of 'superior elements' within the lower classes 'possessing residues suitable for exercising the functions of government and willing enough to use force'. Pareto describes this process as historically inevitable and natural:

> In virtue of class-circulation, the governing élite is always in a state of slow and continuous transformation. It flows on like a river, never being today what it was yesterday. From time to time sudden and violent disturbances occur. There is a flood – the river overflows its banks. Afterwards, the new governing élite again resume its slow transformation. The flood has subsided, the river is again flowing normally (Pareto, 1963, pp. 1430–1).

Revolutions thus restore society to its former equilibrium and prevent its total disintegration. The role of conflict and force is crucial in those situations in which class mobility has slowed down or ceased altogether. Normally the distribution of residues work to produce a dynamic equilibrium. Pareto's conception of system and change is thus superficially similar to Marx's notion that social stability is augmented to the degree that the dominant class assimilates the best brains from the lower classes. 'It is far more difficult to overthrow a governing class when it successfully assimilates most of the individuals in the subject class who show those same talents, are adept in those same arts, and might therefore become the leaders of (the subject class)', for 'left without leadership, without talent, disorganised the subject class is almost always powerless to set up any lasting régime' (Pareto, 1963, pp. 1516–17). Domination is thus defined in terms of the ability of the ruling class judiciously to employ a mixture of force and fraud, a Machiavellian conception which ignores the subjective, consensual component that is so important for Weber.

In general, the most enduring ruling class would combine Class I and Class II residues. Pareto distinguishes two classes of individuals, the lions and the foxes whose actions dominate the political sphere. Lions, as the term suggests, are prepared to employ force in pursuit of their interests and are strong in Class II residues, of loyalty to family and group, solidarity and patriotism; foxes are less direct in their methods, employ innovation and scheming, attaining their ends through cleverness and the manipulation and control of economic and political institutions. Foxes are more likely to maintain power through ideology and propaganda, by combining and recombining different ideas. Class II residues, however, are clearly more important and Pareto emphasises that they 'constitute the foundations of society and stimulate the belligerent spirit that preserves it'. Thus the preponderance of Class II residues will support the pretensions of the lower classes who will inevitably replace the governing class of foxes in which Class I residues have grown stronger while Class II have grown weaker. In this situation the ruling class becomes less and less capable of resorting to force and an unstable equilibrium results. Modern mass democracy is identified by Pareto as a form of society in which the governing class is 'overrich in Class I residues' but 'woefully lacking in Class II'. The result is widespread corruption, 'spineless humanitarianism', degeneration of character and the creation of 'an opening for those who have both the will and the power to use violence in shaking off the yoke of the ruling class' (Pareto, 1963, pp. 1824, 1556, 1797).

Class circulation is thus the master key for understanding the history of civilisation. The residues and derivations, because they embody action, provide the 'energy' which produces change within the social system. Society is thus determined by the ways in which the various elements act on each other; and society as a system, as a whole, acts on the elements themselves. Social structures are never randomly produced but flow from the immanent, structured properties of the system. Thus change is not external but emerges from within the elements that constitute the social system. Whereas positivism conceived society as the product of external relations between different elements acting mechanically on each other, Pareto grasped the immanent active properties of the constituent elements of the social system. Nevertheless, Pareto's sociology is ultimately a dead-end. For although the residues are unevenly distributed throughout a population, their universal and static qualities obfuscates rather than clarifies the complex structures of modern industrial societies. Typical of Pareto's method is his attempt to explain the economic development of Germany and France during the late nineteenth century as the result of the weakness or the intensity of Class I and Class II residues: whole peoples, whole social classes, are analysed in terms of the abstract category of residues, the inner, structural complexity of social classes and social groups, which Simmel's sociology brings out so vividly, reduced to essentialist socio-psychological forces. Pareto's social theory is less a sociological explanation of human society and its historically specific modes of development, than an all-embracing speculative philosophy of history. The richness and diversity of human culture are assimilated to a psychological theory of the human subject, in which action is stripped of its social and communicative properties and yoked to a pessimistic and deterministic notion of the social system.

6
The Sociology of Class and Domination

The foundations of sociological theory were laid down in the work of Durkheim, Weber and Simmel. For these sociologists the object of study was industrial society and particularly the problems of social cohesion, legitimacy and democracy. They were concerned with the conflicts and tensions generated within civil society by bureaucratisation, rationalisation, alienation and rapid social change in the transition from pre-industrial to large-scale industrial, urban communities and cultures. Social development was analysed in implicit dialectical terms: increasing social complexity, autonomous individuality and richness of culture on the one hand, collectivism, conformity and sterile, calculative culture on the other. Society was theorised both synchronically and diachronically; society was a structure loosely integrated around values and human action. Weber, Simmel, and to a lesser extent, Durkheim, in examining society as a structure and as a process involving active human subjects, were led to explore the objective, institutional, basis of authority and domination in its bearing on human action.

Although the concept of domination and its relation with economic and social institutions had been analysed by Saint-Simon and Alexis de Tocqueville (1805–59) from the standpoint of the political after-effects of the French revolution, it was Marx who provided the first systematic theorisation and sociological account of domination in capitalist industrial society. Comte and Spencer contributed few insights into the sociological study of social conflict, class structure and the distribution of power: organicist evolutionism, with its concern for social order, consensus and equilibrium deflected attention away from the role of force, conflict and ideology in social life (other than as the struggle for existence), assuming social order to be unproblematical (the result of individual interests synthesised into a universal good by the operation of the hidden hand of the market economy) or imposed autocratically from above (Comte's Positivist Church). The shift of emphasis from the concept of social differentiation to the concept of the division of labour in Marx, Durkheim, Weber and Simmel focused attention on the cleavages of interest within industrial society and the conflicts engendered by class division.

Marx's theory of domination

Marx was not the first writer to emphasise the class nature of industrial society or the conflicts generated between dominant and subordinate classes. 'What I did that was new', he wrote, 'was to prove, (1) that the existence of classes is only bound up with particular historical phases in the development of production, (2) that the class struggle necessarily leads to the dictatorship of the proletariat, (3) that this dictatorship itself only constitutes the transition to the abolition of all classes and to a classless society' (Marx and Engels, n.d. p. 86). In this formulation (itself made during private correspondence and therefore never intended for publication) Marx advanced a dogmatic notion of the centralising role of the state in the transition to socialism. And in *The Communist Manifesto* Marx and Engels described the modern state as a 'committee for managing the common affairs of the whole bourgeoisie', defining political power as 'the organised power of one class for oppressing another'. The implication in this formulation is that power flows from the ownership of economic resources and is simply a reflection of class interests. Class domination is thus the product of class antagonisms based on economic inequality, and while Marx emphasises that economic inequality and exploitation were characteristic of all modes of production beyond simple tribal communism, it was only capitalism which transformed all social relations into economic relations. In pre-capitalist society the social relations of serf and landowner, for example, functioned through a personal as well as an economic nexus: the class domination of the landowner was based on feudal ties of bondage and vassallage, personal elements which capitalism destroys, 'the motley feudal ties that bound man to his "natural superiors"', leaving only naked self-interest as the bond between individuals. It is in this sense that Marx wrote of class relations under capitalism becoming 'simplified' and 'universalised' with the result that power was increasingly concentrated in the major economic and political institutions.

Marx distinguished between three modes of domination: economic, social and political. Economic and social domination refers to the ways in which *capital* determines the functioning of institutions generally, while political domination refers to the ways in which the state creates and maintains the legal framework for bourgeois rule. Although Marx never used the term 'ideological domination', it is implicit in his analysis of ideology, referring essentially to the need for legitimation within capitalism with the rise of democratic institutions.

In *Capital* Marx depicted capitalist society as a system in which capital acts as an independent force, the capitalist class directly appropriating the whole surplus labour and surplus product in ways which augment the 'domination of capital over labour'. Like Saint-Simon, Marx argued that political institutions expressed basic economic interests; a relation of strict functional correspondence characterised economic and political institutions. Thus in *The Communist Manifesto* a simple, reciprocal base-superstructure model of political power is advanced in which the state – 'political society' – is conceptualised as an ideological institution which supports and defends the rights of private property. The state is a class state. But, in his later, historical writings, especially those analysing contemporary British and French history, Marx developed a more complex model of power, distinguishing between the different fractions within a dominant class and suggesting that the state apparatus was often controlled, not by the bourgeoisie, but by what he called 'a governing class'.

Thus in his analysis of the British political system Marx argued that although the Tory party remained the party of the nobility, it nevertheless carried out the policies of the bourgeoisie: 'The whole aristocracy is convinced of the need to govern in the interests of the bourgeoisie; but at the same time it is determined not to allow the latter to take charge of the matter itself' (Marx and Engels, 1962, pp. 351–8). The dominant class consists of its ruling and non-ruling fractions: the ruling class – the governing class – exercises power through the state on behalf of an economically dominant class such as the nineteenth-century English bourgeoisie. In a similar way Engels describes the German Junkers as the governing class of a Germany which was industrialising and transforming itself into a modern bourgeois society: the conflict of interests between the rising bourgeoisie and the emerging proletariat were overcome by raising the state apparatus over the whole society.

In the *Grundrisse* Marx noted that this internal complexity of class existed at the economic level also: as profit consisted of two separate forms of revenue, the existence of financial and industrial capitalists 'express nothing other than this fact' (Marx, 1973). The dominant class is therefore never a homogeneous whole but a structure of different and potentially conflicting interests. There is no simple mechanical relation, therefore, between class power and economic dominance: power is mediated through political institutions which, developing at a different tempo from the economic forces succeed in exercising an autonomy in respect of class interests.

The state and class domination

From certain of Marx's writings the theory of domination appears as unproblematic: power is the reflection within political society of economic structure. But in analysing the theory of domination as it developed within Marx's work, it becomes clearly essential to distinguish Marx's polemical writings from his historical and scientific works; and further, to distinguish Marx's works from those of Engels.

In general, Engels held to a crude, reductionist theory of domination and his popular summaries of Marxism such as the *Anti-Duhring* and *Socialism: Scientific and Utopian*, together with his historical studies such as *The Origin of the Family, Private Property and the State* tend to restate the position outlined in *The Communist Manifesto*. It should also be emphasised that Marx's concept of the state outlined in his early writings (1841–5) differs from the standpoint of *The Communist Manifesto*: in the former the state is identified with the realm of alienation, founded on the contradiction between public and private life, general and particular interests. In 1844 Marx argued that the unsocial nature of life in civil society, the egoism engendered by the forces of private property, trade and industry constituted the 'natural foundations' of the modern state. The state is not simply the form of organisation that the bourgeois class necessarily adopts to guarantee its property and interests, but an institution which develops out of the alienated social relations of civil society.

Marx's most important works on the state, however, are the historical studies: *The Eighteenth Brumaire of Louis Bonaparte* (1852), *The Class Struggles in France* (1850) and his analyses of the Paris Commune (1871–2). He originally intended to complete his study of capitalism with a final volume devoted to the state but died before finishing the economic analysis. In this sense, therefore, there exists no theory of the state in Marx's work or any analysis of the state system comparable to Marx's economic analysis. Perhaps for this reason it is a relatively simple task to find a number of different concepts of the state ranging from the notion of state as class power to the state as autonomous institution. Bearing in mind, therefore, that Marx failed to develop a coherent theory of capitalist domination the theory of the state can best be approached by focusing on two related, although contradictory themes: that human emancipation depends on civil society being independent of state domination; and the argument that the abolition of capitalism necessarily involves centralised authority.

In Marx's early writings the state is separated from civil society: the state expresses the condition of civil society and is indeed described as its 'official expression'. In his essay, 'On the Jewish Question', Marx accepts Hegel's concept of civil society describing its creation as 'the achievement of the modern world' but he criticised Hegel for defining the state as the institution, together with bureaucracy, which produces social cohesion. Although Hegel's notion of civil society had been largely derived from the writings of the eighteenth-century historians and political economists, he was particularly critical of Adam Smith's depiction of civil society as a harmonious sphere in which conflicting individual interests were synthesised into a unity by the workings of a 'hidden hand'. Hegel defined civil society rather differently as comprising institutions which, by themselves, were incapable of producing social order and unity. Some of these ideas passed into Marx's theory of the state and civil society; Marx's early writings depict the working class as wholly alienated, outside society, their integration possible only through a total revolution and, by implication, the workings of a beneficial state. In *Capital* Marx drew a different picture: the industrial working classes succeed in developing their own characteristic institutions which mediate the relation of class and state, institutions centred in civil society and democratically organised. Marx's analysis of the social relations of capitalism thus suggest the possibility that the working class, through its democratic institutions, can lay the basis for socialist transformation.

It is this latter theme that indicates an anarchist element in Marx's thought and his writings on the Paris Commune are particularly eloquent in defending this standpoint. Nevertheless, the influential Marxist theory of the state, the bourgeois state as embodiment of class power which can be changed only by the centralised socialist state – Marxist–Leninism that is – derives more from Engel's writings than from Marx. Engels declared unequivocally that in 'the last instance' the economic is decisive, a reductionist argument which leads him to characterise the state as the embodiment, in a highly concentrated form, of 'the economic needs of the class controlling production', its historical development the automatic product of economic forces. The modern state, he argued, is the organisation which 'bourgeois society takes on in order to support the external conditions of the capitalist mode of production against encroachments of workers as well as individual capitalists'. For Engels, the state was simply 'a capitalist machine, the State of the capitalists, the ideal personification of the total national capital' (Marx and Engels, 1962, Vol. 2, pp. 148–9). In the 'last instance' the state reflects the economic needs of the class which controls production, an external, coercive apparatus for maintaining class domination.

Engels's formulation suggests that in capitalist society the state is fully and consciously controlled by the economically dominant class. The political structure, therefore, enjoys no autonomy but is simply an ephiphenomenal form of the economic order. Similar arguments inform Marx's own writings, especially *The German Ideology*, which describes the historical evolution of the modern state in terms of the division of labour and mode of production, the separate spheres of administration (law, army, police, civil service) which emerge from the increasingly specialist division of work creating a sense of national unity, an 'illusory community' which seeks to conceal the facts of class struggle and conflicting material interests: 'The state is the form in which the individuals of a ruling class assert their common interests . . . [it] acts as an intermediary in the formation of all communal institutions and gives them political form' (Marx and Engels, 1964).

By the end of the 1840s Marx had yet to work out his theory of social change, surplus value and exploitation: the analysis of capitalism turned on a polarised model of conflict between two classes. This dichotomic model of class structure and social formation underwent profound change in his work of the 1850s and 1860s. One of the most significant historical developments which occurred during the course of the nineteenth century, especially in the advanced capitalist countries, was the increasing centralised nature of capitalism as a system. Marx integrated these developments into his theoretical model of capitalism. He argued that although previous revolutions, such as the French Revolution, had embraced the ideals of freedom and democracy against authoritarian power, the actual results were always 'a perfecting' of the state. The centralised state machine had originally been forged during the period of Absolute Monarchy 'as a weapon of nascent modern society in its struggle of emancipation from feudalism', and although the French Revolution had sought to create national unity necessary for the growth of bourgeois society, this development could be effected only by enlarging the powers of the institution which the ideals of 1789, liberalism and freedom, opposed (Marx and Engels, 1971, p. 149). In the years between the publication of

The Communist Manifesto and the analysis of the failure of the Paris Commune Marx gradually abandoned the reductionist standpoint adopted in the *Manifesto*, with its implication that in socialist revolution the working class would simply take over the existing state machine and use it for the task of reconstruction. In the 'Preface' to the 1872 German edition of the *Manifesto* two crucial changes are apparent:

1. The rapid development of the labour movement resulting from the growth of capitalism had created the potential for democratic change from within civil society itself, through the institutions of the working class.

2. Because of the increasing centralisation of capitalism as an economic system, the state itself becomes more centralised so that the task of socialist transformation is not the reform of the state but its abolition: 'The working class cannot simply lay hold of a ready-made State machinery (as different factions had done in their ascendence to power) and wield it for its own purposes' (Marx and Engels, 1971, p. 270).

Marx's hostility to the state now becomes total: in his writings on the Paris Commune he describes the centralised state machine of modern society as enmeshing 'living civil society like a boa constrictor', functioning as 'a parasitic excrescence on civil society', 'unproductive and mischievous', an 'incubus' which must be 'smashed' (Marx and Engels, 1971, pp. 149–70, 202–3). Whereas in *The Communist Manifesto* and the *Address to the Communist League* (1850) Marx had argued that socialism would necessarily produce further centralisation now he advocated a decentralising transition to socialism.

These political themes are closely bound up with Marx's theoretical analyses of the state as a separate sphere from civil society, partially autonomous from the dominant class yet necessarily linked with it. The bourgeoisie must develop a centralised state structure to facilitate capitalist progress (the state being responsible for communications, education, taxation, foreign trade and law) but because 'the real life' of the bourgeoisie lay in the sphere of civil, rather than political society, the state is always more than a mere agent of this class. This aspect of Marx's theory of domination is especially brought out in his analysis of Bonapartism: in 1851 Louis Bonaparte abolished the Parliamentary institutions of the French bourgeoisie, arrested deputies, deporting socialists and republicans, and outlawed free speech and a free press, all in order to safeguard bourgeois interests from socialism. The bourgeois class consisted of two large factions, the big landed proprietors and the financial and industrial bourgeoisie; the internal divisions of this class, however, obstructed the development of an autonomous, united class-conscious ruling bourgeoisie. Marx attempts to show that the state was not a simple reflection of social forces but rather an example of the separation of the state from society: under the rule of the second Bonaparte, Marx wrote, the state seems 'to have made itself completely independent' so that all classes 'fall on their knees before the rifle butt'. Executive power embraced a broad strata, state officials numbering as many as half a million, and Marx depicts this bureaucratic state machine as an 'appalling parasitic body which enmeshes the body of French society like a net and chokes its pores'. State power soars 'high above society'. This mode of domination emerges historically 'when the proletariat is not ready (or able) and the bourgeoisie has lost the facility of ruling the nation' (Marx and Engels, 1962, Vol. 2, pp. 331–2). Marx is arguing that when no single class enjoys social and political dominance, the state emerges to act as mediator:

> The bourgeoisie confesses that its own interests dictate that it should be delivered from the consequences of its own rule; that, in order to restore tranquility in the country, its bourgeois parliament must, first of all be given its quietus; that, in order to preserve its own social power intact, its political power must be broken; that the individual bourgeois can continue to exploit the other classes and to enjoy undisturbed property, family, religion and order only on condition that their classes be condemned along with the other classes to like political nullity; that in order to save its purse it must forfeit its crown (Marx and Engels, 1962, Vol. 2, p. 288).

In sharp contrast, Marx analysed the events surrounding the Paris Commune to argue that the institutions thrown up spontaneously by the working class organising themselves against the bourgeoisie represented the only authentic alternative to the centralising trends of the modern state. The Paris Commune was essentially the political form of proletarian emancipation, direct democracy characterised by the recall of political representatives, a peoples' army and militia, 'the reabsorption of the State power by society as its own living forces instead of as forces controlling and subduing it, by the popular masses'. The Commune was the 'glorious harbinger' of a new type of society, 'the people acting for itself by itself'. And only the industrial working class could invent and put into practice the concept of Commune, of workers councils (Marx and Engels, 1971, p. 153).

Nevertheless, Marx was sharply critical of the policies pursued by the Commune describing its lack of socialist leadership and coherent socialist ideology: it was not socialist 'nor could it be'. Subsequent generations of Marxists drew the conclusion that a successful proletarian revolution required more than self-governing working-class institutions, but a disciplined revolutionary political party, Marxist theory and a centralised socialist administration. A close analysis of Marx's writings on the Commune, however, suggests that although he saw the events of 1871 as doomed to failure by muddled and incoherent leadership, he nevertheless regarded the Commune as embodying a struggle against the state and the centralising trends of modern society, a reassertion of the independence of civil society.

But Marx's work as a whole, from the philosophical critique of Hegel's authoritarian theory of the state to his hostile criticism of Bakunin's anarchist concept of the state as the source of all problems in capitalist society, is characterised by a sharp tension between a libertarian and democratic temper: the state is as an 'alienated social power' dominating civil society, an authoritarian, centralised structure constituting an essential element of society as a whole. The Commune's policy of democratisation – election to administrative posts, the power of recall and equality of pay – was defined by Marx as part of a process which sought to reverse the historical trend, set in motion by revolutions of the past, which invests the state and its apparatuses with control *over* civil society. But in works such as *The German Ideology*, *The Communist Manifesto* and the *Address to the Communist League* Marx emphasised that the state, founded historically on the division of labour, class interests and class conflict, was effectively the 'official form of social antagonisms in civil society': thus in the transition from capitalism to socialism greater rather than less centralisation would be necessary. A broadly similar standpoint emerges from his criticism of the Marxist programme of the German Social Democratic Party – the Gotha Programme of 1875 – in which he scornfully rejected the concept of 'free state', arguing that the issue was rather one of elaborating the social functions of the state in socialist society analogous to their functions in capitalism. In writings such as these the state is clearly defined as the instrument of class forces, as an integral structure of society: in socialism, therefore, the state, as the dictatorship of the proletariat will dominate civil society disappearing only with the advent of Communism. The state and its organs of repression remain firmly anchored within society. It was only after the experience of the Paris Commune that Marx began to shift his position and hesitantly advance the standpoint of state versus society and emphasise the necessity for civil society to absorb and abolish the distinct organs of political society and reverse the historical trend of increasing centralisation.

But this radical, libertarian strand remained muted: in their published writings both Marx and Engels tended to identify the domination and centralisation of *capital* as the critical issue, the 'despotism of capital' rather than the despotism of the state. This is particularly brought out in Engels's article, 'On Authority' (1872), written polemically against anarchist socialism, in which he explicitly rejected democratic, decentralising forms of authority. 'Wanting to abolish authority in large-scale industry', he wrote, 'is tantamount to wanting to abolish industry itself, to destroy the power loom in order to return to the spinning wheel'. Large-scale industry and social development are impossible without authority: Engels argued that authority was neither good nor bad but relative to the specific social situation. Socialism will effectively transform the political functions of the state 'into the simple administrative functions of watching over the true interests of society'. Engels's formulation asserts the centralising trend of industrialism: authority is imposed from above over civil society and not 'reabsorbed' into its institutional framework (Marx and Engels, 1962, Vol. 2, pp. 636–9).

The theory of class: Weber

Neither Marx nor Weber produced a complete theory of social stratification. Nevertheless, Weber's brief discussion of stratification as a 'multi-dimensional structure' embracing social class, status and party has become a fundamental source of modern social theory.

Weber's interpretation of Marx was based on the contemporary view of Marxism as a form of economic determinism. In general, Weber accepted this interpretation, widely propounded by Marxists such as Kautsky, in which the political was assimilated to the economic. In contrast Weber insisted that the political was not a secondary and derivative phenomenon but an active, autonomous element exercising a critical role in the formation of modern society. He rejected Marx's analysis of capitalism as a system structured in class struggle and internal contradictions, defining capitalism as a rational mode of organisation and thus clearly distinguished from previous social formations. This emphasis on the autonomy of the political and the pervasiveness of rationality within capitalism led Weber to reject the Marxist theory of the state as the instrument of class domination. Before examining Weber's theory of domination, however, it is essential to outline his general perspective on class and power.

Superficially, Weber seems to follow Marx: property, or the lack of it, constitutes 'the basic categories of all class situations' and the factor which produces class 'is unambiguously economic interest'. However, the 'class situation' is differentiated 'according to the kind of services that can be offered in the market'. Here Weber departs from Marx in stressing that skill may constitute a form of property productive of internal class differentiation: those offering services are differentiated 'just as much according to their kinds of services as according to the way in which they make use of these services'. It is 'chance' within the structure of the market which Weber identifies as 'the decisive moment which presents a common condition for the individual's fate'. In this sense class situation is ultimately 'market situation'. Writing of Marx's fragment on class, Weber noted that 'it was intended to deal with the issue of class unity in the face of skill differentials'. Thus Weber distinguished between 'ownership classes' (those who receive rents from the ownership of land, mines, factories) and 'acquisition classes' ('typical entrepreneurs' offering services on the market such as bankers and financiers, as well as members of the 'liberal professions' who enjoy a privileged position through their ability or training). Weber described these groups as 'positively privileged' comparing their market position with 'negatively privileged' groups such as wage-labourers who have neither disposable property nor specialised skills. For Weber, classes never constituted homogeneous wholes but were highly differentiated internally embracing a number of different interests. He argued that the basic tendency of capitalism was the expansion of the 'acquisition classes' with the result a more pluralistic social structure, one increasingly built around educational qualifications.

A pluralistic stratification system thus develops involving complex differentiation within dominant, middle and working classes. Weber described the stratification system within modern capitalism as consisting of working classes, petty bourgeoisie, 'intelligentsia' (a category lacking independent property but whose social position hinges on technical training, such as engineers, bureaucratic officials and other white-collar workers), and finally, a class which occupies a 'privileged position through property and education' (entrepreneurs, etc.). Given this complex stratification system there is clearly no simple relationship between class situation and class consciousness as conceived by Marx. Class constitutes a crucial objective factor in the formation of consciousness, affecting the 'life-chances' of individuals in a variety of ways, but there exists no automatic transposition of so-called economic and class interests into solidaristic class consciousness. Weber rejected the historical relation of class to social change, the concept of historically necessary objective laws of social development. Consciousness, therefore, is structured firmly within the present, within the empirical market situation, and quite

185

clearly Weber's sociology has eliminated such notions as 'class-for-itself' (fully conscious of its historical interests).

Social stratification is further complicated by the existence of 'status groups'. Weber distinguished classes from status groups by arguing that class situation differs from status situation by virtue of 'a specific, positive or negative, social estimation of honour'. Class situation depends on the market; status situation hinges on the judgements which others pass on his, or her social position, thus attributing positive or negative esteem. Because a status group is characterised by a 'specific style of life', comprising social distance and exclusiveness, a repudiation of economic factors as the basis of membership and a commitment to patterns of non-utilitarian consumption, it approximates to a unified social class: 'With some oversimplification, one might thus say that "classes" are stratified according to their relations to the production and acquisition of goods; whereas "status groups" are stratified according to the principles of their *consumption* of goods as represented by special "styles of life".' There is, of course, a close relation between status groups and property and in this respect class and status are linked: an economically ascendent class will, through subsequent generations, achieve the position of a status group. Both propertied and propertyless individuals may belong to the same status group while economically declining groups exercise considerable social influence. Weber's point was that class and status constituted two distinct forms of group formation and organisation: thus although interrelated, class and status are competing structures of stratification relating specifically to the distribution of power. Power is not a separate dimension of stratification; classes, status groups and political parties are all phenomena 'of the distribution of power within a community' (Weber, 1964, pp. 424–9; Gerth and Mills, 1948, pp. 180–95).

Weber's pluralistic model of stratification is theoretically one which assumes the existence of a strong civil society. Power, for example, constitutes an expression of the distribution of interests within civil society; but at the same time power and class cannot be assimilated to economic elements, or political parties be considered solely as the expression of class interests. The principle of autonomy is important for defining the separation from the state and bureaucracy of institutions bound up with class, status and power. For Weber, civil society was a living force: thus theoretically parties can constitute class or status parties but because of the complex nature of industrial society they are more likely to be 'mixed types'. Weber's pluralistic approach to social stratification assumes conflict over interests and a fluid, mobile and open social formation. But, as with Marx, there are tensions between these formulations and Weber's awareness of the centralising trends of modern industrial society.

Capitalism, bureaucracy and democracy: Weber's theory of domination

Throughout his life Weber accepted the necessity for a strong, nation state, its primacy in all social and political spheres. His early studies into the agricultural conditions of Eastern Germany had pointed to the problems caused by an incursion of Polish workers into German territory and their potential threat to German culture. Germany at the end of the nineteenth century had developed into a strong, centralised nation state with its own distinctive national culture. Political unification was achieved during the first stirrings of industrial development and Weber emphasised that if Germany was to become a truly modern industrial nation then it could do so only under the guidance of new political leaders. The *Junker* landowning class still controlled large sections of German political life, yet in Weber's terms they constituted a declining class incapable of generating the necessary dynamic leadership. As for the industrial bourgeoisie Weber depicted this class as cautious and unpolitical, wholly dominated by the *Junkers*. The industrial working class was equally incapable of leadership being an immature class politically, its leaders in the Social Democratic Party contemptuously dismissed as mere journalistic dilettantes. Weber defined a politically mature class as one which repudiated sectional interests in favour of the political power interests of the German nation.

Weber's attitude to questions of power was uncompromising: all modern states, he argued, demanded a structure of domination through which some individuals ruled others.

Weber rejected what he regarded as utopian political concepts such as direct democracy (he discussed the example of Soviets in his essay, 'Parliament and Government in a Reconstructed Germany', written in 1918) on the grounds that in large, complex modern societies such institutions were technically impossible. He accepted the extension of democratic rights in modern societies but argued that the process of democratising society entailed an increasing bureaucratisation and central-isation of power structured in the rational norms of a bureau-cratic state apparatus. In modern society the administrative function is determined by size: the administration of mass structures is radically different from the personalised relation-ships of administration in small associations; administration expands with the result that those with training and experience exercise technical superiority in the carrying out of complex tasks. The classic democratic doctrine, based on the sovereignty of the people, formed no part of Weber's theory of democracy. Writing to Robert Michels, whose book on *Political Parties* (1911) advanced similar arguments on the nature of organisation, Weber asked: 'How much resignation will you still have to put up with? Such concepts as "will of the people", genuine will of the people, have long since ceased to exist for me; they are fictitious. All ideas aiming at abolishing the dominance of men over men are "Utopian" ' (Mommsen, 1974, p. 87).

One of Weber's fundamental arguments was that the rise of modern political parties – itself a democratic development – entailed increasing bureaucratisation and the weakening of human initiative and action. His ideological support for a strong German state and his general distrust of 'mass' democ-racy was closely bound up with his sociological studies of bureaucracy, a legal–rational form of domination described as eliminating all personal, irrational and emotional elements from administration. Bureaucratic administration subordi-nated the individual to the rational, specialised division of labour and an increasing rationalisation of all spheres of social life. Pessimistically Weber described this process in terms of a 'new iron cage of serfdom' and a dehumanised, 'disenchanted world'.

For Weber, Parliamentary Democracy was largely passive in

its effects; the mass of the people were uneducated, politically ignorant and incapable of forming reasoned political judgements. The real objective of democracy was the creation of charismatic leaders who succeed in establishing leadership over the masses not through policies but by their personal qualities. In this way the inherent trends towards bureaucratisation might be checked by the emergence of a powerful personality with extra-mundane gifts who succeeds in integrating the propertyless masses into modern society. Modern mass political parties, however, are based on bureaucratic principles of organisation and the basic trend of modern society is for parties to select their leaders and offer them for election to Parliament: democracy becomes increasingly a mode of selection of leadership.

Weber insisted throughout his writings that the struggle for power was an inherent feature of all social life pervading every sphere of social action. Parties exist to achieve power. It is important to understand Weber's concept of power in this context: he did not accept the crude Marxist position which defined power in terms of economic interests and class structure. Power is defined in social action terms as 'the chance of a man, or of a number of men, to realise their own will in a communal action even against the resistance of others who are participating in their action' (Gerth and Mills, 1948, p. 180). Individuals do not necessarily strive for power merely because of possible economic rewards: power, including economic power, may be valued for itself, or for the social honour it confers. There is thus no single source of power and one of the consequences of Weber's argument is that changes in the economic organisation of society do not automatically result in changes in the distribution of power. Historically the major sociological challenge to this Marxist thesis had originally occurred in the work of the Italian political scientist, Gaetano Mosca (1859–1941). Many of Mosca's themes were developed by Robert Michels (1876–1936) and Max Weber. For Mosca and Michels power flowed from its source in political and bureaucratic organisations; Weber's theory of bureaucratic domination emerged as a more complex development of this theme.

In his *Elementi di Scienza Politica* (translated into English as

The Ruling Class), first published in 1896, Mosca appears
superficially to follow Marx in his argument that 'in all societies
. . . two classes of people appear – a class that rules and a class
that is ruled'. Political power has always been exercised by
organised minorities who impose their rule on the unorganised
masses. His 'political', (or ruling) class, enjoys legal and factual
authority and in democratic societies the selection of candi-
dates by political parties is always the product of organised
minorities. Mosca emphasised that the political class does not
represent economic interests but constitutes an autonomous
social stratum, a natural élite 'whose economic position is
virtually independent of those who hold supreme power and
who have sufficient means to be able to devote a portion of their
time to perfecting their culture and acquiring their interest in
the public weal'. For Mosca, this élite constituted the best
elements of the ruling class. Thus he argued that the stability of
nineteenth-century England had less to do with its Parliamentary institutions than with the continuity of its political
class. The implication is that the state is not an expression of
class interests but an institution resting on moral and material
forces and seeking to achieve unity of all social groups within
the nation (Mosca, 1939, pp. 144–5, 284–92).

Bureaucratic organisation is the key to understanding
political power. Mosca's argument is often couched positivistically in terms of laws – the law of organised minorities – which
have the force of natural laws: thus he departs radically from
Marx's theory of socialism by postulating that 'no social
organisation can be based exclusively on the sentiment of
justice' for human nature is irrational and egoistic, a constant
striving after wealth, power, worldly vanity. Mosca's critique
of socialist collectivism was based partly on his theory of
organisation and an ahistorical notion of human nature.
Democracy thus becomes the rule of organised minorities
which 'in spite of appearances to the contrary, and for all the
legal principles on which government rests . . . still retain the
actual and effective control of the state'. History teaches the
lesson that social progress occurs only if those with power are
controlled and balanced by others who enjoy positions of
absolute independence and no common interest with those who
wield power. It is this mediation of power, Mosca argues,

which tends to disappear with the development of collectivism: a blind belief in the masses can lead only to the destruction of multiple centres of political power (Mosca, 1939, pp. 50–87).

Mosca's pessimistic sociology is thus a critique of so-called mass democracies and the threat posed to governing élites by the rise of bureaucratically organised political parties claiming to represent the interests of the 'irrational' masses. This is one of the themes also of Michels's *Political Parties* (1911) which adumbrates the sociological law of oligarchical inevitability: all organisations, however democratic their ideology, become necessarily oligarchic and bureaucratic. 'As a result of organisation, every party or professional union becomes divided into a minority of directors and a majority of directed'. Basing his arguments on the bureaucratic tendencies of the German Social Democratic Party (the major Marxist political party in Europe at the time of Michels's study, with a nationwide political organisation and deputies in Parliament) Michels sought to show, like Mosca, the inevitable trend to bureaucratic control of the state and the ways this process flowed directly from the organisational requirements of modern, 'mass' society. Michels's 'iron law of oligarchy', working through social institutions, means the rule of the bureaucratic official over democratically elected parliamentary representatives, the growth of authority based on position within a hierarchy of salaried officialdom. Bureaucratic organisation is a natural law which determines the structure of modern political parties and trade unions. Within capitalism administrators increasingly acquire an authority 'at least equal to that possessed by the private owner of capital', while under socialism the ideals of a classless society 'would perish in the moment of its adherents' triumph'. The necessity for bureaucracy gives 'birth to the domination of the elected over the electors, of the mandatories over the mandators, of the delegates over the delegators. *Who says organisation, says oligarchy*' (Michels, 1962, pp. 333–56).

As we have seen, Weber shared Mosca's and Michels's rejection of the 'utopian' ideals of socialism. He argued that the highly specialised division of labour, which forms the backbone of a modern economy, must inevitably lead to greater bureaucratisation: bureaucratic modes of organisation, technically superior to other modes, are essential for large-scale

191

planning and the mobilising of resources. Only through bureaucratic organisation has it been possible to develop the modern polity, economy and technology. The fully developed bureaucratic structure compares with other organisations as the modern machine compares with non-mechanical modes of production. Bureaucracy is characterised by the following characteristics: precision, speed, unambiguity, knowledge of the files, continuity, discretion, unity, strict subordination; the bureaucratic office has a clearly defined sphere of competence, its officials organised in a clearly defined hierarchy of positions, and appointed, not elected, on the basis of technical qualifications. Officials are personally free and subject only to authority in terms of their impersonal bureaucratic obligations. The development of modern society demands this mode of administration for the larger the association, the more complicated its tasks and the more it depends on rational organisation. In this sense the future belongs to bureaucratisation.

For Weber, the increasing bureaucratisation of social life formed the major structural form of modern capitalism: rationalised efficiency which results from bureaucratic organisation enables humanity to develop economically, technologically and politically, but this progress is achieved at some cost, 'a parcelling out of the human soul', a dehumanisation of the subject. As for socialism, rather than decentralising power, it will lead inevitably to a further centralising of institutions and the dictatorship of the bureaucratic official. Weber's pessimism is complete: modern society cannot escape from bureaucratic organisation.

Thus a contradiction is generated between the democratic trends of bourgeois society and the anti-democratic ethos of bureaucratic organisation. In Weber's analysis bureaucracy becomes the major source of authority in the modern world: 'Every domination expresses itself and functions through administration. Every administration, on the other hand, needs domination, because it is always necessary that some powers of command be in the hands of somebody' (Weber, 1954, p. 330). This is what Weber called 'imperative co-ordination', the probability that commands will be obeyed irrespective of their specific content or degree of supervision. Domination is distinguished from power in that domination carries the weight of legitimacy, that individuals obey not because of physical compliance, but through a belief in the validity of norms regulating the command. For Weber, domination was not the simply external fact of an order being obeyed, but involved a subjective component, as if those who are ruled had made the content of the command the basic maxim of their own activity. In this respect Weber differs sharply from Mosca in seeking a voluntaristic basis for power; 'It is an induction from experience', he writes, 'that no system of domination voluntarily limits itself to the appeal to material or affectual or ideal motives as a basis for guaranteeing its continuance. In addition every such system attempts to establish and to cultivate the belief in its "legitimacy" ' (Weber, 1964, p. 325).

Weber identified three ideal types of legitimacy: traditional, resting on a belief in the authority of 'immemorial traditions'; charismatic, based on the prophetic pronouncements of oracles and great leaders invested with 'magical' qualities; and finally, rational, based on a belief in the legality of enacted rules and the right of those in authority to issue commands that have their basis in law. Commands, then, always carry a minimum of voluntary compliance; they are obeyed because of a belief in the legitimacy of the authority. It is, therefore, not a question of an 'organised minority', or élite, imposing its rule on an unorganised mass, but rather of the process of institutionalising the 'inner support' of subjects for the different modes of authority. Weber's sociology of domination is ultimately less concerned with the sources of power in material forces, such as property ownership, than in the ideologies which legitimate different forms of rule.

Modern society is characterised by rational–legal domination centred in bureaucracy. Weber argued that capitalist production created 'an urgent need for stable, strict, intensive and calculable administration'; in the field of administration the choice lay simply 'between bureaucracy and dilettantism'. In his lecture on Socialism, given in 1918, he argued that modern democracy was increasingly a bureaucratised democracy, the administrative staff completely separated from the ownership of property; all bureaucratic enterprises, from factories to armies to schools, based on purely technical norms of efficiency and grounded in rational–legal authority, increasingly separate the individual from the means of work. Socialism would accelerate these trends and prepare the ground for 'a new bondage', a bureaucratic mode of domination stifling all freedom and independent human activity.

Weber's reflections are prescient in the light of later developments within capitalism and state socialist societies, all of which have witnessed an enormous growth in bureaucratic administration. There can be no doubt that Weber was right to emphasise the growing autonomy of the state and the legitimation needs of modern industrial societies: thus while Weber's typology of domination can be criticised for constituting a taxonomy, a formal structure of concepts, rather than a theory which investigates the actual functioning of different modes of domination, including the repressive apparatuses of the state – police, army, etc. – it nevertheless illuminated the necessary subjective element present in structures of authority. In his lecture, 'Politics as a Vocation' (1918), he quotes Trotsky's remark that 'every state is founded on force', but adds that the modern state is never simply a repressive apparatus but a community that successfully claims 'the monopoly of legitimate violence' (Gerth and Mills, 1948, pp. 78–83).

Yet while domination implies a subjective component and a consenting subject, Weber maintained a resolutely pessimistic view of modern democracy. The masses confer legitimacy purely passively: there is little sense of an active relationship between the various groups and classes of civil society and the state apparatus. Weber accepted Michels's theory of mass democracy and the inevitable rule of functionaries. The whole question of popular democratic control is eliminated on the basis that a modern industrial society necessitates bureaucratic administration *from above*. But, as was noted earlier in relation to Weber's theory of stratification, and indeed his theory of bureaucracy, the concept of domination is structured around the existence of an independent civil society. Only from within a strong civil society can the subject actively consent to domination, that is, confer legitimacy through political and social institutions. Weber depicts the technical necessity of rational–legal domination, and thus the emergence of functionaries within the state apparatus controlling modern society; and this, in itself, constitutes a democratic process facilitating mobility and promotion by merit. But this process of rationalisation that seems to lead inevitably to increasing centralisation and the rule of the few over the many, and thus the eclipse of civil society as an independent and living structure, is contradicted by Weber's insistence that social change and thus society itself is the product of human action. Weber failed to reconcile his pessimistic political sociology with his optimistic sociology of social action, for ultimately his sociology of bureaucracy and democracy lacks an adequate theory of civil society.

7
Marxism and Sociology

Marxism after Marx

When Marx died in 1883 Marxism as a distinctive body of knowledge, theory of society and scientific methodology had exercised little influence in the field of the social sciences. Discussion of Marxism was largely confined to the workers' movement and it was not until the 1890s that a wider debate was initiated involving scholars from different areas of the social sciences – economics, history and sociology. The main academic critics of Marxism – Weber, Durkheim, Pareto, Mosca, Croce, Stammler, Sorel – did not set out simply to refute historical materialism but were mainly concerned with the problems which Marx had identified within the social sciences and modern society. This growing interest in Marxism was partly the result of its increasing popularisation in the socialist movement, as well as the importance of socialism itself as an organised political trend based on the principles of class struggle, class consciousness and class solidarity.

Marxism was developed outside the academy by socialist intellectuals who defined it as a natural science of society emphasising the existence of specific laws of social development, the inevitability of class conflict, the polarisation of classes, growing economic crises and eventual collapse of capitalism. At Marx's graveside Engels had declared that as Darwin had discovered 'the law of development of organic nature, so Marx discovered the law of development of human history'. Engels's reference to Darwin and natural history is significant, for the Marxism which developed during the 1880s and 1890s made no distinction between the methods of the natural sciences and those of Marxism. The Marxism of the Second International was particularly positivistic in its early phases. During the 1890s the major political party advocating Marxist theory was the German Social Democratic Party whose leaders, Karl Kautsky (1854–1938) and Eduard Bernstein (1850–1932) enjoyed close ties with Engels; the Social Democrats were responsible for the publication of many of Marx's early and later writings such as the *Theories of Surplus Value*, part of *The German Ideology* and the final volumes of *Capital*. The party, having been legalised in 1890, polled one and a half million votes at the first General Election.

Kautsky, who wrote voluminously on the history of religion, socialism, ethics and economic and political theory – he was described as the 'Pope of Marxism' – represented the orthodox wing of Marxist theory; many of his ideas were shared by the Russian George Plekhanov (1856–1918). More than any other writers Kautsky and Plekhanov transformed Marxism into an integrated world view, defining its basic concepts in positivistic, evolutionary terms arguing that the task of intellectuals was merely to defend Marxist thought from bourgeois theory thus preserving its theoretical purity. Following the inspiration of Engels, in his *Anti-Duhring*, Marxism became codified into a set of rules and general materialist principles applicable to all social and historical phenomena.

During the 1890s the major Marxist works were largely polemical dogmatically defending Marx's method of analysis, his general theory of laws of development and the nature of capitalism as an exploitive system of production. In 1899 Bernstein published his *Evolutionary Socialism* in which he subjected these dogmatic concepts to the test of empirical reality. Contrary to Kautsky and Plekhanov, he argued that the historical development of capitalism did not support Marx's theory of crisis, the notion of inevitable polarisation of classes or the law of the centralisation of capital. The working class was not becoming impoverished, the middle classes were not disappearing, small businesses were developing and there was no evidence that capitalism as a system was doomed to historically inevitable collapse. Bernstein concluded that history demonstrated no 'iron laws', no 'historic necessity'; socialism must be validated, not by appeals to an historically inevitable future, but rather through the ethic of socialism, the *a priori* categories of Kantian moral philosophy in which individuals are regarded, not as means or instruments, but as ends in themselves. For Bernstein the movement was everything; there was no 'ultimate goal'. The political conclusions which Bernstein drew from his analysis came to be known as 'Revisionism', that as capitalism was gradually and peacefully evolving towards a more complex social structure than existed at the time Marx wrote *Capital*, so it was possible to extend democracy, citizenship and equality from within the system itself. The struggle for socialism was thus conceived as a piecemeal, evolutionary process and not as the violent conquest of state power by a disciplined party apparatus.

Bernstein's critique of Marxism was immediately rejected by Kautsky who merely repeated that Marx's analysis of capitalism was correct in virtually every detail: Bernstein had misinterpreted the statistics. The Revisionist controversy is important, however, because it highlighted the weaknesses of Marxism in the light of modern social science. In particular it focused attention on the changes within capitalism since the 1860s that could not be accommodated to the dogmatic prescriptions of orthodox Marxism. For all its claims as a science, Marxism had become ossified into a quasi-religious system which admitted the existence of no facts or historical evidence which might render it untenable. The Revisionist debate reflected many of the criticisms which academic scholars were increasingly levelling at Marxism.

The first significant discussion between Marxists and representatives of 'bourgeois' social science had taken place in 1894 at the first International Congress of Sociology; further debates took place in the 1890s and early years of the twentieth century. The Marxist theory of inevitable social change was particularly criticised, as was the concept of laws of natural necessity and the reduction of the human agent to a product of external conditions. Marxism, it was argued, postulated a rigid, mechanical notion of the relation between the economic 'base' of society and its ideological 'superstructure', a correspondence theory of knowledge which transformed ideas into a passive reflection of class interests. Kautsky developed this model to account for the necessary development of socialist theory itself as occurring outside the workers' movement, the product of intellectuals whose privileged position enabled them to escape from the socio-economic determinism which affected all other groups. The workers attained only a limited consciousness, broadly economic and oriented to trade union matters. As capitalism intensified the objective class struggle through heightened contradictions and tensions, the working class became increasingly receptive to Marxist theory. One important consequence of this élitist position was that the state was defined as an instrument of social transformation, the result of socialist leadership from above. This passive concept of consciousness is central to orthodox Marxism and was further developed by V. I. Lenin (1870–1923) in his theory of the 'vanguard' party discussed below.

Weber, Durkheim and Simmel rejected the Marxist concept of economic laws in favour of a voluntaristic sociology which also took account of the growing complexity, not homogeneity, of modern capitalist society. Criticism of the positivist elements in Marxism, however, did emerge from the Marxist movement itself and was not confined to those intellectuals outside the socialist movement. The Italian Marxist Antonio Labriola (1843–1904) and the French theorist of revolutionary syndical-ism Georges Sorel (1847–1922) sought to combat the concept of Marxism as a self-contained system based on natural laws of development by invoking Vico's dictum that humanity knows only that which it has created. Sorel, who wrote extensively on Marxism during the 1890s and contributing an important essay on Vico, introduced Labriola's work into France especially the *Essays on the Materialist Conception of History* (1896). Sorel, however, was much more concerned with Marxism as a theory of action than Marxism as a theory of totality and it is interesting to see how these two elements were combined in Labriola's work.

Labriola accepted the concept of society as a whole, analysing social classes and individuals as parts developing in relation to the whole; he assimilated, too, the model of base and superstructure in which ideas correspond to specific social conditions. But he went beyond naturalistic Marxism by emphasising the uniqueness of historical formations and rejecting the simple triadic schema of social change –

thesis–antithesis–synthesis – in favour of a theory of change centred on human activity, consciousness and thus praxis. Like Sorel, Labriola attacked the whole notion of economic determinism and the theory that historical change can be explained entirely in terms of the economic factor. He defined the historical process as an historical totality in which intellectual and material culture are organically bound together. Unique historical events cannot be explained away by reference to simple, reciprocal economic causation. Labriola emphasised the economic *structure* of a society as the basis of its organic unity; it was not, therefore, a question of assimilating cultural forces to the economic and defining society in terms of one single *factor*. For Labriola, all elements of material life and intellectual culture were an expression of the historical epoch – an expressive totality – and could not be analysed in positivist terms, as external facts, because of their organic unity in an all-enveloping process of historical development. There was no 'dominant' element as such within this concept of totality: historical events and sociological processes existed in relation to economic forces but could never be reduced to them as mere passive expressions (Labriola, 1967).

Reality is not a given datum but created through human activity; the goal of socialism is not lying in wait in some distant future but result from *praxis*. There is no truth waiting to be discovered only a truth which must be *made*. Sorel praised Labriola's rejection of 'vulgar Marxism' and its crude theory of economic determinism. As the editor of two influential socialist journals, Sorel proposed to examine Marxism in depth and during the late 1890s contributed a number of critical essays on such topical issues as the Revisionist debate, Marxism as a science and the role of ethics in socialist theory. After 1903, however, he became increasingly disillusioned with orthodox Marxism and turned towards revolutionary syndicalism and his theory of the *myth* developed especially in his *Reflections on Violence* (1908).

Orthodox Marxism, Sorel argued, had degenerated into a species of historical fatalism built around the notion of periodic and catastrophic economic crises which supposedly culminate in a general crisis of the whole capitalist system and subsequent political transformation. The reductionist formulas of Kautsky *et al*. ignore the real 'authors' and 'actors' of history and the fact that social relationships are made by men as much as by the development of the productive forces. Sorel was a perceptive critic of vulgar Marxism: his work was influenced by what he called 'the treasures contained in the work of Vico', especially the notion of the social world as the work of humanity and that humanity understands only that which it has created. Thus for Sorel there was no natural history of society, no scientific socialism. In the debate on Revisionism he sided with Bernstein arguing that 'the problem for socialism is to develop in the working classes a superior culture, which would allow them to administer the productive forces . . . Today, the proletariat is far from possessing this culture' (Sorel, 1976, pp. 126, 157–64). Socialism is vindicated, not through appeals to the 'final end' of historical development but by the ethical superiority of proletarian institutions and culture.

Sorel's anti-scientism and his general distrust of theories of social change which minimised or eliminated the active human subject, led him to argue against the holistic approach of Marxist methodology and advocate an atomistic concept of society structured in the voluntaristic practice of actors. His fundamental point was that change occurs through will, collectively organised within the working class, but expressing the contradictions of the present system and a longing for an alternative society. The myth of the general strike functions precisely in this way as a system of images, which invokes through intuition the sentiments oriented towards socialism that form an integral part of working-class experience.

As we shall see below, Sorel's work influenced the Marxism of the Italian Gramsci, especially the critique of scientistic anti-humanist materialism, although in general Sorel's writings exerted little significance for the development of early twentieth-century Marxism.

Marxism as revolutionary consciousness: Lukács and the concept of totality

One of the most important Marxist theorists in the immediate post-1917 period was Georg Lukács (1885–1971). His work includes studies of aesthetics, literature, philosophy, politics and sociology. Lukács turned to Marxism during the First World War: his pre-war writings were informed by a strong anti-positivist outlook influenced by the work of Rickert, Simmel, Weber and Dilthey. In 1915 he belonged to a circle of Hungarian intellectuals which included Karl Mannheim, Arnold Hauser, Bela Bartok, Zoltan Kodaly and Michael Polanyi, all of whom were concerned with the problems of democracy and culture. Joining the Hungarian Communist Party shortly after its founding in 1918, Lukács began writing a series of essays dealing with the question of Marxism and modern bourgeois thought. In 1923 he published *History and Class Consciousness*, subtitled, 'Studies in Marxist Dialectics', a book which has the remarkable distinction of being banned by the Third International as non-Marxist and heretical, and yet a potent influence on the thought of such diverse thinkers as Martin Heidegger, Jean-Paul Sartre, Herbert Marcuse and Lucien Goldmann. *History and Class Consciousness* was directed against the evolutionary positivism that dominated the Marxism of the Second International and was particularly critical of the contribution of Engels to Marxism: Lukács argued that Engels had transformed Marxism from a dialectical into a mechanical social theory in which consciousness became the passive product of external forces, a reflection of objective conditions.

History and Class Consciousness is an attempt to relate Marx's social theory to its Hegelian origins in the concept of totality and dialectical method. Facts do not speak for themselves but have meaning only when integrated into a whole; the fundamental axiom of dialectical method is that the whole is prior to the parts and that the parts themselves must be interpreted in their relation with the whole. For Lukács, the whole has primacy over its parts; the meaning of facts lies in their mediation with the whole. Thus the 'ultimate goal' of the socialist movement is the '*relation to the totality* (to the whole of society seen as a process) through which every aspect of the struggle acquires its revolutionary significance'. The meaning of history, or truth, lies not in the study of the empirical, objective structure of capitalism but in grasping that the working-class movement constitutes the expression of a necessary historical progress. The proletariat simultaneously is both the subject and object of history, the knowing subject which approaches truth through 'knowledge of the real, objective nature of a phenomenon . . . of its historical character and the knowledge of its actual function in the totality of society'. The 'self-knowledge of the proletariat', its awareness of its position in the social structure as an exploited class, 'coincides with knowledge of the whole', its awareness that its class situation can be understood only from the standpoint of the whole society, its system of production and social relations. Thus knowledge of reality is inseparable from the class position of the proletariat (Lukács, 1971, pp. 12–23).

In these formulations Lukács defined Marxism as an ideology but an ideology more advanced theoretically than any other 'style of thought'. Marxism is, therefore, not a systematic body of knowledge based on historically objective laws and the application of natural scientific methodology, but a revolutionary *praxis* in which the individual becomes a subject not an object of the historical process. Marxism is wholly distinct from bourgeois thought, and while bourgeoisie and proletariat share the same social reality, capitalism, they comprehend it differently. Bourgeois thought is profoundly unhistorical accepting the given, empirically immediate forms, thus conceiving change as catastrophe rather than as mediated by the structural principles of the whole. In contrast, proletarian thought is self-knowledge of the real historical situation, comprising a rejection of the immediately given forms of society in favour of the 'immanent meanings' of the historical process as a whole. Lukács concludes that proletarian thought stands 'on a higher scientific plane objectively' than bourgeois thought since it refuses to consider objects in isolation from the total process.

Thus the proletariat comprehends society as a coherent whole and, unlike the bourgeoisie 'aspires towards the truth even in its false consciousness . . . and substantive errors'. Ontologically privileged, the worker is nevertheless transformed into a commodity, into an object by the nature of capitalist production so that his empirical condition corresponds to the capitalist transformation of social relations into relations between objects and things. The fact that labour-power is appropriated as a thing means only that the proletariat, as a class, can achieve a consciousness of its real position. In the act of knowing, subject and object coincide: the cognitive and practical components of knowledge are thus fused within proletarian thought. The proletariat's self-knowledge of society is identical with the revolutionary transformation of capitalism: the movement towards socialism and the consciousness of this movement are one and the same thing. Knowledge is no mere epiphenomena, no simple reflection of external objects but is bound up with the revolutionary practice of the proletariat (Lukács, 1971, Ch. 2).

Lukács's discussion of bourgeois and proletarian thought and his general critique of positivism is linked to his analysis of reification and alienation as critical elements in the formation of consciousness and social theory. Although Marx had discussed alienation in his early writings, the Marxism of the Second International had failed to notice its significance, partly as a result of the unavailability of the texts (many remained unpublished until the 1920s and 1930s), as well as the unreceptive nature of positivist Marxism to non-scientistic concepts as alienation and reification. With his Hegelian and hermeneutic philosophical background, Lukács was able to analyse *Capital* through the categories he discovered in the few texts of Marx's early years which had been published, notably *The Holy Family*. He argues that reification dominates capitalist culture stamping its 'imprint upon the whole consciousness of man', a process which is total:

> Reification is . . . the necessary, immediate reality of every person living in capitalist society. It can be overcome only by *constant and constantly renewed efforts to disrupt the reified structure of existence by concretely relating to the concretely manifested contradictions of the total development, by becoming conscious of these contradictions for the total development* [Lukács's emphasis] (Lukács, 1971, p. 197).

Yet how is it possible for the proletariat to aspire to truth given the total penetration of reification within the culture? Lukács argues that as a commodity, the proletariat embodies the whole process of reification, but because it is an object its class situation drives it towards consciousness, 'the self-consciousness of the object', which enables it to cut through the fetishised nature of capitalism.

In these formulations Lukács comes close to abandoning Marxist materialism altogether. Historically, the worker is not transformed into a *thing*, or mere object, for while the social world of commodities penetrates consciousness, disposing the worker to grasp society as a natural, objective datum, there is always within every situation forces which work against reification. If Lukács's theory was historically accurate, it would be impossible to understand the development of specific working-class institutions such as trade unions or the struggle of the English proletariat against the nineteenth-century Factory Acts: in the most advanced industrial society of the nineteenth century the English working class should have been wholly dominated by reification, yet they created the most powerful trade union movement in the industrialising world and struggled, successfully in many cases, to improve their economic, social and political status. Lukács's conception of reification as a total process flows from his theory of totality, that the whole is prior to its parts which are organically bound together and express the inner core of the whole itself. It should be clear that this conception of totality is neither empirical nor historical but an *historicist* category in which the whole is directly expressive of the historical process. The relation of parts and whole is thus symmetrical rather than uneven and contradictory.

Similarly, in his discussion of class and class consciousness Lukács postulates an abstract and non-historical conception of the relation between social structure and ideology. Class consciousness is equivalent to totality: 'For a class to be ripe for hegemony means that its interests and consciousness enable it to organise the whole of society in accordance with those interests' (Lukács, 1971, p. 52). For Lukács, bourgeois thought fails to grasp society 'from the centre, as a coherent whole', while proletarian thought strives towards a historical understanding of its historical mission as a universal class whose actions will transform the whole. Lukács thus distinguishes 'psychological' from 'imputed' class consciousness, the former consisting of the empirical, day-to-day consciousness of workers which is false and incapable of grasping the whole. 'True' class consciousness is the 'potential' consciousness of a class that corresponds with the Marxist theory of the historical process. Potential consciousness is the 'appropriate and rational reaction' of a class to its historical situation *if* it possessed the necessary knowledge of its relation to the social whole. Employing one of Weber's concepts, Lukács thus writes that 'the objective theory of class consciousness is the theory of its objective possibility' (Lukács, 1971, p. 79).

But what is 'imputed' or 'potential' consciousness? It is obviously more real than everyday consciousness and cannot be reduced to elements of the latter. Yet how is it to be constituted theoretically if not from the empirical forms of consciousness? The answer is the privileged position of intellectuals who genuinely understand the historical process and therefore impute to the proletariat its true consciousness. For Lukács, history is invested with a meaning outside its empirical, concrete determinations, its different phases expressing an essence which is the historical process conceived as a totality. Lukács's critique of positivism thus ends in idealism, the rejection of all principles of verification and empirical evidence as the basis of Marxist theory: totality cannot be reconstructed through its empirical parts, the facts cannot simply be accumulated before the whole emerges. If wholes cannot be structured in terms of the empirical but only in terms of the future, the maturation of the historical process, then all social science would seem superfluous.

Lukács's standpoint is Hegelian, for like Hegel's philosopher who could genuinely interpret the ruses of history, so Lukács's historicism allows scope for the socialist, revolutionary intellectuals to impute consciousness and grasp the meaning of the whole. But the whole must be known before facts can be integrated within it, and the only way that the whole is known is not by empirical method but by accepting the privileged historical standpoint of the proletariat. And, of course, this itself cannot be proved, only accepted as the truth of history.

Culture and domination: Gramsci and the concept of hegemony

Antonio Gramsci (1891–1937) has been described as the most original Marxist theorist of the first half of the twentieth century. Gramsci's work is characterised by a concern with problems of culture and the relation of cultural formations to political domination; the central concept of hegemony has become widely used in the social sciences, as popular a term as that of alienation. Like Lukács, Gramsci defined Marxism in opposition to positivism and all forms of economic determinism emphasising the role of consciousness and the human subject in the making of historical change.

One of the leaders of the Italian Communist Party, Gramsci spent the last years of his short life incarcerated in Mussolini's jails producing, often in elliptical form to avoid prison censorship, reflections and reviews of Marxist theory and the relation between Marxism and political science, sociology, philosophy and history. Arrested in 1926 Gramsci wrote 3000 pages of analysis as well as hundreds of letters: his activity firmly negated the intention of the prosecutor at his trial that 'this brain must be put out of action for twenty years'.

In the years following the Second World War, the Italian Communist Party published much of this material frequently in an abridged form to avoid embarrassing the party's rigid Stalinist standpoint. Not that Gramsci deviated widely from orthodox Leninism: he accepted the necessity for a revolutionary party and rejected his youthful advocacy of workers councils as constituting the basis for a total reorganisation of society. His writings during the great strike wave and factory occupations in Turin during 1919–21 parallel Lenin's reflections on the relation of state and soviets in *The State and Revolution*; influenced especially by the work of Sorel, Gramsci suggested that the working class, through its own independent institutions, can transform social relations from within civil society, and that social change will not be imposed from above through centralised authority. But as Lenin abandoned his concept of Commune state so Gramsci modified his views on working-class spontaneity. In 1924 he wrote that Bolshevism was the first movement to develop the conception of proletarian hegemony; in the *Prison Notebooks* he is more explicit noting that the concept of hegemony represented Lenin's 'greatest theoretical contribution to the philosophy of *praxis*' (Gramsci, 1971, p. 365). Yet there are significant differences between Lenin's notion of the dictatorship of the proletariat, with its assumption of a strong, coercive state apparatus (and which remained central to Lenin's Marxism apart from the single exception of *The State and Revolution*), and Gramsci's theory of hegemony. For Gramsci, hegemony is predicated on a resilient and independent civil society allowing autonomy to 'private institutions' such as education, church, political parties, trade unions, and so on, which form the source of *consent*. Equally, Gramsci's concept of Marxism differs sharply from Leninism being influenced less by Engels, Plekhanov and Kautsky than the anti-positivist elements in Labriola, Sorel and the Italian Hegelian, Benedetto Croce.

For Gramsci, Marxism constituted a form of 'absolute historicism'. All forms of thought and action express a global historical process. Thus philosophy and science are true in the sense that they express the 'real' development of history. Marxism is defined as a world view (a *Weltanschauung*) containing 'in itself all the fundamental elements needed to construct a total and integral conception of the world, a total philosophy and theory of natural science . . . everything that is needed to give life to an integral practical organisation of society, that is, to become a total integral civilization' (Gramsci, 1971, p. 462). Reality is thus always historical, made by active human subjects: science, philosophy, Marxism, are not objective modes of intellectual activity existing in an external relation with the subject but created through the sum of actions which constitutes *praxis*. All elements have meaning in relation to the whole and they are 'true' in that they express the immanent tendencies of the whole itself. Unlike Lukács, Gramsci rejects the dualism of nature and society arguing that the category nature is itself social and historical. Marxism, or as Gramsci phrases it in the *Prison Notebooks*, the philosophy of *praxis*, constitutes the expression of the collective will of the subordinate working class striving to educate and liberate themselves from exploitation and class domination. The historical process is characterised, not simply by economic forces, but by human will, organised into collective forms and becoming 'the driving force of the economy,' moulding 'objective reality' (Gramsci, 1977, p. 35).

Gramsci's emphasis on will, on voluntarism is brought out vividly in one of his first significant articles, his response to the 1917 revolution, called prophetically, 'The Revolution against *Das Kapital*'. Written shortly after the successful October revolution, Gramsci's article argued that the Bolshevik accession to power vindicated Marxism as a non-fatalistic, activist theory built around the concept of 'collective will' rather than objective, 'iron laws'. Throughout his early writings Gramsci continually emphasised the self-activity of the working class, arguing that fatalistic acceptance of the inevitability of socialism condemns the proletariat to passivity and defensive political action. For Gramsci, revolution was not the automatic product of external economic forces but the result of one class establishing a cultural domination over all other classes. A 'rising class', he wrote, will strive to establish its authority over other social strata both through economic, political and military power and 'intellectual and moral leadership'. All revolutions are preceded 'by an intense work of cultural penetration' as the rising class aims to subjugate allied and subordinate strata to its ideas. A dominant class is thus defined as one which saturates civil society with the spirit of its morality, customs, religious and political practices: 'The founding of a ruling class is equivalent to the creation of a *Weltanschauung*.' If the working class are to constitute a dominant class they must establish a culture that commands the support of other strata; its world view, Marxism, is thus not a class ideology as such, but the expression of the immanent structural trends of history. Cultural hegemony is prior to the act of revolution and must be created through collective action. Gramsci thus distinguishes hegemony – associated with consent and equilibrium between social classes – and domination, associated with coercion and the state. Hegemony is created within civil society and the private institutions which mediate the individual and the state; direct domination flows from the state apparatus, coercion through public institutions (Gramsci, 1971, pp. 77–84).

Gramsci first employed the term hegemony in his *Some*

Aspects of the Southern Question (1926), where he said that the proletariat 'can become the leading (*dirigente*) and the dominant class to the extent that it succeeds in creating a system of alliances that allow it to mobilise the majority of the working population against capitalism and the bourgeois state' (Gramsci, 1978, p. 443). Hegemony is effectively a synthesis of political, intellectual and moral leadership in which a class passes from defending its own 'corporate' interests to unifying and directing all other social groups. Two examples from Gramsci's work will illustrate his general argument. He suggests that only the bourgeoisie and proletariat strive to establish hegemony. Feudal society, in contrast to capitalism, is dominated by a closed caste, the dominant classes do not develop an organic passage from the other classes to their own but remain 'technically' and 'ideologically' separate. In contrast, the Jacobins, a specific social group, developed into a hegemonic class by representing all the popular forces ranged against the old regime and organising a national, popular collective will. Thus although possessing certain economic functions related to the developing bourgeois means of production, the Jacobins passed from a merely economic phase of development to an ethical–political stage with their own political party and *Weltanschauung*.

Gramsci, of course, was concerned with the possibility of revolution in the advanced capitalist countries. His analysis of hegemony suggests that the working class are not simply the passive victims of an overpowering structure of bourgeois ideology, but actively acquiesce in the persistence of bourgeois society. In Western Europe civil society is relatively strong thus enabling the bourgeoisie to rule through consent. Gramsci emphasises that hegemony is not wholly consensual but consists of a synthesis of consent and coercion, an equilibrium in which force does not prevail. The distinction between civil and political society is therefore not absolute since the capitalist social formation cannot be broken down into wholly separate and independent institutions. Thus he notes that education, while belonging, as an institution to civil society, is dependent on the state both economically and ideologically. In Hegelian terms, Gramsci argues for the ethical role of the state, that although defending the economic and political interests of the dominant class, the state is nevertheless instrumental in building up the institutions which contribute to the strength of civil society. This is Gramsci's way of expressing the problem of relative autonomy, that the state is not simply the organ one class uses to oppress another but the means whereby a modern complex society is created and legitimised, not through a class ideology, but a bourgeois *Weltanschauung*.

The whole tenor of Gramsci's Marxism was against reductionism of any kind: culture was not simply class culture, the state was not merely a class state, consent was not false consciousness. Hegemony implied a democratic relation between ruled and ruler, the existence of institutions which enable the subordinate groups to articulate their own interests and defend them, to build their own distinctive culture. Thus revolution is not simply the seizure of the state apparatus and the transference of economic forces to a new class: proletarian revolution is a process of mass participation, the exercise of collective will by a class whose culture enables it to become an active subject and hegemonic force thus enlarging civil society and its democratic structures.

Marxism and the sociology of intellectuals: Gramsci

One of Gramsci's most significant contributions to a sociology of modern society and the processes of hegemony was his theory of intellectuals. For Gramsci, intellectuals exercised a critical role in the formation both of ideologies and consent. Social cohesion was as much the function of intellectuals as of social structure. The failure of Marxism in the advanced capitalist societies posed questions both on the role of leadership as well as the function of intellectuals in society as a whole.

Gramsci defined intellectuals sociologically rejecting the conception of intellectual activity as intrinsic to a special social stratum. Such properties, he argued, were characteristic of everyone in society:

What are the 'maximum' limits of acceptance of the term 'intellectuals'? Can one find a unitary criterion to characterise equally all the diverse and disparate activities of intellectuals and

211

to distinguish these at the same time and in an essential way from the activities of other social groupings? The most widespread error of method seems to me that of having looked for this criterion of distinction in the intrinsic nature of intellectual activities, rather than in the ensemble of the system of relations in which these activities . . . have their place within the general complex of social relations . . . All men are intellectuals . . . but not all men have in society the function of intellectuals (Gramsci, 1971, pp. 8–9).

Gramsci thus rejected the idealist notion of 'great intellectuals': intellectuals were defined in terms of knowledge production and work function. Discussing the Italian philosopher, Croce, Gramsci described him as a 'constructor' of ideologies in the interests of the governing class, although 'interests' and 'ideologies' cannot be assimilated mechanistically to class position. Intellectuals produce knowledge and ideologies which are always more than a simple reflection of class interests. As a social stratum intellectuals develop more slowly than other social groups and although giving expression to the interests of a dominant class they equally articulate the cultural traditions of a whole people. The development of capitalism, however, introduces a new type of intellectual, the technical organiser, the specialist who gradually replaces the older, traditional type organising society through the institutions of the state.

Gramsci defined intellectuals, therefore, as those who perform functions of organisation within the realm of production, culture, public administration, a concept wholly opposed to the élitist notion exemplified in Pareto's circulation of élites or Mosca's governing class which effectively divided society into a superior stratum of governors and inferior stratum of the governed. Underpinning Gramsci's theory of intellectuals was his awareness of the specific historical development of bourgeois society towards increasing centralisation – a national educational system, local and national civil service administration, the growth of the church and the professions and especially the rapid development of the state apparatus. In Gramsci's view certain economic 'corporate' classes – classes whose own narrow interests were wholly class conditioned – must necessarily pass into hegemonic classes if they are to become a dominant class. In this process intellectuals play a critical role linking the basic economic structure and basis of a class with the wider cultural institutions:

> Every social group, coming into existence on the original terrain of an essential function in the world of economic production, creates together with itself, organically, one or more strata of intellectuals which give it homogeneity and an awareness of its own function not only in the economic but also in the social and political fields (Gramsci, 1971, p. 5).

Gramsci argues that social classes do not develop their own intellectuals; a social class, striving for hegemony, must transform itself from its original amorphous structure into a homogeneous, ideologically unified group capable of generating, through its allied intellectuals, universal concepts. Intellectuals are defined both in terms of structure and function as well as consciousness.

Gramsci distinguished two types of intellectual: organic and traditional. Organic intellectuals belong to social groups aiming to direct the whole of society, 'experts in legitimation', who emerge as the result of changes in the mode of production; organic intellectuals express the aspirations of a class without themselves constituting a class. In contrast, traditional intellectuals evolve through a process of 'uninterrupted historical continuity' and unlike organic intellectuals are not so closely bound up with the mode of production. Traditional intellectuals are characterised by a caste-like structure; they define themselves independently of the dominant class. Traditional intellectuals are inter-class, existing within the intercises of society, linking the past with the present as an historically continuous process. Organic intellectuals produce ideas which mark a sharp break with the past. Traditional intellectuals include ecclesiastical intellectuals, lawyers, teachers, doctors, their function one of maintaining continuity between one social formation and another. Gramsci cited the eighteenth-century French clergy who, through their function in education and monopoly of religious ideology transformed themselves from traditional intellectuals into the organic intellectuals of the landed aristocracy. Gramsci's point is that any social group

213

striving to establish hegemony must conquer and assimilate the traditional intellectuals. In Italy, the bourgeoisie failed to create a 'hegemonic phase' remaining at the corporate level and thus used Piedmont, the northern monarchical state, as the means of domination. In Germany, the Junkers constituted the traditional intellectuals of the bourgeoisie retaining an independent economic and political base.

Gramsci's examples are hypotheses. He could not conduct empirical research into the complex relation of intellectuals and social structure. His purpose was largely theoretical to show that while all social groups necessarily forge links with different types of intellectuals, only the political party can carry out the task of welding together the organic intellectuals and the traditional intellectuals: 'The party carries out this function in strict dependence on its basic function, which is that of elaborating its own component parts – those elements of a social group which has been born and developed as an "economic" group – and of turning them into qualified political intellectuals, leaders and organisers of all the activities and functions inherent in the organic development of an integral society, both civil and political' (Gramsci, 1971, pp. 16–17). An economic social group – the landed interest, the industrialists, the proletariat – can only develop beyond the specific 'moment of their historical development' and become the agency of national and international activity through the fusion of the two types of intellectual within the structure of a political party.

As 'functionaries of the superstructure', intellectuals mediate the worlds of culture and production producing the ideas which the masses 'spontaneously' accept as legitimate because such ideas express more than the sum of the class interests of the dominant group. In this sense intellectuals are 'organisers' of social hegemony and Gramsci emphasises their critical role in the hegemonic structures of Western European civil societies in which direct forms of domination have been the exception. Gramsci's is not a pessimistic sociology of the intellectual: his concept of modern capitalism was not that of a mass society, although he noted the tendency towards bureaucratisation and centralisation, but a complex structure of independent, 'private' institutions (political parties, trade unions, church, professional associations, etc.) which formed the basis of consent and social hegemony. The vitality of civil society and the persistence of hegemony enabled intellectuals in the advanced capitalist countries to exercise their function as organisers of, and experts in, legitimation without forming a special élite dominating society from above. It thus follows that the proletariat, as a rising class striving for hegemony, must saturate civil society with its own distinct values and culture, not as simple working-class ideas or interests, but universalised as socialism – a world view – which compels the whole society and in particular the traditional intellectuals to accept *actively* the validity and historical necessity of its fundamental principles.

For Gramsci, then, intellectuals are structured in a hierarchy of functions relating to hegemony. At the apex are the creative intellectuals who produce the world views, ideologies and theoretical systems; at the base are administrative intellectuals whose function is one of diffusing the values and culture of the existing hegemony; and finally, in the middle ranges are the organisational intellectuals without which no dominant group could survive. The role of creative intellectuals is more significant in strong civil societies where they work to bring together a number of strata or groups into an 'historical bloc' (i.e. the English industrialists and the aristocracy, the German Junkers and industrialists). Gramsci emphasises that the withdrawal of their allegiance to hegemony will produce an 'organic' crisis, a crisis of authority and the possibility of social disintegration. Creative intellectuals are structurally and ideologically more crucial than the second order intellectuals, although these subaltern groups are functionally necessary if social hegemony is to work adequately and therefore they must be assimilated into the dominant intellectual bloc. In the transition to socialism it thus follows that intellectuals must articulate the consciousness of the working classes and allied groups: Gramsci formulated the concept of the political party as the 'collective intellectual', the institution which synthesises the creative vitality of the masses with the organisational, directing function of the organic intellectuals. Intellectuals are crucial for socialist transformation: it is not a question of the Party dominating the masses from above but rather of a dialectical and democratic relation of party to people. Yet although this formulation opposes authoritarianism and élitism it nevertheless leaves unanswered the question of how a socialist society, based on centralisation and collectivist ideology, can retain an independent civil society and thus autonomous intellectuals. In this sense the collective intellectual suggests an element of totalitarianism within Gramsci's general framework of a democratic socialism structured in the activity and culture of the masses.

Lukács and Gramsci on sociology

Both Lukács and Gramsci defined Marxism as a world view organically bound up with the 'rising' industrial working class. As a science of proletarian revolution Marxism expressed the active elements of human culture, *praxis*, through which human subjects created necessary historical change. Both writers were aware of developments in the field of sociology: Lukács knew the work of Simmel, Weber, Sombart; Gramsci was particularly interested in sociological studies of political parties and problems of methodology and was familiar with the writings of Mosca, Michels, Pareto, Weber, not to mention the nineteenth-century positivist tradition.

Both Gramsci and Lukács tended to identify sociology with positivism: sociology was thus criticised for the elimination of the active subject in favour of external, objective laws which dominate society and the individual. For Lukács, sociology defined the object as given, transforming historical processes into eternal and natural forces; the social world was thus reifed with consciousness reduced to a passive reflection of economic structure. The reification of the historical and social world within bourgeois thought makes it impossible to grasp the connections between the various elements that comprise society and the whole: society as a totality in a constant process of change is absent from bourgeois sociology. Indeed, bourgeois thought splits up social knowledge into separate spheres of inquiry – political economy, history, jurisprudence and sociology. Thus bourgeois thought cannot go beyond the surface of observable facts to determine their relation with the whole: the monographic method, Lukács concludes, the intensive, quantitative study of one element within the whole, constitutes the limit of sociology and confirms its status as ideology. All facts must be interpreted in terms of the historical process as a whole, its objective possibility.

Similarly, Gramsci criticised positivistic sociology for reducing social relations to the status of inviolable natural laws. He was particularly hostile to sociologists such as Michels, for postulating 'iron laws' of organisation that assumed incompetence and passivity on the part of the masses. Hegemony constitutes rather the triumph of consciousness, social action and *will* over external conditions: 'Structure ceases to be an external force', Gramsci wrote, 'which crushes man, assimilates him to itself and makes him passive [but] is transformed into a means of freedom, an instrument to create a new ethico-political form and a source of new initiatives' (Gramsci, 1971, p. 367). Gramsci followed Labriola in rejecting sociology on the basis of its inability to grasp the whole historical process: Labriola had coined the term, the philosophy of *praxis* as the 'essence' of historical materialism, defining it as the 'immanent philosophy' which pervades the entire historical and social individual. As a philosophy of *praxis*, Marxism cannot be reduced to sociology which for Gramsci was a science which sought to discover social facts, the causal relations between them and the general laws of social systems through the methods of the natural sciences. Marxism, as a world view, cannot be schematized into an external body of knowledge structured around the discovery of regular and objective laws since such a standpoint assumes the passivity of the historical subject. Gramsci admitted, however, that statistics were valuable, especially from the point of view of social planning, but his main thrust against sociology, as he conceived it, was that all statistical laws, and predictions based on these laws, defined as natural phenomena, ignored the essential component of all social situations, that of collective will. Reality is constantly changing through *praxis*; it is impossible to predict scientifically the effects of actions or the workings of elements on elements: one can foresee only in the sense that one acts and therefore contributes to the 'predicted' result.

As there were no sociological laws which facilitated prediction as in the natural sciences, so there was no 'Marxist sociology', since reality was always a created reality and the historical process an act of self-knowledge by the proletariat. For Lukács and Gramsci, sociology separated theory from practice: objective laws and objective facts exist only in a process of active mediation involving an historical subject. Ultimately both Lukács and Gramsci argue that historical knowledge is not possible merely as the product of empirical social science: empirical inquiry must be guided by historicism and humanism.

There were attempts from within Marxism to transform Marxism into a sociological system or theory, by the Austro-Marxist school (a term coined by the American socialist, Louis Boudin to describe a group of young Marxists active in the Austrian socialist movement prior to the First World War, the most prominent being Max Adler, Otto Bauer, Rudolf Hilferding and Karl Renner) and the leading Bolshevik theorist, Nikolai Bukharin whose textbook, *Hitorical Materialism*, subtitled *A System of Sociology*, originally published in Russia in 1921, exercised an influential role in the education of leading Marxists inside and outside the Soviet Union. Both Lukács and Gramsci polemicised against Bukharin (1888–1938) precisely because *Historical Materialism* had a greater intellectual impact among Marxists than the more academically oriented work of the Austro-Marxists who, in any case, did not belong to the Third International.

Both Lukács and Gramsci criticised *Historical Materialism* for dividing Marxism into a naturalist scientific sociology, combining history and politics, and a philosophical materialism embracing the theory of knowledge. One of the first Marxists to interpret historical materialism as a form of sociology, Bukharin sought to assimilate the burgeoning sociology of Weber, Simmel, Michels and others, to accommodate twentieth-century Marxism to twentieth-century sociology. He distinguished between 'proletarian science' and 'bourgeois science', the former assimilating the scientific insights of the latter. Yet as Lukács and Gramsci emphasised in their critiques, Bukharin's conception of Marxism is close to 'bourgeois natural scientific materialism' in its attempt to reduce the dialectic to general laws of motion working objectively and independent of human consciousness. In his criticism, Lukács argued that Bukharin's conception eliminated the category of totality from social science, the historical process was no longer grasped as a unifying whole; the relation of parts to whole is conceived mechanically and positivistically. In particular Bukharin's concept of society as a system with its law of equilibrium is close to the formulations of Comte and Pareto in assimilating human activity and human relationships to an underlying and dominating external structure. Lukács was especially critical of Bukharin's scientism, his uncritical acceptance of prediction in social science: only practice, not unmediated facts based on statistics, constitutes proof of empirical propositions, the transformation of reality by human activity and human consciousness. Bukharin's sociologised Marxism, concluded Lukács, was merely a form of 'passive' materialism' that divorces the active subject from the totality of the historical process (Lukács, 1972, pp. 135–42).

Gramsci, too, criticised Bukharin's scientism, for his failure to grasp that all objective economic and sociological phenomena derived from social relationships, human activity, values, culture and consciousness. Bukharin's concept of system, Gramsci argued, fetishised and hypostatised society. For Bukharin, society was defined as a system greater than the sum of its parts; it is not ideology (Lukács) or hegemony (Gramsci) which transforms the different parts into a whole, but a system of mutual interactions between the different members. In this way the subject plays a role but one severely circumscribed by external forces. For Bukharin 'each individual in his development . . . is filled with the influences of his environment, as the skin of a sausage is filled with sausage-meat . . . Like a sponge he constantly absorbs new impressions . . . Each individual at bottom is filled with a social content. The individual himself is a collection of concentrated social influences, united in a small unit' (Bukharin, 1969, p. 98). The parallel between nineteenth-century positivist sociology and Bukharin's Marxist sociology is brought out quite sharply in this formulation. Society is an organism consisting of different structures; the system dominates the individual who is linked to others through mechanical modes of interaction. An homologous relationship subsists between the material and economic 'base', and the culture of society; cultural institutions, ideologies and consciousness are epiphenomenal forces lacking all autonomy. The system normally exists in a state of equilibrium, a situation facilitated by morality and customs which co-ordinate human action to prevent social disintegration. But the existence of class interests and sources of conflict necessarily lead to adjustments and change and, in extreme situations, to revolution.

The important point about Bukharin's mechanistic and abstract concept of society is that it fails totally to develop a theory of civil society and the institutions through which social action occurs, values produced, culture transformed and with it the social individual, social groups and social classes. In Bukharin's formulation the human subject is passive, the product of external forces; social change is the result of a breakdown of equilibrium within the system, of necessary adjustments and thus the development of a new systemic equilibrium. Such ahistorical, excessively abstract and mechanical conceptions of society are strikingly similar to Pareto's *Treatise*, and its concern with developing a general theory of society to the exclusion of any detailed, empirical analysis of any one society and its constituent structures. Abstractly conceived, Bukharin's work fails to grasp, in Marx's and Engels's words, that 'civil society is the true source and theatre of all history' (Marx and Engels, 1964, p. 48).

Marxism and sociology: the Austro-Marxists

It is interesting to compare Bukharin's work with the explicit sociological Marxism of Austro-Marxism. Unlike Bukharin, the Austro-Marxists were mainly concerned with the specific development of capitalism, its class structure, and state institutions: they argued, rather like Weber, that civil society was changing, the class and occupational structure leading to the emergence of a broad middle class including what Renner called 'the service class' (managers and salaried employees), and a shift in authority relations from those based on private property to bureaucracy. Perhaps the most significant empirical study of the school was Hilferding's *Finance Capital*, which influenced Lenin's *Imperialism* in its depiction of modern capitalism as a fusion of banking and industrial capital within a structure dominated by cartels, trusts and monopolies. Hilferding emphasised the role of an increasingly interventionist state which prevented capitalist economic laws working out towards crisis and collapse: his concept of 'organised capitalism' emphasises the close relation between the nation state and private capital. The relation between state and civil society was thus close to the formulations of orthodox Marxism: although aware of the changing nature of capitalism as a social formation, the Austro-Marxists failed to grasp the significance of centralised state power defining the state, not as parasitic on civil society, but rather as an integral element of society.

Their failure to theorise civil society as the object of sociology finds its practical expression in the Austro-Marxists's analysis of Workers Councils. These institutions had developed rapidly in Austria after the end of the First World War, elemental working-class structures challenging the dominance of the state over civil society. But they were conceived by the School as administrative institutions, democratically organised to run production; the council movement was theorised in terms of industrial democracy 'a way of effecting a complete revolution in the relation of the masses to the state, of awakening the initiative and encouraging the most fruitful kinds of spontaneous activity among the workers' (Bottomore and Goode, 1978, pp. 165–7). Thus the socialist programme advocated by the Austro-Marxists was broadly evolutionary, taking over the state apparatus and wielding it for the public good: there was no conception of the state being absorbed and abolished by the democratic institutions of civil society.

Thus although focusing empirically on changes within capitalism, the Austro-Marxists reached similarly élitist conclusions to those of Bukharin and orthodox Marxism. The masses were largely passive; the human subject exercised no decisive role in change other than as determined by external forces. Thus their methodological orientation explicitly rejected the *verstehen* approach of Weber and Simmel arguing for the unity of the natural and cultural sciences: 'Nature and society . . . comprise the causal regularity of events as a whole . . . a social scientific standpoint . . . is logically on the same footing as natural science'. As a 'natural science of social beings

and events' Marxism studied the law-governed interconnectedness of phenomena: the link between the Austro-Marxist
methodology of scientific inquiry and their social reformism is
brought out in Adler's concept of Marxism as 'a system of
sociological knowledge' which grounds socialism 'upon causal
knowledge of the events of social life'. Marxism and sociology
'are one and the same thing', the science 'of the laws of social
life and its causal development', striving 'to deduce the
development of socialism from capitalism as a matter of causal
necessity' (Bottomore and Goode, 1978, pp. 60–4). Defining
society as 'socialised humanity', the Austro-Marxists conceptualised this category as an *a priori*, as a given datum, an essence
which manifests itself through human consciousness. In this
way the active, human element in social development became
assimilated to an underlying fixed structure.

Conclusion

The various attempts to synthesise Marxism with sociology, or
to transform Marxism into a sociological system or theory,
foundered over the failure of Marxism to develop from within
its own framework an adequate sociological concept of civil
society. The institutions of civil society together with the role of
the human subject were yoked to an immanent, historical
economic determinism. The object of study for Marxism was
not that of classical sociology. For although many of its
fundamental principles were anti-democratic, élitist and
deterministic, classical sociology sought to define and articulate the complex, many-sided structures of civil society as they
developed through the transition from pre-industrial to industrial society. Marxism, by emphasising the centralising and
collectivist nature of the emerging industrial, capitalist, social
order tended to assimilate the concept of civil society to
historicism (Lukács, Gramsci) or the economic infrastructure
and the causal laws of the social system (Bukharin). Gramsci's
theorisation of civil society gives his work a sociological
dimension but his historicism pulls it back towards orthodox
Marxism. Early twentieth-century Marxist thought could not
account for the complexity of industrial capitalism: Marxist

theorists increasingly turned to sociology for concepts and theories of social structure and social change absent from Marxist discourse.

One result was the problematic nature of Marxism itself: to what extent could Marxist thought assimilate sociological concepts and yet remain distinctively Marxist? And if Marxism was turned into a sociological system what happened to its status as a revolutionary science? Many of these issues were to be raised in the subsequent development of Marxism: but with the consolidation of the Soviet state in the 1920s and, following the Second World War, the formation of similar totalitarian systems in Eastern Europe, the paths of Marxism and sociology diverged. Marxism became synonymous with Stalinism, sociology with pluralism and democracy. Part III will explore these issues.

PART III
MODERN SOCIOLOGY

8
Functionalism

Functionalism as a distinct methodology and theory of society originated first in the work of Comte, Spencer and Durkheim, and secondly, in late nineteenth-century and early twentieth-century anthropology especially the writings of A. R. Radcliffe-Brown (1881–1955) and Bronislaw Malinowski (1884–1942). Durkheim is often cited as the dominant influence on the development of sociological functionalism for his argument that social institutions exist solely to fulfil specific social needs. 'All moral systems', he argued, constitute 'a function of the social organisation', and apart from 'abnormal cases' every society develops a morality necessary for its adequate functioning (Durkheim, 1953, p. 56). In *The Rules of Sociological Method* he explicitly argued that the function of a social fact is social in that it necessarily produces socially useful effects. Thus:

> . . . to explain a social phenomenon the efficient cause which produces it and the function it fulfills must be investigated separately (Durkheim, 1982, p. 123).

For Durkheim, cause and function related to specific ends, especially those concerned with social solidarity and the maintenance of society as an organic whole. Durkheim's holistic functionalism sought to explain social facts not solely by focusing on the cause on which they depended but by showing their function 'in the establishment of . . . general harmony' (Durkheim, 1982, p. 125). Thus in analysing the division of labour Durkheim established its efficient cause as increasing moral and material density, and its function as the social need it fulfilled, that is, to integrate the social struture of modern industrial society.

Durkheim was particularly concerned to show that the function of social facts was moral: social institutions 'normally' worked to promote the goals of social solidarity. Morality thus constituted a structure of social functions which embodied the collective conscience of society as a whole. Education and religion functioned in this way promoting moral values which integrated different individuals into the social collectivity. Similarly, crime, as a 'normal' and 'healthy' feature of all societies functions both to reinforce collective sentiments and to facilitate 'the normal evolution of morality and law'. Durkheim argued that the existence of criminal behaviour constituted an index of the flexibility of the *conscience collective*. A normal level of crime indicates that the collective conscience lacks the total authority to 'suppress' all 'divergencies' within society. Crime itself reflects the existence of social conditions which enables individuals to express themselves as individuals: 'If there were no crimes, this condition would not be fulfilled . . . collective sentiments would have attained a degree of intensity unparalleled in history . . . The authority which the moral conscience enjoys must not be excessive for otherwise no one would dare to attack it, and it would petrify too easily into an immutable form'. The existence of crime, therefore, shows that the collective sentiments are not too strong as to crush all sense of individuality and originality (Durkheim, 1982, p. 101).

Durkheim's functional approach to the study of institutions, while remaining tenuously within the framework of nineteenth-century evolutionism, tended to emphasise the synchronic, structural dimensions of society at the expense of the diachronic, the genetic and historical: the concept of society as a differentiated and integrated whole, in which the various elements exercise interdependent functions to sustain a complex unity, has the effect of separating 'function' from 'development' generating abstract, ahistorical social typologies such as mechanical and organic solidarity. In a broadly similar vein Malinowski and Radcliffe-Brown, in their studies of Pacific tribal communities (Trobriand and Andaman Islanders), rejected the evolutionary and diffusionist approach and argued for structural and systemic analysis. Rather than pose the question, how did this particular institution or custom originate, they asked how does it fit into the broader context, how does the part relate to the whole. In contrast to American cultural anthropology and German ethnology, early twentieth-century British anthropology developed a distinctive sociological approach to the analysis of social structure, defining society as an integrated system.

Radcliffe-Brown specifically abandoned the search for *origins*, the historical past of institutions and customs, arguing that each culture constitutes 'a functionally interrelated system' in which 'general laws or functions' operate (Radcliffe-Brown, 1952, p. 180). Anthropology, declared Malinowski, should deal with the totality of social, cultural and psychological elements of communal life 'for they are so interwoven that not one can be understood without taking into consideration all the others' (Malinowski, 1922, p. xvi). In this way magic was analysed as fulfilling 'an indispensable function' in primitive societies through satisfying a social need 'which cannot be satisfied by any other factors of primitive civilisation', while the function of the funeral ceremony 'is the part it plays in the social life as a whole and therefore the contribution it makes to the maintenance of the structural continuity'. For Radcliffe-Brown, a social system, that is, 'the total social structure of a society together with the totality of social usages', constituted 'a functional unity', a condition in which all parts 'work together with a sufficient degree of harmony or internal consistency, i.e. without producing persistent conflicts which can neither be resolved nor regulated'. Culture was thus an integrated whole: to explain any belief, rule, custom or institution demanded an analysis which linked the element functionally with the *structure* of the culture as a system (Radcliffe-Brown, 1952, ch. 9).

This model of society stresses the elements of harmony and consistency not those of conflict and contradiction. The functional unity of a system is defined in terms of social order. In defining society in holistic terms functionalism implies that as everything within the system is necessarily functional for the whole then change, based on conflict, must be conceived as a threat to the basis of the system itself. The tendency to regard functionalism as a conservative sociological theory largely stems from its central concern with integration and the analogy of society as a human organism in which social 'health' is identified with social order and 'disease' with social conflict. Thus the major problem in *The Division of Labour* lay in reconciling the increasing social differentiation of the advanced societies with the need for social integration, a means of regulating 'insatiable desires and appetites'. The function of the division of labour, Durkheim argued, as with elements of the human organism, was normally one of promoting unity, but its 'abnormal' form functioned to create dissension and conflict eventuating in a widespread state of anomie. Durkheim's holistic functionalism, concerned particularly with problems of social order, can be seen, however, as one attempt to develop an objective science of society which rejected the nominalist conception of society as constituted in individuals and explanation of social phenomena in psychological terms.

Given its early development in Durkheim's sociology functionalism was barely a significant presence in the mainstream of European sociology during the first years of the twentieth century. The early American sociologists – Albion Small, Robert Park, Charles Cooley and W. I. Thomas – were attracted to the individualistic, psychological approach of Tarde, and Simmel's theory of sociation, both, of course, criticised by Durkheim for a failure to grasp society as a collective phenomenon. American individualism, combined with empiricism and social psychology, effectively precluded the development of a *theory* of society in the manner of the European sociologists: a collectivist conception of society did, however, emerge in America during the 1930s in the form of a dogmatic Marxism although it failed to strike deep roots in American intellectual culture. Sociological functionalism developed as the major sociological paradigm after the Second World War, the first significant holistic conception of society developed by American sociology. In Kingsley Davis's *Human Society* (1949) society was defined in macrosociological terms with the main focus on integration and survival and the relation of parts to whole; and in the work of Talcott Parsons (1902–79) functionalism became codified into a form of systems analysis.

Talcott Parsons is the major figure in the transition from the predominantly individualistic social psychological theory of early American sociology to its post-war holistic, anti-psychological standpoint. Parsons was the first American sociologist to develop a coherent theory of society conceived as a whole in opposition to the dominant mode of anti-theoretical sociological empiricism. Yet Parsons's work during the 1930s, culminating in his *The Structure of Social Action* (1937), was not strictly speaking functionalist at all but a development of the anti-utilitarian, voluntaristic theory of action in which Weber and Durkheim were singled out for their insight that social integration is centred around a core of common norms and values accepted as legitimate by the members of society.

Parsons's theory of action, which explicitly relegated Marx to a minor position in the history of social theory, emphasised the need for central values at a time in American history – the Depression years of the 1930s – when American values appeared to be under strain. Parsons's voluntarism clearly opposed what he regarded as deterministic Marxist theories of inevitable class conflict, class ideologies and class struggle. For Parsons, the answer to social disorganisation lay in the furthering of moral values which would bind society together as a cohesive unity; and by emphasising the voluntaristic aspects of action, Parsons focused on the need for individuals to act and thus create the conditions necessary for social regeneration.

During the period following the end of the Second World War, however, beginning with his article, 'The Present Position and Prospects of Systematic Theory in Sociology' (1945), Parsons's action approach became a systems approach which diminished the voluntaristic element. Whereas in *The Structure of Social Action* Parsons's starting point was the 'unit' act, in books such as *The Social System* (1951), the starting point was that of 'the empirical system' and social structure focusing particularly on 'the integration of the motivation of actors with the normative cultural standards which integrate the action system'. In his later work Parsons attempted increasingly to link the actor with the social structure within the framework of system defined in anti-voluntaristic functionalist terms.

By the 1950s sociological functionalism was increasingly regarded not simply as one of many sociological approaches but *the* sociological method. In his 1959 paper, 'The Myth of Functional Analysis as a Special Method in Sociology and

Anthropology', Kingsley Davis proclaimed that functionalism was simply the method employed by all social scientists irrespective of whether they called themselves functionalists or not. Functionalism, he noted, was a method which related parts to whole and one part to another, a method characteristic of any science and if 'there is a functional method, it is simply the method of sociological analysis'. Critics of functionalism, however, have suggested that far from constituting an objectively neutral methodology for the social sciences, functionalism is simply an expression of conservative ideology. In seeking to explain the need for social stability and social order, sociological functionalism fails to provide an adequate analysis of social change and social conflict; the historical basis of society as a *process* and structure is assimilated to a static concept of social solidarity and social consensus. Functionalism, wrote Alvin Gouldner, in his extended critique of Parsons, 'resonates sentiments that favour the preservation of privilege ... A social theory that takes as its central problem the maintenance of social order' and is thus 'more ideologically congenial to those who have more to lose' (Gouldner, 1971, pp. 253–4).

Gouldner's critique of functionalism, especially the work of Parsons, is broadly similar to C. Wright Mills's criticism during the 1950s which defined functionalism as an example of 'grand theory' reflecting the dominant values of American capitalism and which failed to account for the reality of power in society. In his analysis of Parsons in *The Sociological Imagination* (1959), for example, Mills argued that the 'normative order' which Parsons identified as the basis of every social system ultimately fails to explain the simple fact that in all societies some individuals make decisions while others obey them: Parsons's theory suggests that individuals virtually govern themselves through a social consensus which pre-empts any consideration that consent might be manipulated (Mills, 1959, ch. 2).

In general these criticisms miss the point: it is one thing to argue against the later Parsons that the human subject has disappeared within the framework of the social theory, and another to charge functionalism with a lack of substantive concern with power. Functionalism cannot be dismissed for ignoring power in society and the problems of social conflict and of 'vested interests'; Parsons's work includes many discussions of the sources of conflict and power, while his argument that in explaining social order he simultaneously focuses on those elements likely to produce social instability, a lack of cohesion and thus the possibilities of social change, is clearly persuasive in the sense that any sociological theory must incorporate analysis of both dynamics and statics. It is in this spirit that R. K. Merton has argued that far from embodying a conservative ideology, sociological functionalism can be radical and critical by pointing to the failures and weaknesses, the 'malfunctioning' of specific institutions for satisfying the collective needs of society. The introduction of concepts such as 'functional alternatives', 'dysfunctions' and 'moving equilibrium', and the identification, in some functionalist writings, of 'the postitive functions of social conflict', its creative role in systemic change, have tended to weaken the general criticism of functionalism as a theory of system maintenance and cohesion. Thus, for Merton, functionalism is methodologically neutral given an ideological colouring only by the politically motivated. Functional analysis, he writes, does not entail any specific ideological commitment which 'is not to say that such commitments are not often implicit in the works of functional analysts' but that they remain 'extraneous rather than intrinsic to functional theory' (Merton, 1957, pp. 38–43).

What, then, is sociological functionalism?

Sociological functionalism: general features

The basic characteristics of sociological functionalism can be briefly summarised:

1. Societies are wholes, systems of interrelated parts. Each part has meaning only in terms of its relation with the whole performing a specific function within the system; society is thus a system of interdependent elements all of which contribute to the integration and adaptation of the system as a whole. Social causation is thus multiple and reciprocal.

2. The concept of system, derived as a sociological concept from Pareto, is central to all forms of sociological functionalism.

It is the functional relation of parts to whole which distinguishes functionalism from other holistic approaches. Society is thus defined as a structure of elements possessing a patterned form; the point of departure is the system as a whole and those factors essential for its survival, evolution and adequate functioning. Systemic functionalism can be distinguished from general functionalism: systemic functionalism begins from the assumption that all elements contribute to maintaining the whole, while general functionalism is concerned only with the empirical functions of different items which may or may not contribute to maintaining the whole. Both types of functionalism, however, are concerned with what Merton describes as 'observable objective consequences', not 'subjective dispositions' (i.e. motives and purposes), which effectively constitute the basis of function.

3. All elements which make up the social system are indispensable to the extent that they perform special functions related to the 'needs' of the system as a system. Parsonian functionalism has developed the notion of functional prerequisites of social systems which 'refer broadly to the things that must get done in any society if it is to continue as a going concern, i.e. the generalised conditions necessary for the maintenance of the system concerned'. The functional prerequisites have included provision for an adequate relationship of the individual to the environment, role differentiation and role assignment, communication, shared cognitive orientations and articulated goals, normative regulation of means, the regulation of affective expression, socialisation and social control of deviant behaviour. Many of these functional prerequisites are implied in any concept of society and are therefore tautologous: all societies must have modes of socialisation and means of communication since without these society as a concept would be impossible, irrespective of whether the theoretical standpoint is functionalism, social action, sociological nominalism or Marxism. Parsons, however, has regrouped the prerequisites under four headings: Adaptation, Goal Attainment, Integration, and Latency (AGIL for short). Adaptation refers to activities by which the system adapts to its environment modifying, controlling it in terms of the needs of the system; Goal Attainment refers to the mobilising of resources to attain

specific goals and seeking such goals methodologically; Integration refers to the solidarity of the system, its survival as a cohesive whole; and finally, Latency, which refers to the accumulations and distribution of energy which takes the form of motivation (Parsons, 1967). In his later writings Parsons refers to the fourth variable as *pattern maintenance* or *tension management*. Although the emphasis is clearly on social cohesion and stability, change is present in the form of structural differentiation which enables a social system to respond to its needs; with increasing complexity societies evolve new modes of integration.

4. Nevertheless, integration of all parts of the system – the sub-systems – is never 'perfect'. Merton describes the postulate of universal functionalism as an ideal never found in reality: Durkheim's work, for example, stressed the instability, the extremely fragile nature of social solidarity within the advanced societies and the consequent problems of the integration of the individual into the social whole. The basic tendency of social systems is towards equilibrium and a harmonious balance between its various institutions. Elements of 'mal-integration' will, however, always be present hence the importance of social control mechanisms.

5. Deviance, tension and strains exist as 'dysfunctional' elements which tend to become institutionalised or resolved in the direction of social integration and equilibrium.

6. Social change is adaptive and gradual. If there is rapid social change it occurs within the cultural rather than within the economic institutions. Even rapid social change has a tendency to leave the basic institutional framework intact.

7. Social integration is achieved essentially through value consensus, 'shared cognitive orientations', that is, through a pervasive set of principles which legitimise the existing social, economic and political structure.

A distinction has sometimes been made between *general* and *normative* functionalism. The latter, associated especially with the work of Parsons, postulates 'shared value elements' as constituting the basis of social cohesion and consensus; society is defined as a system of interdependent parts. Normative functionalism emphasises the contribution of value consensus to the maintenance of an integrated, equilibrated social system. Normative functionalism attempts to synthesise Durkheim's concept of society as 'normally' integrated through shared values with Weber's action theory, the individual and the collectivity, emphasising the centrality to functionalist analysis of social roles, social processes, social norms and institutions all contributing to social control. Both types of functionalism are concerned with defining society as a system in which socialisation is the key element thus giving rise to the criticism that functionalism, in minimising individuality and 'eccentricity' (or defining the latter as deviant behaviour) works with an oversocialised conception of humanity. It is true that general functionalism minimises the functional integration of parts and postulates the dysfunctional consequences of differing and sometimes opposing values. But this distinction seems exaggerated: the work of so-called general functionalists – Davis and Merton for example – differs only in degree, not in kind, from normative functionalism. As will be argued below, both types of functionalism postulate the view that social integration is a consequence of both normative and structural forces and cannot be reduced to one or the other.

The concept of system

The concept of society as a system is most elaborately developed in Parsonian functionalism. Repudiating the atomistic, individualistic theorising of early American sociology, Parsons consistently argued that a theory of society cannot be built up from facts; the data of social science itself must begin from theory, derive from theory: a fact is always a statement of experience couched in terms of a conceptual scheme. Facts never reproduce an external objectivity; theory is essential and it is theory on a grand scale clearly different from Merton's more modest 'theories of the middle range'. Parsons's concept of system differentiates his functionalist approach from Merton's general functionalism. In *The Social System* the concept of system is linked with two analytically distinct systems, personality and culture. The social system consists of actors interacting in a socio-cultural situation, a process mediated by 'a

236

system of culturally structured and shared symbols'. Parsons notes that every social system consists of four major sub-systems, kinship, social stratification, power and religion. The kinship system is the main socialising agency, stratification the means of distributing rewards within a differentiated social structure, and these two sub-systems effectively reinforce the pattern of inequality in society:

> The consequence of this is that the combination of an occupationally differentiated industrial system and a significantly solidary kinship system must be a system of stratification in which the children of the more highly placed come to have differential advantages, by virtue of their ascribed kinship status, not shared by those lower down (Parsons, 1951, p. 161).

These internal sub-systems, the economy, the polity, socialisation and societal community (stratification, power, kinship, religion) are further sub-divided into the sub-systems of action (AGIL). Parsons, of course, is not defining society in terms of the interactions of individuals, or the totality of such interactions structurally patterned: society is defined in terms of the structure which links individuals with the whole, a systemic approach that emphasises the factor of motivation, that actors pursue goals within the framework of voluntaristic elements that is neither reducible to individuals or atomistic interaction.

For Parsons, system is an indispensable master concept, its meaning directly bound up with its relation to the concept 'environment'. The concept of sub-system enables Parsons to treat the individual in relation to this environment while still remaining part of a system of action. The system is thus highly centralised and organised around values as distinct from interests: there is little awareness of possible conflicting social worlds, with their own distinctive culture and values, within a social system, that a social system, while retaining its wholeness, may lack a coherent, unifying *centre*. The biological organism or system necessarily adapts to its environment. But the social system is made by humanity, social groups and social classes each seeking to establish their own identity within the social whole and striving to remain autonomous in terms of their institutions and values. In Parsonian functionalism there is no sense of society as a decentred, polyphonic structure built upon the basis of different interests *and* values. Rather, the system tends to total coherence possessing an inbuilt equilibrium which Parsons emphasises is constantly undergoing change – the 'moving equilibrium':

> The social system's own equilibrium is itself made up of many subequilibriums within and cutting across one another, with numerous personality systems more or less in internal equilibrium, making up different equilibrated systems such as kinship groups, social strata, churches, sects, economic enterprises, and government bodies. All enter into a huge moving equilibrium in which instabilities in one sub-system in the personality or social sphere are communicated simultaneously to both levels, either disequilibrating the larger system or part of it, until either a re-equilibrium takes place or the total equilibrium changes its form (Parsons and Shils, 1962, pp. 226–7).

Parsons's imagery does present problems when related to his concern with 'voluntarism' and social action. When he writes of the 'in-puts' and 'out-puts' of sub-systems and systems, for example, he seems to be rejecting normative functionalism in favour of what might be termed 'cybernetic functionalism' in which society has become a self-contained and self-equilibrating system. Parsons's work is dominated by a reified and dehumanised theory of society in which the process of equilibrium takes place outside human action and independently of consciousness, interests and struggle. Nevertheless, even here, Parsons is careful to qualify the usage of his concepts: equilibrium is not an empirical fact or reality for no society is equilibrated in the sense that its parts 'fit' together in complete harmony. Equilibrium is a heuristic device which is employed in conjunction with the concept of inertia: the absence of change within a system of action results in stasis, but in reality systems of action are constantly modified and changed by processes involving communication, decision-making and differentiation. This aspect is especially marked in Parsons's analysis of integration: since no system can be perfectly integrated it becomes essential to create institutions that mediate the possible conflict of interests, the 'internal conflict and other failures of co-ordination'; the integrative sub-system thus functions to adapt individuals to the 'goals of the social system' by generating legitimate values, 'the institutionalisation of value-patterns which define the main structural outline of society' bringing ' "into line" the behaviour of system units in accordance with the integrative needs of the system, to check or reverse disruptive tendencies to deviant behaviour and to promote the condition of harmonious co-operation' (Parsons and Smelser, 1959, pp. 16–23).

Equilibrium of *all parts of the social system* comprises the normal condition of human society, with conflict, although present, an essentially residual and abnormal element. Society is thus characterised by the existence of 'value orientations' held by certain 'solidary groupings' (professional occupations such as scientists) which, over time, pass into the 'value system' of the whole society. Parsons defines value system as 'the set of normative judgements held by the members of the society who define, . . . what to them is a good society' (Parsons, 1951, pp. 36–7). But not all members of a society would necessarily agree on what constitutes the 'good society'. In any case, Parsons's own approach seems to give individuals little choice in the matter: norms, values and collective goals govern and control individual behaviour and he follows Durkheim in emphasising the need to control the individual; collective and social, not personal goals motivate and orientate the individual to the social system. Internalising the collective goals the individual is thus socialised and social order augmented, a standpoint which suggests a passive not active relation of the individual actor to values, the internalisation of norms approaching simple habit formation and thus conformism to the status quo. Through explicit socialising agencies such as family, school and community the actor successfully internalises societal goals so that social order, far from being problematical is 'normal'. Like Durkheim, Parsons emphasises that constraint is not forced on the individual but develops organically from the collective conscience, that is, from society. 'In this way', he writes, 'the moral component of the *conscience collective* is social' comprising common, shared values internalised through the agencies of socialisation (Parsons, 1967, pp. 27–9).

Culture is a critical element in this process. Writing on

Marx, Parsons argues that an inadequate theory of personality led Marx to misunderstand that action 'is a function of the *organisation* of behaviour . . . in terms of generalised codes that permit the programming of widely varying particulars'; it is these 'cultural codes' which underlie the 'normative components of societies'. For, contrary to Marx's materialist theory, society is not dominated by social and class conflict; Durkheim's concept of organic solidarity is recommended as a more fruitful way of understanding modern society. For lacking adequate concepts of order and personality Marxist materialism must fail to explain what Parsons calls 'directionality of orientations to work and enterprise' – this being accomplished in Weber's study of Protestantism and capitalism. Thus remaining 'psychologically naïve' Marx's social theory failed to account for the significance of cultural factors in the maintenance of social order, social integration and equilibrium (Parsons, 1967, pp. 123–35).

Parsons's critique of Marx undoubtedly focuses on one of the major weaknesses of historical materialism as it developed in the analysis of modern capitalism (*Capital*) and became codified into a world view by later generations of Marxists. The voluntaristic element is assimilated to underlying laws and external structures: yet this is precisely Parsons's own theoretical position. For example, although dismissing Marxism for its notion of class conflict and structural contradiction, Parsons advances concepts such as 'strains', 'tensions' and notes that in modern society there is 'widespread' anomie all of which suggests the possibility of structural conflict. It is, nevertheless, the system which produces strains and tensions, the failure of its regulative, socialising institutions: within the closed field of the system there is virtually no scope for autonomous social action because there are no sources of legitimate opposition to the all-embracing central values, no institutional means for expressing the possibilities of social alternatives other than in the form of 'deviance'. Parsonian functionalism has successfully effaced the human subject from social theory other than as supports of the *system*.

Functionalism and the dialectic of social life: Merton

Writing on the functional necessity of religion for modern industrial society, Parsons accepted Durkheim's correlation of morality with the sacred noting his 'important insight' into the 'exceedingly close integration of the system of religious symbols of a society and the patterns sanctioned by the common moral sentiments of the members of the community' (Parsons, 1954, p. 206). In a similar vein two representatives of general functionalism write:

> The reason why religion is necessary is apparently to be found in the fact that human society achieves its unity primarily through the possession by its members of certain ultimate values and ends in common. Although these values and ends are subjective, they influence behaviour, and their integration enables this society to operate as a system . . . Even in a secularised society some system must exist for the integration of ultimate values, for their ritualistic expression, and for the emotional adjustments required by disappointment, death and disaster (Davis and Moore, 1969, p. 499).

Criticising this extreme functional interpretation of religion, R. K. Merton (1910–   ) has argued that although some kind of moral agency is functionally indispensable for society, religion can be both functionally unifying and dysfunctional. He points out that the Durkheimian orientation of functionalist analysis is one rooted in the function of religion in non-literate societies and thus the effective absence of several religions. In modern society the tendency is for a plurality of religions and an increasing secularisation of values and beliefs, processes which raise serious questions on the function of religion *as such* to promote or produce structural unity. 'In what sense does religion make for integration of the larger society, if the content of its doctrine and values is at odds with the content of other, non-religious values held by many people in the same society?' In non-literate societies there is usually a single religion which can thus be taken as a model of functional unity. Merton goes on to suggest that in modern societies the concept of 'functional alternative', or 'functional substitute', may be of more value in analysing the relation of values to social cohesion. Although

241

this still assumes the centrality of religious values for the concept of social unity it raises the question of the degree of unity found in the social and historical world.

Merton argues that the postulate of total functional unity is clearly contrary to social reality and an obstacle to social analysis, diverting attention from 'possible disparate consequences of a given social or cultural item' for the various social groups and individual members of groups. All human societies are integrated but few societies are characterised by that '*high* degree of integration in which *every* culturally standardised activity or belief is functional for the society as a whole'. Rejecting the whole notion of functional unity, or functional indispensability of elements, Merton advances the argument of a *net balance of functional consequences* which 'avoids the tendency of functional analysis to concentrate on positive functions' and focus on possible dysfunctional consequences. A major theorem of functional analysis, Merton concludes, is '*just as the same item may have multiple functions, so may the same function be diversely fulfilled by alternative items*'.

Merton defines function objectively as the 'observed consequences' which 'make for the adaptation or adjustment of a given system', while dysfunction is defined as the consequences which reduce the possibility of adjustment and adaptation. Further modifying the functional theory of coherence of systems, Merton distinguishes manifest from latent functions, the former consisting of the objective consequences facilitating adjustment and adaptation of the system and which are 'intended and recognised' by individuals, while latent functions are unintended or unrecognised. As an example he cites Thorstein Veblen's analysis of 'conspicuous consumption', human activity, which functions both to satisfy the needs of the individual consumers (manifest function) and to enhance social status since goods are bought not because of their utility but for their expensiveness (latent function). In this way what may appear to be irrational behaviour by members of different social groups to outsiders is actually functional for the group itself. For Merton latent functions constitute a significant development of sociological theory since they challenge all commonsense knowledge and focus on the 'hidden' components of processes (Merton, 1957, pp. 27–33, 51–8, 65–71).

Merton has sought to introduce a more flexible form of functionalist analysis, but in doing so has confused the distinction between actor and system: the concept of manifest function assumes some awareness on the part of the actor of the actual consequences of action. But does this imply that the actor is equally aware of the consequences for the system as a whole? Unanticipated consequences of action defined as latent functions are clearly systemic in nature linking the individual social actions collectively with society as a whole. Thus although he avoids employing the concept of system arguing that sociological analysis must begin from the 'units' or 'items' rather than from the system as a whole, Merton's notion of social structure, with its interdependence of parts, implies a systemic and deterministic approach. This is particularly brought out in his analysis of the latent functions of the phenomenon of 'Bossism' or 'political racketeering' in American society.

Superficially the illegitimate political machine violates all accepted legal and moral norms yet it succeeds in carrying out 'positive functions' inadequately fulfilled by other legitimate structures. Merton argues that the political machine functions first as a means of centralising the scattered bases of political power (officially devolved by the democratic ethos of the American Constitution), and secondly, to provide assistance for certain deprived sub-groups whose access to legitimate channels is restricted. The 'corrupt political machine' effectively 'fulfils the basic function of providing avenues of social mobility for the otherwise disadvantaged . . . in a society which places a high premium on economic affluence and social ascent for all its members'. 'Bossism' is therefore not merely the means 'of self-aggrandizement for profit-hungry and power-hungry individuals, but . . . an organised provision for subgroups otherwise excluded from or handicapped in the race for "getting ahead" '. Moral disapproval is irrelevant for an understanding of the structural and functional role of the political machine (Merton, 1957).

Bossism as a structure persists, therefore, not through fulfilling a vital need for the system as a whole, but for the reciprocal relationship it generates with smaller units. It is this 'norm of reciprocity' which enables the element to enjoy autonomy; the relation of part to whole is uneven rather than symmetrical. Nevertheless, the part, or sub-system, can be understood ultimately only in terms of the wider system. In this way unintended consequences are assimilated to an underlying structure similar to Smith's 'hidden hand' and Marx's dialectic of history. 'Bossism' is more than simple corruption but a process which functions at both the micro and macrolevel of the social system, its latent functions dependent on the failure of other institutions within the social whole. Merton's concept of latent function is therefore predicated on systemic analysis; it also minimises the role of the subject since it is the system itself which determines the functions, and thus the ends, unintended or not, of institutions at the microlevel.

The conservative implications of Merton's functionalism are thus clear: 'Bossism' is *explained away* by focusing on its effects on those individuals immediately involved in its workings: but the existence of widespread political corruption constitutes a threat to the legitimacy of the democratic political order and its persistence must ultimately weaken belief in democratic processes in society as a whole. Merton's functionalism fails to incorporate a genetic dimension so that social structures are never concretely related to interests and ideology. Historically, political 'Bossism' develops out of the weaknesses of civil society and a failure to thoroughly democratise society as a whole. Merton's analysis accepts *as given* what should be explained: that élitism, in whatever form, functions to promote specific interests against other opposed interests by organising society *from above*. The analysis assumes a passive population, subjects who can be manipulated by élites towards ends neither acknowledge.

Similar criticisms can be brought against one of Merton's most significant contributions to functionalism, the study of anomie and social structure. Here he presents a typology of individual adaptations to the disjunction 'between culturally induced high aspirations and socially structured obstacles to realisation of these aspirations', between the officially sanctioned cultural goal of monetary success (although Merton emphasises that American culture defines other success goals) and the legitimate institutional means of achieving such goals. Culture generates motivation; social structure constitutes the means of satisfying aspirations. But not everyone can be successful: anomie is likely to result when an acute disjunction exists between the cultural norms and goals and 'the socially structured capacities of members of the group to act in accord with them'. Merton thus considers five modes of adaptation:* (1) conformity to the goals and the institutional means, the most common form without which no society could survive; (2) innovation, in which the goals are accepted but non-institutional means employed for their realisation, such as white-collar crime, or the Robber Barons; (3) ritualistic adaptation in which the goals are 'scaled down' but the means accepted as legitimate thus allaying status anxiety – the ritualist is one who continues to follow compulsively institutional norms, e.g. the conformist bureaucrat; (4) retreatism is the rejection of both goals and means so while individuals may have assimilated both as norms, failure or frustration can lead to defeatism, quietism and resignation, the individual escaping into the private world of drug addiction, chronic alcoholism or vagabondage; and finally, (5) rebellion, a combination of accepting and rejecting the goals and the means, as with revolutionaries who seek to set up an entirely new society, or those who have become resentful and discontented with their failure to achieve the goals (Merton, 1957, ch. 4).

Merton argues that every society generates norms governing conduct but they differ 'in the degree to which the folkways, mores and institutional controls are effectively integrated with the goals which stand high in the hierarchy of cultural values'. Not everyone can be upwardly mobile or follow a middle-class life-style. Within Merton's model there are similar assumptions to those made by Durkheim on the nature of humanity –

* **A typology of modes of individual adaptation**
  + signifies acceptance, − signifies rejection

Modes of Adaptation	Cultural Goals	Institutionalised Means
Conformity	+	+
Innovation	+	−
Ritualism	−	+
Retreatism	−	−
Rebellion	±	±

245

striving competitively for success rather than co-operating with others – and the function of institutions to maintain social stability and thus the status quo. Merton's analysis is effectively couched at the level of system: it assumes the necessity for a systemic ideology which is accepted uncritically and passively as the norm by the population; institutions function not to mediate ideology but to serve as neutral means for the realisation of ideological goals. But individuals are not passively socialised into the dominant cultural norms: social class, family, trade unions, and other institutions function as mediators of 'official culture', generating co-operative values which may well include a rejection of the dominant goals and institutionalised means as defined by Merton. But this activity cannot be accommodated easily to Merton's typology which assumes that social stability, or equilibrium of the social system, to rest on an 'oversocialised' notion of humanity (Merton, 1957, pp. 77–8).

Functionalism, social conflict and social change

One of the most persistent criticisms of sociological functionalism, as it developed into the dominant paradigm of American sociology during the 1940s and 1950s, was its failure to explain social change and the persistence of social conflict within the advanced societies. Yet Parsons has not shirked from analysing the problem of social change, revolution and anomie. In his discussion of German fascism, written during the 1940s, he described Nazism as 'one of the most critical . . . social events of our times' (Parsons, 1954, ch. 6) while in *The Social System* a substantial part of the chapter on social change was devoted to analysing Russian communism and the 1917 revolution. In every social system, Parsons has argued, equilibrium is always precarious and its breakdown as 'scientifically important a phenomenon as its preservation' (Parsons, 1951, p. 338).

Parsons's analysis of German fascism is based on the assumption that in modern society the common value-system is always likely to break down and produce the 'strains' which result in disequilibrium and anomie. A revolutionary movement is one consequence of such strains, strains which gain ascendancy only if a number of specific conditions exist such as 'the presence in the population of sufficiently intense, widely spread and properly distributed alienative motivational elements'. Nazism succeeded because the rapid industrial and technological development of Germany created strains within the cultural sub-system leading to 'widespread insecurity' and 'a good deal of free floating aggression, a tendency to unstable emotionalism and susceptibility to emotionalised propaganda'. In short, a process of rationalisation, a 'secularisation of religious values', undermined 'traditional and conservative systems of symbols', producing 'imperfectly integrated institutional structures, ideological definitions of the situation and the psychological reaction patterns typical of anomie'. Parsons analyses fascism and communism as movements exemplifying a 'romantic' revolt against 'the whole tendency of rationalisation in the Western World'. Rapid social change produces a state of instability in which norms no longer regulate society; anomie results with fascism and communism emerging as mass movements able to canalise the 'free floating aggression' engendered by technology, urbanism and industry (Parsons, 1954, pp. 104–41).

Parsons is thus proposing a theory of cultural determinism. Although critical of Marx for failing to develop a theory of motivation, Parsons effectively proposes that a conjunction of certain cultural elements determined that Germany deviated from the 'normal' Western path of industrial evolution. His analysis of Bolshevism is couched similarly in terms of an equilibrium model leaving no room for human *praxis*: the events in Russia, as with those in Germany, were inescapable. Revolutionary movements are notably 'ambivalent in structure' fusing together utopian and realist elements, and although beginning from a perspective of total, uncompromising criticism of the existing social system, are increasingly forced to accommodate themselves to 'reality' after the revolution. No society, Parsons writes, can 'become stabilised on the basis that a fundamentally ambivalent motivational structure towards its central values and ideology became the norm'. The central values of the old society reassert themselves. Differential payments in industry and a rigid system of stratification emerge as 'the need for adaptive structures in the light of fundamental functional requirements ... and the re-emergence of conformity needs associated with the old society as such'. There is thus continuity in change and Parsons concludes his analysis with the hope that industrialisation will bring with it 'a universalistic-achievement pattern' of motivation to transform Soviet Russia into a broadly similar social system as America (Parsons, 1951, pp. 523–33).

Similarly, Parsons has never denied the factual existence of conflict in modern society: 'Class conflict certainly exists ... class conflict is endemic in our modern industrial type of society.' The point, however, is that class conflict for Parsons and other functionalists does not constitute the dominant structural element in a system of social stratification (Parsons, 1954, pp. 329–33). Conflict is not conceived as a source of change but rather as an indication of a breakdown of social control, a deviant response to inequalities of income, status and power. Parsons's equilibrium model minimises the importance of power and conflict; it does not deny the factual significance of these elements. Similarly, sociological conflict theory makes frequent reference to consensus and equilibrium. Both Parsons and Merton repudiate the argument that sociology can thus be divided into those theories which emphasise conflict and those which stress consensus. Using the analogy of biology Parsons notes that there are not two distinct theories referring to the health of the organism on the one hand, and its pathology on the other (Parsons, 1975). Nevertheless, a tradition has developed within sociology which accepts this dichotomy.

Sociological conflict theory developed originally during the late nineteenth century largely in response to Marxist class conflict theory: the major figures such as Gumplowicz, Ratzenhofer and Novicow were conservative theorists working within the organicist and Social Darwinist tradition. Early twentieth-century conflict theorists, such as the Americans, Veblen, Ross and Small, rejected the organicist model and emphasised the constitutive role played by social conflict for social life generally. In contrast, sociological functionalism has tended to categorise conflict as dysfunctional, or as a 'disease', thereby shifting attention away from its important constitutive role in the formation and maintenance of social structures.

Thus Lewis Coser in his *The Functions of Social Conflict* (1954), working within the formal sociological tradition of Georg Simmel for whom conflict constituted the 'essence' of social life, argued that social conflict functioned positively in terms of social structure. Criticising Parson's 'static' equilibrium model he suggests that 'conflict, rather than being disruptive and dissociating, may indeed be a means of balancing and hence maintaining a society as going concern'. Rather than tearing society apart, conflict performs 'group maintaining functions in so far as it regulates systems of relationships', functioning as 'safety valve' mechanism producing an 'equilibrating and stabilising impact'. Conflict creates new norms and values, re-establishes unity between different groups and the boundaries between them, and redresses potentially disruptive inequalities in power and authority. A society lacking conflict ossifies and stagnates; societies in which conflict has become institutionalised are correspondingly more stable and integrated than those with rigid structures:

> By permitting immediate and direct expression of rival claims, such social systems are able to readjust their structures by eliminating the sources of dissatisfaction. The multiple conflicts which they experience may serve to eliminate the causes for dissociation and to re-establish unity. These systems avail themselves, through the toleration and institutionalisation of conflict, of an important stabilising mechanism (Coser, 1956, pp. 153–5).

Coser's functional approach to conflict is primarily based on the assumption that institutionalised conflict will make a positive contribution to the adaptive capacity of the social system always providing that the social structure is sufficiently elastic. Social change occurs only when the conflict relations within a society co-operate with the unifying forces:

> What threatens the equilibrium of such a structure is not conflict as such, but the rigidity itself which permits hostilities to accumulate and to be channelled along one major line of cleavage once they break out in conflict (Coser, 1956, p. 157).

Pluralistic, democratic and open societies thus allow for underlying social change to develop through a process of

249

institutionalising conflict: conflict establishes social unity and maintains a balance within the social structure. Coser's concern is not with systemic conflict, with basic contradictions within the system itself and thus the possibility of revolutionary change, but conflict as antagonisms between different parts of the system, such as social groups, communities, political parties. Nevertheless, Coser's general conclusion is of great significance: change *of* or *within* a system is closely bound up with the degree of cohesion that the system has attained. Capitalist democracies, with their strong institutional structures based in civil society, 'tolerate' and 'creatively utilise' group conflict; totalitarian societies are incapable of responding to conflict in this limited sense since the means of expressing diverging interests and values are virtually absent in a situation of an ideologically closed 'consensus'.

In its historical development sociological functionalism failed to confront the problem of social conflict, its social bases and relation with social change. This is not to suggest, however, that functionalism cannot account for social change: the difficulty is that functionalism defines change from within the closed field of the system, as the product of disjunctions between culture and social structure, or of strains and tensions which develop independently of groups or class interests, culture and ideology. Talcott Parsons's belated rediscovery of evolutionism in his 1964 paper, 'Evolutionary Universals in Society', does not advance much beyond the systemic formalism of his earlier work. The terms remain as before – 'adaptive capacity', 'system-needs' – but now combined with an evolutionary framework which emphasises the significance of cultural diffusion and two critical universal evolutionary universals, 'a well-marked system of social stratification' and a system of 'cultural legitimation'. Parsons's evolutionary schema, which culminates in the modern democratic polity, characteristically underemphasises the structural significance of conflict and power, ideology and culture of the lower social strata.

In general, functionalism assimilates conflict to an underlying process which effectively strips it of all active human components. In particular, functionalist theories of social change minimise the important reciprocal relationship be-

250

tween the institutions, or structures, and the human agents who comprise them; change is thus conceptualised as the disintegration of structural equilibrium and not as the result of a crisis in reciprocity and the corresponding changes in consciousness and values of the human subjects. At least on this level the frequent comparison between Marxism and functionalism is valid for both tend to reify society as an external system structured in equilibrium and hegemony, a whole superior to its parts; and both seek to eliminate the active human subject as the source of social relationships and social change.

Functionalism and stratification

In 1945 Kingsley Davis and Wilbert Moore published their paper, 'Some Principles of Stratification', in which they sought to elaborate a functionalist theory of social stratification. Their work proved to be one of the most widely discussed contributions to sociology; any debate on the nature of social stratification in modern industrial society would include some discussion of Davis and Moore.

Their starting point, unexceptionable in itself, was the proposition that no known society was classless. All human societies, they argued, were characterised by structures of inequality which comprised universal and variable features. All social systems must develop some means of allocating individuals to specific occupational positions some of which are more functionally important than others. If societies are to survive, then a functionally efficient means of fitting talented individuals to occupations must develop. Stratification is a system which determines that individuals are trained to the limit of their inherent ability to fill functionally essential positions which reward them with high remuneration and status. Stratification constitutes the mechanism 'by which societies ensure that the most important positions are conscientiously filled by the most qualified persons'. In this way individuals are motivated and placed in the social structure with the inevitable result of structured social inequality. Stratification effectively means inequality:

> Social inequality is thus an unconsciously evolved device by which societies . . . differentiate persons in terms of both prestige and esteem (Davis and Moore, 1969, p. 497).

Although stratification and inequality are universal, their forms vary from one society to another depending on the level of social development, scarcity of resources and thus the need for special skills and talent (teachers are less functionally important in non-literate cultures than advanced industrial societies for example).

Davis and Moore's thesis hinges on two basic propositions: (1) the factual existence of functionally important occupations, and (2) the need for an adequate reward system which will motivate the most talented individuals to seek essential training. In his *Human Society* Davis modified the argument that stratification functions as the sole mechanism allocating talented individuals to social position by noting the important role played by birth and inheritance as elements in determining role position. But in general this is not seen as a great problem since the development of industrial society weakens the influence of inherited wealth and status. But it leaves open the problem of defining functionally important position. It could be argued, for example, that doctors are functionally more important than nurses in that their training and expertise enables them to fulfil the work tasks of nurses, but that nurses could not work as doctors. Comparable examples could be cited although in the long run the profession of doctors could not survive without the profession of nurses. They are both functionally necessary to each other because they involve a reciprocal relationship. To argue that doctors and other comparable higher professions require a high level of material rewards because of long, 'expensive' and 'burdensome' training ignores the equally 'burdensome' training undergone by nurses and others.

Historically, the higher professions have been associated with the upper strata of society: remuneration and status are less connected with *function* than with socio-cultural antecedents. The anti-historical, non-genetic nature of functionalism leads to explanations of social phenomenon which assume that their present form is their natural form. Can one really argue that plumbers are less functionally significant for industrial society than Professors of Divinity? Or electricians, or train drivers? How is talent to be measured? Many critics of functionalism have noted that social structures function to limit the inherent potential of individuals through various mechanisms associated with social class, education and the dominant culture. And what of motivation? Is this not also determined by the ways in which individuals define themselves in relation to others and to society as a whole? Motivation is not a neutral element but influenced by the class structure, culture and ideology.

The concept of functionally important position relates to the general functionalist argument that stratification works to integrate the social system around a core of values which legitimate existing inequality. This is the essence of the functionalist theory of stratification. Its undoubted truth, that a complex division of labour demands an efficient means of allocating individuals to necessary occupations which results in some degree of unequal reward, is common to all theories of class from Smith to Marx to Weber. Functionalism departs fundamentally from these writers by eliminating power and class interests as important and enduring structural principles in the formation of inequality. There is a great deal of evidence, much of it historical in character, which points to the divisive nature of stratification and the unequal distribution of power in modern industrial societies. It is over these issues that functionalism founders as a sociological explanation, attributing 'needs' to society as if society constituted an active subject rather than an historical system, a structure and a process which changes through the 'needs' and interests of actors or subjects.

9
Self, Society and the Sociology of Everyday Life

Action theory and the concept of self: the early and later Parsons

A major problem of classical sociology was the contradiction between its emphasis on the concept of society as a system or structure governed by objective laws, and the role of the subject, or actor, in the making of social structure and social change. A tension was generated within classical sociology between the concepts of subject and structure, voluntarism and determinism. Marxism, Functionalism and Sociological Positivism tended to assimilate the active role of the subject to an underlying economic, socio-cultural system. Social action theory, as it developed in the work of Simmel and Weber, sought to redefine the object of sociology as the study of human interaction. Talcott Parsons's *The Structure of Social Action* (1937) advanced the argument that a voluntaristic theory of action constituted the major preoccupation of Weber, Durkheim and Pareto, and although there were important differences between these sociologists, working apart from each other in their own distinctive national cultures, a real convergence of sociological theory was nevertheless taking place. For Parsons, the history of sociology was not a history of competing and opposing schools, 'that there are as many systems of sociological theory as there are sociologists, that there is no common basis, that all is arbitrary and subjective', but rather the development of 'a substantial common basis of theory' and 'sound theoretical foundations on which to build' (Parsons, 1961a, pp. 774–5). This convergence of sociological theory is towards a 'generalised theory of action'.

Parsons's broad argument was that a sociological theory of action could not develop on the basis of nineteenth-century positivism with its belief in the methods of the natural sciences. The stability of society, the existence of social order, cannot be explained solely in terms of natural laws. Social order has its basis both in the objective structure of society and in the subjective actions of individuals as they internalise the values of the culture. Thus utilitarian philosophy, with its conception of individuals seeking their own interests, embodied a strong action element. But utilitarian philosophy could not account for the persistence of social order through its central precepts of the randomness of ends, the rational orientation of individuals to such ends based on knowledge of the situation, and an atomistic conception of society. It was not sufficient for Bentham and the classical political economists to cite the 'hidden hand' which fused individual interests and ends with the interests of society as a whole and collective ends or, as with Spencer, to postulate a social contract existing between individuals as forming the basis of social order. Utilitarian rationality assumed that social order was possible through (1) the rational recognition of a natural identity of interests thus neatly solving the problem of a possible conflict of ends; and (2) the voluntarist postulate of a social contract which assumed that humanity consciously recognise the utility of government and social stability. Parsons argued that the whole utilitarian doctrine, built around an atomistic conception of society and rational norms which govern the means–ends relationship, was inherently unstable since it assumed that ends were both random and atomistic. All departures from the rational norms were regarded as irrational.

In contrast, Durkheim, Weber, Pareto and to a lesser extent Tönnies and Simmel, were concerned, not with 'interests' defined atomistically, but with the norms regulating human action which, internalised by the actor, were regarded as putatively desirable and therefore worthy to be realised. The voluntaristic theory of action thus refers to a process whereby the subject actively consents to the legitimacy of specific values. The norms regulating human action are therefore not external forces or constraints (as was the case with nineteenth-century positivism and Durkheim's early work) but elements organically bound up with the human actor. There is, in other words, an active not passive or adaptive relation between individuals and norms: the relation is both creative and voluntaristic.

For Parsons, however, human action is characterised by its systemic nature. The notion of human action as a system is central to Parsons's argument that late nineteenth-century sociological theory exhibited a movement towards convergence: thus although human action assumes motives, goals and wishes it can be studied scientifically only through objective, systemic analysis. The influence of Pareto on Parsons's thought is clearly in evidence here since neither Durkheim nor Weber developed a notion of system in this sense. Action constitutes a system: society is a system of action. And in the same way as the particle relates to classical physics so does the 'unit act' relate to the social system: as particles 'can be defined only in terms of their properties, mass, velocity, location in space, direction of motion, etc., so the units of action systems . . . have certain basic properties without which it is not possible to conceive of the unit as "existing" '. All action constitutes a structure of unit-acts involving actors. An act, therefore, involves an agent, an end to which the process of action is oriented and a situation (the 'conditions of action') involving elements some of which the actor may control and others over which he/she has no control. Within the situation there is always a choice of alternative means to ends, a 'normative orientation of action' (Parsons, 1961a, pp. 43–4).

A system of action can thus be broken down into parts or smaller 'sub-systems'. The unit-act is the smallest unit of an action system. A system of action constitutes an organisation of the interactions between actor and situation. Social action is built around rules, norms and patterns. It was Durkheim who particularly stressed the processes whereby collective representations become internalised by individuals to promote social order and a personality structure adequate to the social structure. Parsons argues that Durkheim's critique of positivism led him to define the social milieu in terms of an integrated system of norms which involve 'the existence of a common system of ultimate-value attitudes'. A common value system is one which is institutionalised. Action is thus objectively and subjectively institutionalised:

> The most fundamental theorem of the theory of action seems to me to be that the *structure* of systems of action *consists* in institutionalised (in social and cultural systems) and/or internalised (in personalities and organisms) patterns of cultural meaning (Parsons, 1961d, p. 342).

Thus ritual is a system of action involving sacred things performed without any utilitarian calculation of advantage and related to a symbolic means–ends relationship. Thus although the source of the sacred is the supernatural 'our symbolic representations of it are sacred things' and 'the attitude of respect to them is, along with respect for moral obligations, a manifestation of our ultimate-value attitudes which are social in so far as they are common' (Parsons, 1961a, pp. 709–13).

As an action theorist Parsons was concerned with the universality of action, the relation of the human agent or personality to the social system. *The Structure of Social Action* examined the possibilities of action in the social world by rejecting the extreme voluntarism of utilitarianism, with its focus on the freely choosing actor, and the determinism of positivism, with its emphasis on causes and effects. In short, Parsons attempted to analyse the subjective element of human society as an objective structure: ends, means and conditions were all theorised from the point of view of the actor and also as external datums. As I have already noted (pp. 230–1), in his later writings – *Toward a General Theory of Action* (1951) and *The Social System* (1951), for example, – action is redefined in systemic terms. The motivation of the actor in terms of goal attainment is determined by the 'needs' of the socio-cultural system. The voluntaristic component is thus diminished: the meaning of action is located within the system and not from the standpoint of the actor. Action is organised as a necessary function of the actor's relation to the situation. The social system is thus defined as

. . . a plurality of individual actors interacting with each other in a situation which has at least a physical or environmental aspect, actors who are motivated in terms of a tendency to the 'optimization of gratification' and whose relation to their situations, including each other, is defined and mediated in terms of culturally structured and shared symbols (Parsons, 1951, pp. 5–6).

In his explicitly functionalist writings Parsons describes action systems in terms of roles, stable patterns of behaviour bearing a specific status such as 'father', 'businessman', 'professional', etc. Although in his functionalist works, action and system are combined, as was noted in Chapter 8, Parsons tends to emphasise the predominant role of the system over the subject and propose a concept of closed rather than open system. Although the theory of action can be seen as a critique of nineteenth-century positivist reductionism, an attempt to bring back the human subject into sociological theory and define society in terms of everyday human actions saturated with meaning, it has led, in Parsons's work, to a reified notion of society and a conservative concept of personality. As a system of action the human personality is mediated and stabilised by a common culture involving language and socialisation: moral standards and '*all the components of the common culture* are internalised as part of the personality structure'. Thus moral standards constitute the core of 'the stabilising mechanisms of the system of social interaction' (Parsons, 1964, pp. 20–2). There is thus a 'fit' between the type of personality and the type of social structure, a standpoint difficult to reconcile with the voluntaristic and creative theory of social action outlined in Parsons's early work. *The Structure of Social Action* made no reference to Freud or Mead, but in his later writings Parsons has stressed both the importance of Mead's 'symbolic interactionist' sociology and, more significantly, the convergence of thought in Freud and Durkheim.

It is Freud, however, who has exercised the greatest influence on Parsons's concept of personality and its relation to the social system. Freud's great discovery 'of the internalisation of moral values as an essential part of the structure of the personality itself' converged with Durkheim's theory of the socially integrative role of moral norms. 'This convergence, from two quite distinct and independent starting points, deserves to be ranked as one of the truly fundamental landmarks of the development of modern social science' (Parsons, 1964, pp. 18–19). Nevertheless, Freud is criticised for an excessive emphasis on the individual and for failing to analyse personality as it interacts with others to form a system. The personality system is defined by Parsons as a system of action which functions in a relatively autonomous way in relation to its dynamic structure and needs. For Parsons, the personality does not internalise social objects individually, but rather assimilates systems of interaction between social objects. Many of Freud's basic psycho-analytical concepts – id, super-ego, ego, the Oedipus complex – are redefined sociologically by Parsons: the function of the super-ego, for example, is limited almost entirely to internalising patterns of social interaction and social roles, an integrative mechanism which exercises control over the personality. Similarly, the Oedipal phase of human development is linked specifically with industrial society and the nuclear family: in Freud's work the Oedipal phase was defined as a fixed, universal phenomenon of all human societies.

Freud's contribution to social theory will be discussed in the next section of this chapter. In relation to Parsons's attempt to sociologise psycho-analytic theory it is worth noting, however, that many of Freud's basic concepts are made to conform with a model of social integration that eliminates negative and contradictory elements. The concept of self, for example, is stripped of Freud's emphasis on the repression of instinctual drives; human sexuality is reduced to a matter of social role and social order. A fundamental harmony is assumed to subsist between the personality and the social system. Thus the development of personality, the stages through which it passes, is separated from Freud's notion of instincts or drives and from the repressive nature of culture. For Freud, socialisation was deeply problematical, but for Parsons it constituted an integrating and harmonious process of learning experiences and internalisation of dominant values.

Psycho-analysis and self: Freud

The science of psycho-analysis was officially inaugurated in 1908 with the formation of the Vienna Psycho-Analytical Society; in the same year the first international Psycho-Analytical Congress was held. Of those participating in the Vienna society the most important figure was Sigmund Freud (1856–1939). A contemporary of Durkheim, Weber and Pareto, Freud drew attention to the significant role played by non-rational elements in human action and culture. Like Weber and Pareto, Freud was deeply sceptical of such notions as the perfectability of humanity, nineteenth-century theories of progress and the claims of mass, popular democracy.

Freud's first interests had been in the general area of the physiology of the nervous system. He studied hysteria and its treatment through hypnosis. In the course of the 1890s he developed the technique of 'free association' in which patients were encouraged to say whatever came into their thoughts no matter how ludicrous or obscene. Many of Freud's patients mentioned sexual experiences and sexual problems and this led him to conclude that hysteria was not simply a biological malfunctioning of the organism but the result of sexual repression. Freud's emphasis on the role of sexuality in the aetiology of the neuroses differentiated his approach from orthodox psychology: through free association the patient recalled early childhood sexual experiences which had been subsequently censored by the mind. Freud thus advanced the argument that hysteria was the result of childhood sexual seduction carried out either by an adult or older child. But from 1900 onwards, especially with the publication of *The Interpretation of Dreams* (1900), *The Psychopathology of Everyday Life* (1901) and *Three Essays in the Theory of Sexuality* (1905), he argued that neuroses involved both the whole human personality and unconscious elements.

Freud rejected both the rationalist and mechanistic concepts of personality: no mental phenomenon was accidental or irrational but the effect of a complex process of causation. Symptoms were meaningful in relation to the patient's unconscious. Similarly, the apparently random actions of everyday life such as slips of the tongue, jokes, and forgetting of names together with dreams, equally involved unconscious elements in their causation: dreams and jokes became meaningful only when they were integrated into another structure which in Freud's theory was the structure of the unconscious mind. Freud also argued against a simple cause and effect model: mental phenomena were 'overdetermined', the combination of many elements and not the products of a straightforward process of reciprocal causation. Thus dreams may have several meanings and fulfil a number of different wishes; an element within a dream will combine a number of quite different features of many elements. And because a dream condenses a number of experiences into single composite figures and censors, those elements which might disturb sleep itself, the manifest content of the dream (what the individual remembers) is less significant than its latent content (the underlying structure which gives the dream its meaning or meanings). Freud regarded *The Interpretation of Dreams* as forming the basis of the psycho-analytical method and his most important work: the analysis of dreams, he argued, provided evidence of the deeper structure of the human mind:

It was discovered one day that the pathological symptoms of certain neurotic patients have a sense. On this discovery the psycho-analytic method of treatment was founded. It happened in the course of this treatment that patients, instead of bringing forward their symptoms, brought forward dreams. A suspicion thus arose that the dreams too had sense (Freud, 1953, Vol. XV, p. 83).

Dream interpretation was thus 'the royal road to a knowledge of the unconscious activities of the mind'. The true meaning, or meanings, of a dream emerge only by analysing the complex ways whereby the dream wishes are distorted by 'dream-work'. Sleep relaxes control over the unconscious: dream-work functions to disguise the 'forbidden' and repressed elements of the unconscious as they surface within the dream. Thus dreams are censored by the processes of *condensation* and *displacement* (that is, by fusing a number of different traits into a composite figure, and by making emotionally significant elements insignificant).

Freud's theory of the self was built around the necessity for society to repress specific instinctual drives which then found their expression in dreams, symbols and fantasies. For Freud, the human organism was characterised by a tension between the 'pleasure principle' (the sexual instincts) and the 'reality principle' (the drive for self-preservation). The pleasure principle was related to sexual energy (or libido) which is constantly seeking release and gratification. Libido was diffused throughout the whole of human organism and sexuality embraced pleasurable bodily sensation as well as the 'sublimation' of feelings such as tenderness and friendship. The process of becoming social – the reality principle – involved the repression of instinctual sexuality. In *Civilisation and its Discontents* (1930) Freud drew attention to the inevitable conflict between civilised culture (industry, technology, education and art) and the irrational drives of Eros – sexuality – and Thanatos – the instincts of destruction and death. The nature of modern society demanded the renunciation of both instincts in the interests of social order. The result was widespread guilt and mental illness.

Freud's psychological theory of personality assumes a sociological dimension in terms of the mechanism whereby individuals internalise cultural values and norms, thus becoming social beings. In 1922 he published *The Ego and the Id* in which the human personality was described as a system comprising three autonomous and conflicting levels – id, ego and super-ego. The id is essentially amoral, instinctual and dominated by the pleasure principle. Reality is defined narcissistically as the extension of itself. In the process of adjusting to reality, however, the personality becomes differentiated into ego and super-ego. The ego, or self, develops first its primary function to protect and maintain the individual through adaption to the environment. But the ego as such cannot cope with the demands of a complex culture and thus the super-ego emerges as the moral conscience of the personality or the 'ego-ideal', remaining partly unconscious although controlling the actions of the individual *from within*.

Freud's main concern was with the super-ego and its relation with family structure. Initially the child takes both parents, but especially one, as the object of its erotic wishes. 'As a rule a father prefers his daughter and a mother her son; the child reacts to this by wishing, if he is a son, to take his father's place, and if she is a daughter, her mother's.' The resolution of these incestuous desires takes the form of the Oedipus complex in boys and the Electra complex in girls. But Freud was mostly concerned with the Oedipus complex, a term derived from Sophocles's play *Oedipus Rex* in which the king kills his father and marries his mother in ignorance of both identities. Sexual identity is not a given datum; human nature is basically bisexual. It is the object-choice and its resolution which for Freud determines the sexual character of individuals. Libido passes through a number of different stages in its maturation: the phallic phase for males, for example, begins roughly at the age of three years with awareness of, and interest in, the penis: this leads to an infantile desire for the mother and jealousy of the father. But the erotic feelings for the mother (pleasure principle) comes into conflict with the authority and fear of the father (reality principle, the fear being that of castration). The child abandons his desire for the mother by assimilating the father's male authority. In this way the super-ego develops out of the Oedipus complex: a strong parental influence and notion of self has been integrated into the structure of the personality. The female attachment to the father, which in Freud's interpretation is loosely based on the Greek myth of Electra who sought the death of her mother, Clytemnestra, is resolved by an acceptance of castration (in Freud's view girls develop penis envy) and a turning towards the father.

The development of the super-ego is thus closely bound up with the sense of guilt which the child experiences as the result of his or her erotic desire for the mother or father. The Oedipus complex exerts a more powerful influence on the process of assimilating parental values: thus Freud concludes that males develop a stronger super-ego than females. This is, perhaps, one of Freud's more speculative notions comparable to the 'primal horde' thesis of *Totem and Taboo* (1913) and his theory of religion as 'the universal obsessional neurosis of humanity' in *The Future of an Illusion* (1927). For Freud, the Oedipus complex is a universal phenomenon found in all human societies and social groups. Anthropologists, such as Malinowski in his study of the Trobriand Islanders in *Sex and Repression in Savage Society* (1937) concluded that family structure differed sharply from that implied in the theory of the Oedipus complex: social status and property is inherited not from the child's father but from the maternal uncle, and in general the father plays a far less significant role in the socialisation of the child than is the case with the middle-class European family.

Freud's significance for sociological theory, however, does not depend on the validity of his quasi-mystical notions of cultural development – the struggle between the life and death instincts, for example – and ahistorical categories such as the Oedipus complex, but in his attempt to develop an action concept of personality, with its emphasis on energy, and a notion of a creative self. The role of irrational, unconscious forces in the formation of self and society further suggests the potential absence of harmony between the individual and society. Ultimately, however, the relation of self to the social system and to everyday life, including ideological influences, remains absent from Freud's theory.

The social self: Mead and symbolic interactionism

Although the dominant trend of late nineteenth-century and early twentieth-century social theory was towards developing a concept of action, none of the major sociologists discussed by Parsons in *The Structure of Social Action* constructed an adequate notion of self. The self was defined anonymously as a disembodied actor assimilating norms and producing meanings in relation to the wider, macrosociological system. The self as a distinctive social being, as the source of action and energy, existed implicitly as the necessary voluntaristic component of an anti-positivist sociology. The self was defined in terms of institutions, ideologies, culture: but its rich complexity, its many-sided aspects, its forms of action and consciousness were largely absent. Only Simmel's sociology with its basis in sociation and interaction approached an adequate theory of the living, active social subject. And it was Simmel, not Durkheim, Weber or Pareto, who exerted the greatest influence on the theory of the self which developed in the social psychology, or social behaviourism, of G. H. Mead (1863–1931).

For much of his academic life Mead taught at the University

of Chicago. The first major school of American sociology developed at the University of Chicago in the work of Robert Park, who had studied with Simmel in Germany, W. I. Thomas, Florian Znaneicki and many others all of whom were largely concerned with micro rather than macrosociological issues especially the study of social interaction in the city, the process of urbanism and the ways in which individuals construct reality. Thus Thomas and Znaniecki argued that since the personal element is a constitutive factor of every social occurrence, 'social science cannot remain on the surface . . . but must reach the actual human experiences and attitudes which constitute the full, live and actual reality beneath the formal organisation of social institutions' (Thomas and Znaniecki, 1927, Vol. 2, p. 1834). The Chicago based *American Journal of Sociology* had published a number of Simmel's essays before 1914 while the first major textbook in American sociology, *Introduction to the Science of Sociology* (1921) written by Park together with E. W. Burgess, contained more references to Simmel than to any other European sociologist. Simmel's emphasis on the importance of subjectivity in social life and the deeply alienating nature of modern urban society found a ready response in the Chicago school's focus on the rootlessness of American culture, the increasing isolation of individuals from community and primary groups. 'It is plausible', writes Rock, 'that the greatly accelerated processes of capitalism in early twentieth-century America gave ontological primacy to the individual above all other categories. Theories which centred . . . on the European forms of class, could be discounted as irrelevant. The self became chiefly problematic' (Rock, 1979, pp. 95–6). But although problematic the self was not integrated within a sociological theory of society as a system: the Chicago school tended to define society atomistically. Indeed, the only available theory of the subject which conceived the self anti-atomistically, as a structure, derived from the social psychological approach of Mead.

Mead published very little during his lifetime; his influence on his contemporaries flowed from his lecture courses and scattered articles. After his death the lectures were published in book form, *Mind, Self and Society* (1934), *Movements of Thought in the Nineteenth Century* (1936), *The Philosophy of the Act* (1938) and his work reached a wider audience. Mead is important because he broke from the mechanical and passive notions of self and consciousness which had dominated early twentieth-century American psychology and sociology. Mead attempted to examine the genesis of the self both in terms of its practical social experience (its external aspects), as well as its experience as consciousness (its inner aspects). The intellectual influences on Mead's thought were numerous and varied: the philosophy of pragmatism (John Dewey, William James), Darwinian evolutionism, German idealism, nineteenth-century Romanticism and the sociology of Charles Cooley. Thus although the self was partly biological in that its development was dependent on the central nervous system it was only by adapting to its environment, and struggling continually to control it, that the human organism comes to identify itself as a subject. German idealism (Hegel, Fichte) and Romanticism had both emphasised the significance of a constituting subject in the formation and development of culture, but failed to ground it materialistically in the day-to-day experience of ordinary humanity. Mead criticised Cooley, for example, for a similar failure, a too-subjectivist notion of the self.

Charles Cooley (1864–1929) rejected the dualism of individual and society arguing that they both constituted 'collective' and 'distributive' aspects of the same phenomena. The self arises out of a process of communication with others and society as a whole: the 'I' is impossible without the 'you', the 'he', without the 'they'. In his most famous formulation Cooley described the genesis of a 'looking-glass self' which consisted of 'the imagination of our appearance to the other person, the imagination of his judgment of that appearance, and some sort of self-feeling, such as pride or mortification'. Society, however, and its 'solid facts' were ultimately constituted in 'the imaginations which people have of one another' (Cooley, 1902, pp. 184, 121). By defining the self almost entirely in terms of those ideas which others entertain of it, Cooley slipped into mentalism, society defined psychologically as a psychical whole. Mead, in his assessment of Cooley's contribution to American social theory wrote:

His method was that of an introspection which recognised the mind as the *locus* of the selves that act upon each other, but the methodological problem of the objectification of this mind he pushed aside as metaphysical . . . [But] in the process of communication there appears a social world of selves standing on the same level of immediate reality as that of the physical world that surround us. It is out of this social world that the inner experience arises which we term psychical . . . the *locus* of society is not in the mind . . . though what goes on in the inner forum of our experience is essential to meaningful communication (Mead, 1964, pp. 304–5).

For Mead, both mind and self were the social creations of everyday life: 'Human society as we know it could not exist without minds and selves, since all of its most characteristic features presuppose the possession of minds and selves by its individual members' (Mead, 1934, p. 227). Humanity, through mind and self, had the capacity to reason and to reflect. Two elements of the self which Mead analysed in great detail were its reflexive nature and ability to develop symbolic forms of communication. Moreover, the self exists only in relation to social groups 'because the individual himself belongs to a social structure, a social order' (Mead, 1934, pp. 1–7). Mind and self, consciousness and action, were thus collaborative not individual phenomena involving social roles, social relations and social institutions.

Mead was concerned with analysing the patterns of interaction, the social acts which constituted the basis of human society. Reality was not a fixed datum but constantly shifting as actors – selves – create new roles and new meanings, defining their situation in a variety of different ways all of which were 'real' to them. Communication is effected through 'significant gestures', self-conscious acts which distinguish human from non-human behaviour. The acts of dogs, about to fight each other, consist of what Mead called 'a conversation of gestures' but not of significant gestures: the animals instinctively react and adjust to the situation. Significant gestures are full of meaning because they involve ideas communicated through a system of universal symbols such as language. In this way human beings interpret the actions of others. Mead emphasised that the capacity of individuals to communicate through vocal gestures was closely linked to the evolution of society in which co-operative activity increasingly became the norm. Social acts were defined as acts involving the co-operation of more than one person within a framework of the group.

The self is thus individual only through its reciprocal relations with others and with the community. The self is both a subject and an object, the 'I' as the subject which thinks and acts, the 'Me' as the individual's awareness of self as an object in the world existing for others. Mead's notion of the 'I' is both biological and social, a synthesis of organic drives and social experience; it is not, therefore, easily separated from the 'Me'. Mead's emphasis on the role of language in the formation of the self, however, suggests that the 'Me' aspect of self arises out of dialogic speech acts, out of discourse, 'the inner flow of speech'. There is no 'I' or 'Me' in a conversation of gestures: it is only through dialogic communication that self-consciousness develops:

> The 'I' is the response of the organism to the attitudes of the others; the 'me' is the organised set of attitudes of others which one himself assumes. The attitudes of the others constitute the organised 'me', and then one reacts towards that as an 'I' (Mead, 1934).

A self exists, only then, when it interacts with itself and the other selves of the community: the self arises 'through its ability to take the attitude of the group to which he belongs' and assimilate the group's social habits, the common attitudes of the community (Mead, 1964, pp. 33–4). The individual takes not simply the attitudes of others towards him/her but seeks to integrate the 'whole social process' into individual experience. The self is finally organised into a unity by this 'generalised other'.

Thus the young girl who takes the role of mother, conversing with herself and acting towards herself as she believes mothers do, has succeeded in getting outside herself by adopting the role of a 'significant other'. For Mead, as for Freud, childhood constituted the first stage in the formation of the self: the second stage Mead described as the 'game' (as distinct from the 'play' of the first stage where individual roles are internalised) in which the child takes a collective role, the 'generalised other', the organised group. Mead illustrated this process in terms of a baseball team: the individual player must take account of the role of the whole team, its structure as a team, as a whole, which is always involved in his individual action. (Other examples were the family, education, political parties, trade unions, etc.)

Mead's theory of the self represented a marked advance on previous sociologies of the actor: the act and the self were structures bound up with social structure yet creative and reflexive. But as Mead's work became widely known during the 1940s and 1950s it was increasingly appropriated by social theorists who tended to stress the passive nature of roles and diminish the active properties of self. The 'Me' dominated the 'I' in the interests of the social system and social order. Yet there is a sense in which Mead's work inclines in this direction: through his emphasis on the collective community as a unity, a structure of commonly shared values, Mead's theory of self approaches a conservative standpoint. There is, for example, no awareness in his writings of the repressive character of culture – the generalised other – and the potential conflict between the creative, voluntaristic aspect of the self and the collective, conformist nature of modern industrial society. Mead's fundamental concepts assume a common core of values which arise spontaneously from within the common culture and community. It is the strong sense of community which effectively overrides the possibility of conflicting and alternative values.

Nevertheless, Mead's emphasis on the potential creativity of the subject constitutes a significant corrective to mechanistic and reified notions of self and society. In particular, the category of meaning is located within the common symbols of social groups and their modes of interaction. Other symbolic interactionists (the term was coined by Herbert Blumer in 1937) developed many of Mead's ideas concerning the role of gestures and speech in the formation and structure of human society. Mead's voluntarism and concern with the dialogic nature of everyday life stand opposed to the dominant assumptions of structural functionalism which one critic has conveniently summarised as 'the oversocialised conception of man' (Wrong, 1976). Thus for Herbert Blumer meaning is not a property intrinsic to an object but constructed through the interactions of group members. It is this notion of meaning as inter-subjective which links symbolic interactionism, in its Meadian and post-Meadian phases, with sociological phenomenology.

Sociological phenomenology: Schutz and the reality of everyday life

In the historical development of a voluntaristic sociological theory of action the work of Alfred Schutz (1899–1959) occupies as important a place as that of Freud and Mead. Like Mead, Schutz emphasised the creative and active role of the subject; social reality is a process constantly reconstructed through the everyday action of individuals. Schutz follows Weber in rejecting positivist methods for the exploration of social and cultural life, arguing that the object of sociology is the meaning-endowing actions of human agents.

Schutz's first significant work, *The Phenomenology of the Social World*, published in Germany in 1932 (and translated into English in 1967), set out to establish a distinctive phenomenological approach to the study of society. Schutz was influenced by the phenomenological philosophy of Edmund Husserl (1859–1938) whose work was primarily concerned with the structure of consciousness and the relation between subjectivity and scientific method. In his various writings Husserl advanced the argument that all the sciences had their basis in the pre-scientific world (*Lebenswelt*) of a common humanity. For Husserl, reality was 'intentional' in the sense that the human subject directed his/her consciousness to objects. Experience was always intentional and all modes of consciousness involved consciousness of objects: it was through the activity of consciousness that the objects acquired a structure and a meaning. Thus the meaning of an object was not inherent in the object itself but located in the inner life of the subject. But the subjective life-world, the consciousness, con-sisted of numerous accumulated experiences and pre-suppositions which hinder the process of understanding. Husserl thus advocated the method of 'phenomenological reduction' whereby consciousness abandons all ideas about the external world and its objects. Consciousness would become a pure consciousness. In this way society, culture, history are 'bracketed away', put on one side as it were, so that knowledge is the product of the 'intentionality' of the 'pure consciousness'.

Husserl called this procedure the *epoché*, a suspension of belief in the objects of experience: what is left afterwards is the 'transcendent ego', the pure consciousness free to discover its 'true' meaning, its essence. As Schutz described it: Husserl's 'transcendental phenomenological reduction . . . must deprive the world which formerly, within the natural attitude, was simply posited as being, of just this posited being . . . what is grasped in the epoché is the pure life of consciousness in which and through which the whole objective world exists for me . . . I abstain from belief in the being of this world, and I direct my view exclusively to my consciousness of the world' (Schutz, 1978, p. 124). Schutz's sociological version of this phenomenological reduction was to bracket away all scientific presuppositions about the socio-historical world: sociology must begin its task of analysis and understanding not from a conception of a world 'out there', but from the actions and consciousness of subjects who strive to construct and make sense of reality. Meaning is thus not waiting passively to be discovered but requires active construction.

Schutz defined the 'life-world' as a continuous flow of experience and action; the actor rarely reflects on this process. Now whereas Husserl had sought to purify consciousness of all empirical elements, Schutz starts from these experiences, from everyday life, common sense, the social actions of ordinary individuals. Social science begins from the 'taken-for-granted' self-evident nature of the social world that is the marked characteristic of those individuals who remain 'within the natural attitude'. The natural attitude is one which accepts the reality of the everyday world suspending all doubt that it can be other than it is. To understand this ordinary world the social scientist must account for the ways in which individuals define and reflect upon their situation and action (the actor's intentions and purposes), as well as examining its structure.

Schutz defines the everyday world as inter-subjective: the world is not private but shared with others, a plurality of interacting actors whose presence influences the development of ourselves. Social reality is thus the sum total of all the objects

271

and occurrences within the social world. But this world has a structure – it is not an atomistic world – built around social relationships which involve various modes of communication. An actor has to make sense of the actions of others by learning to interpret what the action is about. To do this requires a stock of commonsense knowledge, commonsense understanding, which enables the individual to structure the social world in terms of 'meaningful configurations' such as ideal types or typifications. Schutz distinguishes between first order typifications (e.g. the act of posting a letter which assumes knowledge of specific types involved in the action, postmen, sorters, etc.) from second order typifications which the sociologist employs to analyse and reconstitute reality.

The stock of knowledge is based on individual experience which has, over time, become 'sedimented', congealed within the culture of the life-world and communicated through language since only a small fraction of the totality of such knowledge can exist in the consciousness of a single individual. The actor's stock of knowledge is simply taken for granted, practical, relating to how the world works. Thus the everyday world has its own distinctive structure which to a great extent coheres around the notions of 'cookery book' knowledge or recipe knowledge in which action becomes 'reduced to automatic habits of unquestioned platitudes' (Schutz, 1972, pp. 142–3). For Schutz, knowledge is defined by 'interests', usually practical in nature, which are bound up with an individual's 'project'. The life-world is, therefore, further structured into domains or 'zones of relevance' which relate to certain group associations (marriage, business enterprises, clubs). The life-process is made up of these changing systems of relevance for individuals. In undertaking a project the actor is necessarily bound to a system of relevances intrinsic to the project. It is this process which enables the individual to select and interpret: 'All facts are from the outset, facts selected from a universal context by the activities of our mind. They are therefore always interpreted facts.' The individual thus structures the life-world through consciousness: the stock of knowledge, typifications and relevance constitute the categories through which the consciousness organises reality. Schutz's formulation is thus similar to Kant's analysis of causality, time

272

and space as immanent categories of the mind which organise external matter rather than as elements intrinsic to the object.

Schutz's description of the life-world emphasises the importance of shared meanings, the notion of the world as 'ours' rather than 'mine', a linguistic community existing through mutual symbols:

> Our everyday world is, from the outset, an intersubjective world of culture. It is intersubjective because we live in it as men among other men, bound to them through common influence and work, understanding others and being an object of understanding for others. It is a world of culture because, from the outset, the life-world is a universe of significations to us, i.e. a framework of meaning which we have to interpret, and of interrelations of meaning which we institute only through our action in this life-world. It is a world of culture also because we are always conscious of its *historicity*, which we encounter in tradition and habituality . . . the men to whom I stand in relationships are my kind, my friends, or strangers. Language is not a substratum of philosophical or grammatical considerations for me, but a means for expressing my intentions or understanding the intentions of Others. Only in reference to me does that relation to Others obtain its specific meaning which I designate with the word 'We' (Schutz, 1978, pp. 134–5).

It is this 'We' relationship which constitutes the basic structure of everyday life; all other relationships depend on and relate to it. Schutz argues that the social world, centred around the individual, consists of a web of relationships ranging from the immediate, personal and unique (relations with *consociates* such as family and friends) to the indirect and more anonymous 'They' relations (with *contemporaries*, *predecessors* and *successors*). Knowledge of contemporaries is largely inferential and discursive based on typical not unique features. The pure 'We' relation, in contrast, 'involves our awareness of each other's presence and also the knowledge of each that the other is aware of him' (Schutz, 1972, pp. 142–3, 168).

For Schutz, then, society constitutes a structure of 'multiple realities' cohering around different 'zones of relevance', interests, consociates, etc. It is not strictly speaking a world of objects but one constructed by the active subject. Schutz's social world lacks a fixed centre other than the vague notion of social order. It is a social world made meaningful through language, rules, roles, statuses. But it is a stable and conformist world:

> In order to find my bearings within the social group, I have to know the different ways of dressing and behaving, the manifold insignia, emblems, tools etc. which are considered by the group as indicating social status and are therefore socially approved as relevant (Schutz, 1962–6, Vol. 1, p. 350).

The social world is not therefore an objective system or structure; the social world flows from the shared stock of knowledge and common assumptions of different social groups and communities. Nevertheless, Schutz maintains that meaning forms an integral part of the interaction process and to this extent his sociology is objective: consciousness and action are meaningful in their relation with social structure and institutions.

Objectivity, however, increasingly becomes problematical in the further development of phenomenology and interactionism. This is especially the case with ethnomethodology which shares with phenomenology a concern with ordinary routine existence as the object of study and the inter-subjective nature of meaning. Developed initially by Harold Garfinkel during the 1960s, ethnomethodology (ethno – referring to the stock of commonsense knowledge available to individuals; method – referring to the strategies whereby the acting subject makes sense of the social world and seeks to communicate meaning) focused on 'practical actions as contingent ongoing accomplishments of organised artful practices of everyday life' (Garfinkel, 1967, p. 11). In effect, ethnomethodology sought to reveal the implicit rules and planful nature of everyday life. The everyday world consists of reflexive social acts which embody a variety of meanings depending on the specific context. Garfinkel uses the term 'indexicality' to refer to the context-bound nature of meaning: there is no objective meaning. By constructing meaning ordinary individuals are effectively 'doing sociology' and in this sense there is little to choose between the sociology of the professional and the lay public. Social science itself is a practical accomplishment.

This is to abandon all hope for a sociology grounded in the complex relation of self to society, subject to structure. Ethnomethodology is the final trivialisation of voluntarist sociology: social structure, culture and ideology are dissolved into the atomised relations of individuals freely constructing meanings. The everyday world is a system comprising community, culture and action: meaning is both constructed and given, related both to the specific situation and the wider social whole. In the next chapter the holistic social theory of structuralism is examined as one example of a modern sociological theory which rejects the notion of subject and constituting self.

10
Structuralism

The last chapter examined the development of a humanist sociology centred on the notion of a creative human subject. Symbolic interactionism and sociological phenomenology are sociologies which reject the large-scale systemic objectivism of positivism and functionalism. One of the major weaknesses, however, of this subject-centred sociology lies in its failure to explicate, both theoretically and historically, the relation of objective structure – society as a system – to human action and human agency. In Parsons's work, for example, the voluntaristic component of the theory of action is ultimately assimilated to the underlying needs of the social system. Similarly, some forms of Marxism focus on the structural determinations of social systems and objective laws of social development to the detriment of the active subject and a voluntaristic theory of action. Both functionalism and Marxism are characterised by an insistence on the objectivity of social structure: societies are not simple aggregates but structures consisting of elements which have their meaning only in relation to the whole.

Since the 1950s a new sociological theory has emerged which shares many of the holistic assumptions of functionalism and Marxism. Originating in the study of languages, structuralism has exerted an enormous influence in the social sciences especially in the work of Lévi-Strauss (anthropology), Roland Barthes, Julia Krestiva (semiotics and literary theory), Althusser, Poulantzas (Marxism and sociology) Godelier (economics), Foucault (philosophy and the history of science), and Lacan (psycho-analysis). Although these theorists disagree about the exact nature of structuralism there is, nevertheless, a broad consensus that a structuralist approach to the study of human society and culture involves the notion of wholes (a structure is not a simple aggregate of elements), the idea of transformation (structures are dynamic, not static, governed by laws which determine the ways that new elements are introduced into the structure and changed) and the concept of self-regulation (the meaning of a structure is self-contained in relation to its internal laws and rules). Where structuralism differs from functionalism and positivist Marxism is in its rejection of objective social facts and a concept of society as an objective, non-problematic external datum. Social facts have to be reconstituted in a theoretical discourse if they are to have any meaning at all. In short, structuralism defines reality in terms of the relations between elements, not in terms of things and social facts. Its basic principle is that the observable is meaningful only in so far as it can be related to an underlying structure or order.

The development of structuralism: Saussure

The founder of modern structuralism was Ferdinand de Saussure (1857–1913), a Swiss linguist who taught in Paris between 1881 and 1891 and whose most significant work, *Course in General Linguistics* (based on lectures given at the University of Geneva between 1906 and 1911), was published after his death. An expert in Indo-European languages, Saussure worked on a general theory of languages during the 1890s and he followed Durkheim in regarding language as an example of a social fact. Durkheim, of course, did not regard social facts as simple, naturalistic datums but rather as elements related to morality and collective representations.

The contemporary French linguist, Antoine Meillet, who studied with Saussure and Durkheim, noted the significance of Durkheim's sociology for Saussure's theory of language. And Saussure himself followed the debate between Durkheim and Tarde (which we discussed in Chapter 4) on the nature of sociological method. Saussure accepted Durkheim's methodological collectivism not Tarde's methodological individualism: thus he distinguished between language (*langue*) and speech (*parole*) in terms of the collectivist character of *langue* and the individualistic speech – utterances of *parole*. For Saussure, language constituted a collective representation, an abstract system of linguistic rules which governed concrete language use, a formal and coherent structure, the product 'of the collective mind and linguistic groups' (Saussure, 1974, p. 5). Saussure rejected nineteenth-century reductionist accounts of language arguing against historical, psychological and causal explanations. Language was not reducible to the psychology of speakers or the historical evolution of society. As a social fact, exercising constraint on individuals, language constituted a definite system, or structure, which existed independently of individual speakers whose utterances were merely an imperfect reflection of the whole. No one could retain the whole of a language system just as no one could know the legal system as a whole: language, like law, exists in everyday life within the consciousness of individuals constraining their actions, its concrete forms meaningful only in relation to its structure as a whole, as a collective representation.

Saussure drew an important distinction between the study of language conceived synchronically (its existence at a specific moment in terms of its functioning as a system) and diachronically (its development through time, that is, historically). 'The opposition between the two viewpoints', he argued, 'is absolute and allows no compromise.' Synchronic linguistics 'will be concerned with the logical and psychological relations that bind together co-existing terms and form a system in the collective mind of speakers' while diachronic linguistics studies 'relations that bind together successive terms not perceived by the collective mind but substituted for each other without forming a system' (Saussure, 1974, pp. 99–100). By psychology Saussure meant collective, not individual psychology although he remained uncertain of the exact nature of a psychology of language. His main focus was on synchronic linguistics the study of which he frequently compared with the game of chess. Chess is meaningful only in terms of its internal rules, its grammar, its network of relationships in which the value of a single piece depends on its relation with the whole; and to move a single piece is to alter the relation of the other elements to the whole. To understand chess, in other words, it is necessary to account for it as a system: 'The respective value of the pieces depends on their position on the chessboard just as each linguistic term derives its value from its opposition to all the other terms.' The synchronic facts of a language, like the synchronic facts of chess, are characterised by their systemic nature. To adopt a diachronic perspective is not to observe language as a system but rather as 'a series of events that modify it' (Saussure, 1974, pp. 88–91). The facts of diachronic, historical linguistics lack a systematic character and are thus of secondary importance in the study of language. Language is a system where all parts can, and must, be considered in their synchronic solidity.

For Saussure language formed part of the science of semiology – defined as a branch of social psychology concerned with analysing the 'life of signs' in society – which he conceived as a dynamic and transformative science. As a sign-system language did not 'mirror' an external reality (as the positivists believed) but constituted a 'field' of signification which sought to organise the world and define reality. Language comprised two components, the *signifier* (or *signifiant* in French) and the *signified* (or *signifié*), that is, the sound image and the concept or meaning. The linguistic sign was thus the unity of signifier and signified. One of Saussure's most important insights was that the linguistic sign was purely arbitrary; there was no natural only a conventional link between the signifier and the thing signified:

> The idea of 'sister' is not linked by any inner relationship to the succession of sounds s-ö-r which serves as its signifier in French; that it could be represented equally by just any other sequence is proved by differences among languages and by the very existence of different languages: the signified 'ox' has as its signifier b-o-f on one side of the border and o-k-s (Ochs) on the other (Saussure, 1974, pp. 67–8).

Saussure drew an important conclusion from his argument that it was linguistic convention which determined the arbitrary nature of the sign: there was no necessary relation between the sign and the reality to which it alluded. Language thus articulates human experience rather than simply reflecting it. It is through the linguistic sign that differences between objects are made and the world of reality organised into a meaningful structure. Language was not, therefore, a fixed and eternal essence but grounded in arbitrariness and difference. 'A linguistic system is a series of differences of sound combined with a series of differences of ideas.' The sound image 'chair', for example, is identified by differentiating it from 'pair', 'spare', etc.; and the meaning of 'chair' hinges on its difference from 'table', 'bed', etc. Without difference there is no meaning. The units that comprise a system of language acquire their meaning from their formal position, location and function within the whole. Saussure's central argument, therefore, was that language was produced socially as a collective phenomenon, independent of human will and intentions, a system irreducible to individual utterances. Speech and communication were thus made possible because of an underlying linguistic code, a system of collective norms which give meaning to specific verbal acts. Although Saussure did not employ the concept of structure, his theory of language is structural: to explain and understand an individual utterance it must be related to the 'hidden' system of functions, norms and categories. Thus Sassure abandoned causal explanation in favour of synchronic analysis of the position and function of elements within a system. The rules of language thus explain how language itself is simultaneously unknown and present, hidden from consciousness yet structuring human action.

Post-Saussurian structuralism: language and culture

Saussure's *Course in General Linguistics* was not published until 1916. His concept of language as a self-contained system and advocacy of synchronic over diachronic analysis influenced the development of language studies and more particularly of literary and cultural theory. In Russia between 1916 and 1930 a number of scholars, specialists in linguistics, philology and cultural history attempted to develop what they called a science of literature based on the concept of the immanent laws of literary form. Literature was defined as the transformation of practical, everyday speech into poetic language through the use of specific literary devices and constructions. The result was an autonomous, artistic object, an organised whole. Describing themselves as 'formalists' these Russian scholars defined the task of criticism as the discovery of the laws of poetic language. Like Saussure they rejected genetic, diachronic modes of explanation focusing instead on the ahistorical, synchronic nature of literary forms.

By the end of the 1920s, however, Russian Formalism was no longer an acceptable academic activity; the Soviet authorities, increasingly dogmatic in their Marxism, branded the movement as a form of alien bourgeois ideology. The leading Formalists (Roman Jakobson, Victor Shklovsky, Yuri Tynyanov, Mikhail Bakhtin, Vladimer Propp) were forced either into an accommodation with Soviet ideology (although the work of Bakhtin had already suggested a synthesis of Formalism and Marxism) or exile to Western Europe. The majority remained in Russia: Jakobson moved to Czechoslovakia where he joined the Prague Linguistic Circle. During the 1930s the Prague School, creatively assimilating Formalism into their theory of semiology, developed the structuralist approach to the study of language, culture and aesthetics. One of the major figures of the Prague School was the sociologist, Jan Mukarovsky (1891–1975) whose work in the sociology of culture exemplified a distinctive structuralist approach. Defining art as a 'semiological fact' Mukarovsky advocated the concept of structure, rather than form, totality or wholeness, to describe the inner unification of a cultural object through the mutual relations of its parts in which harmony as well as conflict and contradiction played a role.

In the development of structuralism two distinct trends are apparent. The first follows Saussure's separation of synchronic from diachronic analysis; while the other seeks a more historically grounded approach. An example of the former is Propp's study of fairy tales (*The Morphology of the Fairy Tale*, 1928) which later influenced the structural anthropology of Claude Lévi-Strauss. In his research, Propp advocated the primacy of the synchronic over the genetic arguing that in the analysis of fairy tales it was possible to identify a limited number of functions (thirty-one) which could then be organised into an underlying system or structure. In this way fairy stories, which originated in widely differing cultures, could be classified since the multiplicity of characters is in direct contrast to the limited number of functions which the characters exercise in the course of the action.

In contrast to Propp's synchronic analysis, Bakhtin (1895–1975) developed an historical structuralism. Bakhtin began from a critique of Saussure which was published in Russia during the 1920s. Language was not an abstract, linguistic system, as Saussure had argued, but essentially historical acquiring its living forms 'in concrete verbal communication'. Saussure's separation of utterance (*parole*) from language (*langue*) postulated the view of language as a product passively assimilated by individuals and not 'a function of the speaker'.. Saussure's dualism was rejected. Indeed, orthodox linguistics was criticised for a failure to examine dialogic relations, the linguistic interaction of different speakers. Saussure's binary opposition of a 'pure' language and an 'impure', historically specific, utterance was overcome through defining the word as dialogic. This is one of Bakhtin's most significant contributions to structuralist thought. He wrote: 'Language is alive only in the dialogic intercourse of those who make use of it. Dialogic intercourse is the genuine sphere of the life of language [which] is permeated by dialogic relationships' (Bakhtin/Volosinov, 1973, pp. 102–3). Semantic and logical relations of language lack the dialogic aspect until they become utterances and embody the positions of various speakers.

Bakhtin applied these concepts to the study of the novel which he defined as a literary genre that sought to represent the multiplicity of the languages of a specific era and thus all the social and ideological 'voices' claiming to be significant. He was particularly concerned with analysing the relation between cultural forms and the broader structure of popular culture. In one of his most significant sociological studies, *Rabelais and His World* (1940) he argued that writers such as Boccaccio, Cervantes, Shakespeare and Rabelais developed their artistic techniques and vision historically from the depths of a folk culture which 'shaped during many centuries . . . had defended the people's creativity in non-official forms, in verbal expression or spectacle'. Bakhtin shows in rich detail the organic relation of the 'popular–festive images' associated with the 'unofficial culture' of popular festivals and carnivals with Rabelais's 'grotesque realist' literary form:

> Thanks to this process, popular–festive images became a powerful means of grasping reality; they served as a basis for an authentic and deep realism. Popular imagery did not reflect the naturalistic, fleeting, meaningless, and scattered aspect of reality but the very process of becoming, its meaning and direction (Bakhtin, 1968, p. 72).

Bakhtin's extraordinary detailed analysis of Rabelais's novel, *Gargantua and Pantagruel*, its verbal imagery and the relation of its different parts to the whole is structured around the key element of carnival. As an archaic element in the process of cultural continuity with its origins in pre-industrial folk-culture, carnival cannot be assimilated to the economic system or defined as a reflection or reproduction of an historically given reality: carnivalesque literature does not signify ideology but the universal elements within popular, democratic culture. Carnival is an inherent element in human culture although its forms vary historically: it constitutes an alternative reality to official culture with its panoply of ecclesiastical and political cults and ceremonies:

> A boundless world of humorous forms and manifestations opposed the official and serious tone . . . of feudal culture. In spite of their variety, folk festivities of the carnival type, the comic rites and cults, the clowns and fools, giants, dwarfs and jugglers, the vast and manifold literature of parody – all . . . belong to one culture of folk carnival humour (Bakhtin, 1968, p. 4).

Carnival functioned to liberate humanity from the established order; it was 'the suspension of all hierarchical rank, privilege, norms and prohibitions . . . hostile to all that was immortalised and completed'. The unofficial popular culture emphasised equality of human relationships and defined humanity in dynamic, not fixed, secular terms. Folk laughter is identified as the laughter of the whole community, simultaneously mocking, triumphant, derisory, assertive, denying, burying, reviving. As part of the carnival crowd the individual 'is aware of being a member of a continually growing and renewed people' in which folk laughter represents an element of victory 'over super-natural laws . . . the sacred . . . death', over everything which is oppressive and restrictive.

In Bakhtin's analysis popular culture is a living and open structure which liberates the individual from dogmatism and fanaticism. Perhaps the most striking feature of Bakhtin's analysis is the emphasis he places on the ambivalence of laughter and its role in culture. Laughter, he argues, refuses to allow seriousness to atrophy but seeks to maintain its unfinal-ised and open form. Thus the unity which characterises the human community is not imposed from above but flows organically from the depths of a popular and democratic culture. The development of capitalism, the growth of bureauc-racy and the trend to rationalisation in culture tend to separate popular culture from the human community, although the implication of Bakhtin's work – the wider study of culture and languages – suggests the persistence of an open-ended, polyphonic culture within modern societies.

Bakhtin's theory of the dialogic, unfinalised nature of the human community and the complex ways in which this structure informs the work of specific writers represents one of the most important contributions to the development of a diachronically grounded structuralism. Similarly, Mukarovsky in his sociological studies of culture – especially *Aesthetic Function, Norm and Value* (1934) – advanced a concept of art as semiotic fact based on the social and historical relation of speakers to the human collectivity. Like Bakhtin, Mukarovsky defined art as a system of autonomous signs regulated by a set of norms valid for a particular community which the art-work actively implements. A sign-system, such as literature, was both a mode of communication and an aesthetic structure characterised by a hierarchy of elements which cohered around a 'dominant'. (The concept of the 'dominant' was advanced by Jakobson and bears a strong similarity with the notion of a 'structure in dominance' which Althusser developed later: see below pp. 289–91.) Mukarovsky's concept of structure embraces all the relations within a system. He argued that an aesthetic work was one in which the *aesthetic function* was dominant so that the message communicated by the art-object was 'literary' and 'artistic'.

Thus for Mukarovsky, an aesthetic attitude was not a given fact but always oriented to the sign; and the sign referred to things other than itself. These were the codes through which the sign-system worked, essentially social and thus changing as society itself changed. More precisely, the aesthetic constituted a function and not an inherent property of the art-work. The aesthetic was thus connected both with the internal organisation of art, in which it exercised a dominant influence, and social life in which it played a secondary function. Mukarovsky concluded that it was impossible to distinguish art clearly from non-art: in architecture, music and literature, for example, the practical and aesthetic functions co-existed in a mutually dynamic relationship; and in literature the practical–communicative function frequently dominated the aesthetic function.

Mukarovsky's structuralism dispensed with the notion of the subject. The genesis of art-forms depended on supra-individual structures rooted in collective social life; the individual writer or artist was merely the passive vehicle for these forces. The genetic structuralism of Lucien Goldmann (1913–70) follows Mukarovsky's emphasis on the collective nature of art and Bakhtin's broad, humanist perspective. Goldmann was largely influenced by the early writings of Lukács, especially *History and Class Consciousness*, from which he derived the concepts of world vision, totality, consciousness, and the Swiss psychologist, Jean Piaget from whose work he adapted the notions of significant structure, function and structuration/destructuration. As we have seen, structuralism developed first in the areas of linguistics, literary and aesthetic studies, and Goldmann followed this tradition in his sociology of literature. (His major work was a study of the philosophy of Pascal and the dramas of Racine, *The Hidden God* published in 1956; he also wrote on Malraux, Genet, Heidegger, Enlightenment philosophy and was highly critical of other, contemporary forms of non-genetic structuralism.)

Basic to Goldmann's sociology was a conception of structure created and transformed by human activity. Structures were *made* through the *praxis* of the human subject. But the subject is not an individual but a collective category, a social group which constitutes the true source of cultural creation. This *collective subject* is, like cultural creation, a significant structure. All major cultural forms embody a significant structure, a world view which expresses the 'collective consciousness' of a significant social group. The world view unites the various elements and levels of a cultural form into unity and coherence. Thus Goldmann's sociology of literature begins by analysing the immanent structure of an art-work – the work as a whole – and then relates it to a social group. Since the art-work expresses the tendencies, actions and values of the collective subject it bears a functional relation with it. Thus to understand the totality of a literary work it is necessary to explain its historical genesis in the social life of the group. The cultural objects are analysed both synchronically (the work as a whole) and diachronically (the products of human action). Structures are meaningful only in relation to human action and communication. Purely diachronic study, Goldmann argues, 'which forgoes systems and structures, is scientifically impossible and inadequate', for reality is constantly undergoing a process of structuration and destructuration:

> History is the object of structuring processes and these cannot be studied if one has not first established models. Inversely, however, structures are only provisional, the result of men's behaviour in precise and concrete situations which they themselves transform within given structures. In this way they create new structures (Goldmann, 1980, p. 50).

Goldmann's emphasis on the creative, human dimension of structure distinguishes his approach from that of his contemporary, Roland Barthes (1915–80). Goldmann's genetic structuralism owed little to linguistic theory: defining structuralism in 1967, Barthes stressed its origin in the methods of linguistics.

Structuralism had been introduced into France by Lévi-Strauss whose structural anthropology was deeply influenced by Jakobson and Saussure. In his analysis of kinship relationships, for example, Lévi-Strauss argued that they form a system and are structured like a language: each item has meaning only in terms of its relation with the whole. But it was not until the 1960s that structuralism became a major presence within

French intellectual life. Barthes became associated with this development through his studies of mass culture and general semiotic theory. He defined semiology as the scientific study of human actions and objects in relation to an underlying system of rules and differences that enable a signifying process to take place. Culture consists of signifying phenomena and Barthes describes two such signifying systems, fashion and food. In his *Système de la mode* (1967) Barthes described fashion as a system which has the effect of naturalising the conventions on which the system itself rests. Underlying the *parole* of fashion and food is a distinctive code, or *langue*, defining which garment suits a particular event and the items of food that together constitute a 'course'. The cultural code is the system of distinctions and conventions which generate meaning for the members of different social groups.

One of Barthes early works in semiotic analysis was his study of mass culture, *Mythologies* (1957), in which he discussed the signifying systems of striptease, cars, margarine, detergents and toys. Describing these products of mass culture as 'collective representations', sign-systems, Barthes suggested that their function was to 'mystify' the true nature of modern capitalist society. On one level of signification soup was simply soup and French wine merely good wine; but as signs they communicate secondary meanings so that wine is not one drink among others but a sign of the superior French way of life, the drinking itself constituting a ritual, collective act producing a sense of social solidarity. Similarly, Barthes analysed the cover of the magazine *Paris-Match* in which a black soldier, in French uniform salutes the French flag: the first level of signification is a French soldier saluting the national flag, but the second level of meaning is the French Empire, lacking racial discrimination with its virtues exemplified by the zeal of the black soldier serving his alleged colonial oppressors: 'I am therefore . . . faced with a greater semiological system: there is a signifier, itself already formed with a previous system (*a black soldier is giving the French salute*); there is a signified (it is here a purposeful mixture of Frenchness and militariness); finally, there is a presence of the signified through the signifier' (Barthes, 1973, p. 116). It is at the second level of signification that the object or event becomes myth seeking to present its conventions (in photography, food, fashion, for example) as natural datums. As such, fashion signifies the cultural importance of the insignificant, the slight differences in dress; but as a signifying system fashion communicates secondary and ideological meanings.

For Barthes, bourgeois culture is built around these mythical, ideological meanings, generating norms which appear as facts of nature:

> The whole of France is steeped in this anonymous ideology: our press . . . films . . . theatre . . . the garments we wear, everything in everyday life, is dependent on the representation which the bourgeoisie *has and makes us have* of the relations between man and the world. These 'normalised' forms attract little attention, by the very fact of their extension, in which their origin is easily lost . . . bourgeois norms are experienced as the evident laws of a natural order (Barthes, 1973, p. 140).

As a means of communication myth is thus a language which generates its own meanings. Meaning is not determined by the voluntaristic actions and intentions of the subject or speaker but produced by the system itself. Barthes's semiotics is thus broadly anti-historical, anti-genetic and anti-humanist, the triumph of the system over the subject.

Marxism and structuralism

During the course of the 1960s a distinctive form of Marxist structuralism, resolutely anti-humanist, developed in France. Its leading theoretician was the Communist Party philosopher, Louis Althusser. In a series of essays and analyses Althusser proposed a radically new, scientific 'reading' of Marx. Influenced by structural linguistics and the scientific rationalism of Gaston Bachelard, Althusser criticised all forms of positivist/empiricist Marxism as well as the idealist, humanist-centred approach of Lukács, the Frankfurt School and those contemporary Marxists, such as Sartre, for whom Marxism was the philosophy of *praxis*.

For Althusser, Marxism was the science of social formations, the study of the inner logic, the relations between its various

levels, or structures. The specific nature of a social formation –
capitalism, socialism, etc. – cannot be analysed in terms of
subjects or social action but only from the standpoint of a
complex totality which consists of economic, political–legal
and ideological structures or 'practices'. Althusser rejected the
base-superstructure model of orthodox Marxism because it
suggested an essentialist notion of society, that the social
totality *expresses* a single dominant element, the labour–capital
relation or the alienation of humanity. This 'expressive totality'
is ultimately Hegelian since it conveys the notion of unity
produced through a single essence. Althusser's concept of
totality, in contrast, emphasises the multiplicity of economic,
political and ideological structures, their relative autonomy
and, employing a concept derived from Freud, *overdetermination*.
Thus the most basic contradiction, the capital–labour contradiction, 'is never simple, but always specified by the historically
concrete forms and circumstances in which it is exercised . . .
specified by forms of the superstructure (the State, dominant
ideology, religion . . .); specified by the internal and external
historical situation'. Contradictions are not pure but are
overdetermined, that is, determined and determining 'in one
and the same movement'. Hegelian philosophy and humanist
Marxism tended only to assimilate the complex diversity of 'a
historically given society' to a single substance, or element,
which functioned to determine all other elements of as well as
the social whole itself (Althusser, 1969, pp. 106–13).

There is thus uneven development between the various levels
of a social formation; the structure and its effects determine
each other with totality defined in terms of its effects. Social
formations are asymmetrical in their structure. But what of the
relation between the economy and the superstructure? Is the
economic merely one structure among many or is it, as Marx,
Engels and other Marxists have held, dominant? Althusser
suggests that although the social formation comprises relatively autonomous levels or structures, 'in the last instance' the
economic determines which specific structure is dominant.
This notion of a 'structure in dominance' allows Althusser to
maintain the traditional Marxist emphasis on the primacy of
the economic while at the same time advancing a pluralist
conception of the social formation.

One result of Althusser's work has been an increasing emphasis in Marxist theory on the concept of mode of production and its relation with the superstructure, and the theory of ideology. For Althusser, the mode of production constitutes a number of different structures including the economic. It is the way in which these structures are combined which differentiates one mode of production from another. For example, the capitalist mode of production consists of a specific economic structure (the labourer, means of production, etc.) and a rational, legal system which forms part of the super-structure. The economic structure determines the specificity of the various laws which relate to property and contract. A different combination of economy and law subsists within a socialist mode of production, the socialised economic relations determining a different set of legal principles and rights. Nevertheless, the legal system, as a structure of ideology, is relatively autonomous constituting a distinct level of the social formation. But as E. P. Thompson, in his extended critique of Althusser, has pointed out, such a formal, synchronic approach fails to grasp that law, as an historical phenomenon, was not part of a separate level but always 'imbricated within the mode of production and productive relations themselves . . . [intruding] . . . with religion . . . an arm of politics . . . [and] it was an academic discipline, subjected to the rigour of its own autonomous logic' (Thompson, 1978, p. 288). Because Althusser's structuralism has separated the human subject and human action from the structures themselves, one consequence is the reification of the social formation and its levels, the dominance of the system over the individual, and a tendency for the system itself to remain closed, emptied of all dialogic communicative relations. Structures, after all, do not make laws or change them.

The rigidity of Althusser's Marxism is particularly brought out in his analysis of ideology. The traditional Marxist definition of ideology as a 'false consciousness' (adumbrated in Marx's early work, especially *The German Ideology*), a distorted picture of the external world, illusory and unreal, is rejected by Althusser for its non-scientific humanism. Such a theory of ideology is centred on the notion of a 'constituting subject' and the assumption that knowledge, formed and reflected in human consciousness, develops only through the experiences of this subject. The true source of ideology is neither experience nor the subject, but objective, material reality; as an objective structure ideology cannot be reduced to the actions and consciousness of the subject. Ideology is thus defined as 'a system of representations', 'images and concepts' which 'impose' themselves as structures on social classes and individuals. Making a distinction between 'real objects' and 'objects of knowledge', Althusser located ideology as a real object forming an 'instance' of the social totality, a partly autonomous structure irreducible to the economic or political levels. Ideology is thus a system through which the individual exists as a social being, a 'lived' relation between the individual and the world, a relation which

> . . . only appears as *'conscious'* on condition that it is *unconscious* . . . not a simple relation but a relation between relations, a second degree relation. In ideology men do indeed express, not the relation between them and their conditions of existence, but *the way* they live the relation between them and their conditions of existence: this presupposes both a real relation and 'an imaginary, lived' relation (Althusser, 1969, p. 233).

Representing the 'imaginary' relations of individuals to the 'real' conditions of their existence, ideology forms an essential element of all social formations (including Socialism and Communism) since social cohesion is only possible through the 'practico-social' functions of ideology. Althusser here distinguishes science from ideology: science is 'theoretical knowledge', a system of concepts, a discourse which produces the objects of knowledge and which leads ultimately to the framing of scientific generalities. There is thus an important difference between theoretical knowledge and knowledge of the external world: the former does not depend on external proofs for its validity since it is purely theoretical; the latter is involved with ideology and thus the practico-social function dominates the theoretical function.

Ideology is produced, therefore, not by the intentions of subjects but by institutions, specific apparatuses which, in modern capitalism, are increasingly state organs. Ideology is anchored within institutions which themselves are the products of ideology. In his essay, 'Ideology and Ideological State Apparatuses' (1971), Althusser, responding to criticisms that his Marxist theory of ideology underemphasised the role of class struggle, argued that ideology constituted the 'site' of class conflict. Distinguishing between the Ideological State Apparatus (consisting of religious, educational, cultural institutions as well as political parties) and the Repressive State Apparatus (consisting of the institutions of coercion such as the army, police, judiciary) Althusser argued that the Ideological State Apparatuses 'largely secure the reproduction specifically of the relations of production, behind a "shield" provided by the repressive State apparatus'. In pre-capitalist societies the Church functioned as the dominant ideological apparatus. In modern capitalism the educational institutions have become the dominant ideological apparatus:

> It takes children from every class at infant school age, and then for years, the years in which the child is most vulnerable; squeezed between the family State apparatus and the educational State apparatus, it drums into them, whether it uses new or old methods, a certain amount of 'know-how' wrapped in the ruling ideology (French, arithmetic, natural history, the sciences, literature) or simply the ruling ideology in its pure state (ethics, civic instruction, philosophy) (Althusser, 1971).

For Althusser, the ideological state apparatuses perpetuate submission to the established order reproducing the relations of production. But the model of society which Althusser proposes in this formulation comes close to a totalitarian system in which a process of complete ideological indoctrination into a dominant ideology is secured both by the passivity of an atomised population and the absence of alternative structures. Althusser's structuralist concept of ideology is historically and sociologically inadequate: the 'private' institutions which form part of the ideological state apparatus are centred in civil society and cannot be assimilated to state practices in the way that Althusser suggests. In capitalist society education is governed both by ideological assumptions and practices as well as by its own specific laws and values, that is, education is both dependent on the mode of production and class structure, and yet partly autonomous in terms of its immanent properties.

Ultimately, however, Althusser's structuralism constitutes the most strenuous rejection of the social-humanist and dialogic tradition of sociological theory. The social world was not, and is not, made by humanity: men and women are the supports of external structures and there is no room in Althusser's system for 'voluntarism'. Yet without the active subject how can the development of the concept of workers' council or soviet be explained sociologically? The concept of council was not produced simply by intellectuals but arose simultaneously with the institution itself in Paris in 1871, and Russia in 1905 and 1917. The decentralising, plebeian democracy enshrined in workers' councils was the product of working-class activity and culture. Both the concept and the institution can be grasped sociologically only by positing an acting subject. In Althusser's formulations, however, concepts are elaborated independently of human experience and *praxis*. Knowledge is produced through a process of 'theoretical practice' in which the raw materials of science – 'the abstract, part-ideological, part-scientific generalities' – become transformed into genuine concepts. But theoretical practice, defined in this excessively abstract form, cannot possibly accommodate the specific genesis of concepts such as workers' councils. There is a dialogic relation between concepts and culture, theory and society which escapes the formalist rigidity of Althusserian structuralism.

The absence of a genetic, historical dimension is particularly brought out in the sociological studies of class, power and the state by Nicos Poulantzas (Poulantzas, 1973, 1975). Unlike Althusser, Poulantzas is wholly concerned with empirical processes, institutions and the specific functioning of a social formation. Yet his work remains excessively abstract and ahistorical. In general his formulations do not advance much beyond Marx's notions of the partial autonomy of the state and culture and his general argument that as a system capitalism develops through the operations of an underlying structure. But Marx's voluntarism, the emphasis on the making of social institutions, is flatly rejected as humanist ideology.

11
The Sociology of Knowledge and Culture

The sociology of knowledge and sociological theory

It was the German sociologist, Max Scheler (1874–1928) who
coined the term, the sociology of knowledge (*Wissenssoziologie*)
in 1924. Its basic elements were defined as the collective, social
nature of knowledge, the sociological distribution of knowledge
through specific social institutions such as schools and news-
papers, and the reality of social interests in the formation of
different kinds of knowledge. All mental acts, wrote Scheler,
were 'necessarily sociologically co-conditioned ... by the
structure of society' (Scheler, in Curtis and Petras, 1970,
pp. 170–5). The sociology of knowledge was, therefore, not
merely a sociological version of the history of ideas, but rather
an attempt to trace, as systematically as possible, the social
location of different forms of knowledge examining their genesis
in relation to specific social structural elements: strictly
speaking it is not concerned with the truth of ideas but with
their social function and relation with social groups and
interests. The sociology of knowledge studies both truth and
error as forms of thought which are both socially conditioned.
As R. K. Merton has argued, 'as long as attention was focussed
on the social determinants of ideology, illusion, myth, and
moral norms, the sociology of knowledge could not emerge ...
The sociology of knowledge came into being with the signal
hypothesis that even truths were to be held socially account-
able, were to be related to the historical society in which they
emerged' (Merton, 1957, pp. 459–60).

294

In general, nineteenth-century sociological positivism, with its central belief that science constituted the secure foundations of true knowledge, failed to develop an adequate concept of ideology or to theorise the relation of thought itself to social structure. Within the framework of evolutionary theory error and illusion were elements which the law of development itself would ultimately eradicate. Marx was the first major social theorist to suggest a systematic approach to the analysis of the production of thought, of the relation between forms of knowledge (ideology) and different types of society. In *The German Ideology* he proposed a mechanical model of the social production of ideas in which class interest and mode of production determined the structure of thought within different epochs. Economic theory, religion, political and social ideas, and law were classified as forms of ideology reflecting the values of specific groups: thus eighteenth-century French materialist philosophy corresponded directly with the secular interests of the rising bourgeoisie; nineteenth-century political economy was the expression of the economic needs of a dominant bourgeoisie. Although as I have suggested in Chapter 3, Marx modified many of his early, mechanistic formulations, especially those related to his model of 'base' and 'superstructure', his basic proposition that knowledge or ideology, a collective and not individual product, necessarily bound up in its genesis and structure with definite social groups, classes and interests, stimulated a later generation of sociologists to study thought as a social, not *a priori* category.

Durkheim, like Marx, defined thought in social terms as a collective phenomenon expressed in collective representations such as religion, corporations, etc. In his analysis of primitive social organisation – the studies of *Primitive Classification* (with Marcel Mauss, 1899) and *The Elementary Forms of the Religious Life* (1912) – based on anthropological evidence from studies of the Zuni and Sioux Indians as well as the Australian aborigines, Durkheim argued that the principle of classification derived from the division of society into clans. The basic structure of society determined the structure of human thought: the categories of time, space, number were social and not immanent properties of the mind. Thus the division of the year into months, weeks, days corresponded directly to the periodical recurrence of certain rites, feasts, public ceremonies; the calendar was the expression of this rhythm in collective social life, 'made in the image of social phenomena'. The categories of logical thought were thus traced to the existence of hierarchies of superiors and inferiors in social life. Forms of knowledge were functional for society in the sense that communication between individuals was possible only because they shared in the collective representations: 'Thus society could not abandon the categories to the free choice of the individual without abandoning itself. If it is to live there is not merely need of a satisfactory moral conformity, but also there is a minimum of logical conformity beyond which it cannot safely go' (Durkheim, 1961, pp. 9–17). For Durkheim, knowledge was bound up with the requirements of social order in that the mental categories which comprised the structure of the collective representations derived from the fundamental principle of social cohesion. Durkheim went on to suggest that with the development of more complex societies, thought itself becomes detached from its social origins striving towards autonomy and objectivity. Thus Durkheim and Mauss assumed that the system of classification, characteristic of primitive social organisation, cannot form the basis of a sociological explanation of modern thought.

Durkheim's assimilation of knowledge and its categories to an underlying system based on the collectivity tends to negate the active role of ideas themselves and to diminish the practical involvement of human subjects in the formation of thought-products. In contrast, Weber's sociology of religion emphasised the action element in forms of ideology: Pietism, Calvinism, Catholicism, Taoism, Confucianism were religious ideologies, or world views, closely linked with specific types of social group which provide the necessary psychological motivation either for individuals to advance the values of capital accumulation or turn to other-worldly activity. Religious ideologies were not, therefore, illusions, false consciousness, or mere epiphenomenal forms reflecting simple group interests, but complex structures of thought through which the individual oriented him/herself to reality and defined the nature of that reality.

Thus the foundations of a sociology of knowledge were laid

by Marx, Weber and Durkheim. The theory of ideology was, of course, central to this development. But a sociological theory of ideology could not emerge until the nineteenth-century positivist 'world view' was challenged – in the fields of social theory, philosophy, linguistics, psychology – by conflicting discourses or perspectives. 'With increasing social conflict, differences in the values, attitudes and modes of thought of groups develop to the point where the orientation which these groups previously had in common is overshadowed by incompatible differences' (Merton, 1957, p. 457).

For Scheler, the sociological analysis of forms of knowledge served to illuminate what he, and other contemporary sociologists, defined as a crisis of values in a world dominated by such diverse philosophies, sociologies and psychologies as neo-Kantianism, phenomenology, Marxism, psycho-analysis, vitalism and formalism. In the realm of social theory, relativism in epistemology and agnosticism in methodology predominated; while a plurality of world views, socialism, Marxism, liberalism, fascism emerged, each with its particular claim to truth. In opposition to the relativism implicit in Durkheim and Weber and Marx, Scheler argued idealistically for a distinct realm of timeless essences, universal values which transcend specific historical and social reality. 'There are many different truths', he wrote, 'but they all spring from the perception of the one ultimate realm of ideas and value orderings.' The task of the sociology of knowledge was defined as the selection of the truthful, universal elements in each world view and their integration into a total conception (Scheler, 1970). Many of Scheler's metaphysical notions passed into the subsequent development of the sociology of knowledge especially his concern with absolute knowledge, *truth*. Scheler's anti-positivism, Dilthey's conception of 'world view', Marx's theory of ideology were brought together in the sociology of Karl Mannheim (1893–1947) who produced the major European contribution to the sociology of knowledge.

Mannheim: general elements of the sociology of knowledge

Mannheim belonged to a generation of Hungarian intellectuals who were concerned above all with culture and human values: he was a member of a group consisting of Lukács, the art historian, Arnold Hauser, the composer, Bela Bartok and the philosopher, Michael Polyani. Mannheim was particularly influenced by the work of Weber and Simmel on the problems of culture and epistemology. He shared their criticisms of natural science as an inadequate basis for social science, and during the 1920s sought to define an interpretative sociological approach in the analysis of different forms of knowledge. During the period, 1921–9 he wrote a series of essays exploring the possibility of a sociology of knowledge. The most important of these works were 'On the Interpretation of *Weltanschauung*' (1921), 'Historicism' (1924), 'The Problem of a Sociology of Knowledge' (1925), 'Conservative Thought' (1926) and *Ideology and Utopia* (a book of three essays published in 1929).

The broad theme of these works is the collective nature of knowledge (Mannheim employed the concept of collective subject to indicate that a particular thinker does not express an individual but a group or collective standpoint, his/her work expressing external social currents), its classification into distinctive 'styles of thought' (a term derived from art history and encompassing 'bourgeois', 'proletarian' and 'conservative' thought), and its close relation with distinctive social groups. For Mannheim, styles of thought were bound up with the interests of particular groups and the task of analysis involved both an external historical–contextual analysis linking the group's social structure with the thought–product, and an immanent analysis of the inner unity, the 'fundamental impulse' of the whole itself. Styles of thought were totalities which could not be understood sociologically through quantitative means: one of Mannheim's important methodological principles was the impossibility of analysing the complex, the whole, in terms of the simple, the part. Reviewing Lukács's *Theory of the Novel* (in 1920) he argued that the interpretation of cultural objects must work 'from above' since the form of art 'is only an abstract component of the full spiritual content . . . an interpretation of the abstract part is justified and possible only by proceeding from the whole' (Wolff, 1971, p. 3). It is this methodological principle which separates Mannheim's sociology from positivism: interpretation does not render causal explanation superfluous, however, for both are essential components in the analysis of the 'conditions for the actualisation or realisation of a given meaning' (Mannheim, 1952, p. 81).

In his early writings, roughly up to the publication of 'Conservative Thought', Mannheim adopted an interpretative, hermeneutic standpoint. He was concerned primarily with the immanent structure of a cultural form. Thus he wrote that 'the analysis of meanings will be the core of our technique' and advocated both phenomenological (the basic intention underpinning each style of thought) and structural methodology (the relation of knowledge to external elements). A cultural object has three distinct although related levels of meaning which Mannheim identified as objective, expressive and documentary. Thus music has a melodic and harmonic content which can be objectively understood by an observer without any knowledge of the intentions of the composer; and the expressive meaning of music lies in its emotional content which is closely linked to the intentions of the composer. In contrast, documentary meaning relates the whole musical form to the style of thought of a particular epoch seeking to integrate particular cultural phenomena in the larger structure of a world view (Mannheim, 1952, pp. 42–5). Documentary meaning, in short, refers to the global outlook of a world view.

But an immanent approach can easily lead to circularity: 'We understand the whole from the part, and the part from the whole. We derive the "spirit of the epoch" from its individual documentary manifestations – and we interpret the individual documentary manifestations on the basis of what we know about the spirit of the epoch' (Mannheim, 1952, p. 62). To escape from the relativism implicit in these formulations Mannheim advanced a method of analysis which linked the documentary meaning of cultural forms with both the historical and social context and the inner unity of the whole itself. It is this emphasis on the larger meanings of cultural elements, such as different types of knowledge, which dominate Mannheim's later work. For Mannheim, the rapidly changing and dynamic nature of the historical and social context constituted the major problem for the sociology of knowledge. Were all styles of thought relative in terms of their truth content? 'The sociology of knowledge', he wrote, 'is . . . the *systematisation* of the doubt which is to be found in social life as a vague insecurity and uncertainty.' The modern world is to blame for this situation with social life increasingly alienated, disorganised and anarchical. Mannheim wrote gloomily of 'the intellectual twilight which dominates our epoch', the 'appalling trend of modern thought' and the confusion into which social and intellectual life has fallen (Mannheim, 1960, p. 94).

These pessimistic comments are from one of Mannheim's most significant works, *Ideology and Utopia* (1929), in which he confronted the problems of objectivity and perspective that Weber and Lukács had raised in their sharply differing ways. If there is no objective reality but merely the sum of divergent perspectives then how is historical knowledge possible? In opposition to Weber's cultural relativism and sceptical sociology, Mannheim proposed an historicist solution, 'a dynamic conception of the truth', an absolute standard by which to judge the validity of different perspectives. Mannheim adopted the concept of totality arguing that although different types of knowledge are related to different social locations each new perspective which emerges in the course of historical development actually contains new and valuable insights into the nature of historical reality – Marxism emphasised the class struggle, Fascism the element of action in social life, Liberalism the importance of the autonomous individual. Each new perspective synthesises previous perspectives: different 'styles of thought' continually undergo uninterrupted fusion and interpenetration. Thus modern society, although characterised by intense fragmentation and polarisation, nevertheless lays the foundation for 'an ever-widening drive towards a total conception', in that each new perspective uncovers 'an approximate truth' that forms part of a 'larger body of meaning' within the structure of historical reality. All perspectives are necessarily partial 'because historical totality is always too comprehensive to be grasped by any one of the individual points of view which emerge out of it' (Mannheim, 1960, pp. 94–6, 134–5). This is the meaning of Mannheim's 'dynamic conception of truth'. In the essay on 'Historicism', for example, he argued that no single class, or group, could constitute itself as the bearer of the totalising movement of history. The whole can only be grasped by taking all perspectives into account, 'the whole contrapuntal pattern of all the voices'.

Mannheim thus adopts a version of Hegel's 'cunning of reason' in which the historical process immanently transforms ideological and interest-bound thought into objective truth. In *Ideology and Utopia* Marx's theory of ideology is praised for identifying the link between class interests and forms of knowledge. But Marx failed to apply his theory to his own thought and conceived ideology as a 'privileged concept of socialists'. Although an advance on previous theories, the Marxist concept fused two distinct meanings of ideology: the simple (or particular) concept, referring to individual disguises and rationalisations of actions operating on a psychological level; and the total concept which refers to the thought of a social class, or epoch, to styles of thought. The latter meaning is sociological and therefore approximates to the truth. The total concept of ideology is non-evaluative seeking only to elucidate the relation of 'mental structures' to specific 'life-situations'; it enables the sociology of knowledge to explore the social determinants of thought and raise the question of truth and falsity (Mannheim, 1960, pp. 66–72).

All thought is socially determined. However, Mannheim exempts mathematics and the natural sciences from a dependence on social causation. In contrast to 'existentially determined thought' mathematics and the natural sciences are governed by immanent factors so that in the formulation $2 + 2 = 4$ 'there is no indication as to who did the thinking and where'. Many critics have pointed out the weakness of this distinction between formal and historical knowledge: if thought is socially determined then science, the product of human action and culture, is equally determined. In general, Mannheim failed to distinguish clearly between different types of knowledge assuming that political, ethical, historical and religious beliefs were the same as everyday values and ideas. For if knowledge is determined by extra-theoretic factors then logic and science, as well as political philosophy and epistemology, are relative in terms of the truth content.

In his early writings Mannheim had identified the problem of relativism as the basic problem of the sociology of knowledge since it clearly suggested the limits of the sociology of knowledge itself. His solution in *Ideology and Utopia* was to distinguish *relativism* (that all ideas are relative to a situation) from *relationism* (that knowledge, although related to specific contexts, is not thereby invalidated as truthful or not). But as we have seen, ultimately Mannheim adopted an Hegelian historicist standpoint so that although the sociologist of knowledge relates specific forms of thought to specific social locations, the truth content of different perspectives lies in their relation with 'supra-historical' reality. And the task of distilling truth from error in different perspectives was not carried out by history but by intellectuals.

The sociology of intellectuals

In *History and Class Consciousness* Lukács had proposed the radical historicist solution to the problem of historical relativism: the optimum of truth lay with the ontologically privileged proletariat whose world view of Marxism embodied the principle of totality and thus of historical meaning. Like Lukács, Mannheim argued that some social locations enable a social group to understand historical reality at a deeper level than others; not all perspectives are equally valid. Mannheim rejected Lukács's assimilation of truth to class and advanced the view that the task of synthesising different perspectives lay with a privileged social stratum, the 'free-floating intelligentsia' (*freischwebende Intelligenz*), a group unattached to specific social interests and thus intellectually autonomous. Marx's theory of ideology could develop into the sociology of knowledge only through the actions of these independent intellectuals who occupied a social location outside the main institutions of capitalist society.

> It seems inherent in the historical process itself that the narrowness and the limitations which restrict one point of view tend to be corrected by clashing with the opposite points of view. The task of the study of ideology . . . is to understand the narrowness of each

individual point of view and the interplay between these distinctive attitudes in the total social process (Mannheim, 1960, p. 72).

Only the intellectuals can achieve a total perspective and in *Ideology and Utopia* Mannheim adopted Alfred Weber's term describing the intelligentsia as a *'relatively* classless stratum' (Mannheim's emphasis), highly differentiated and unified by the bond of education. Mannheim distinguished between the 'socially unattached intelligentsia' (clergymen, engineers, writers, academics) and the 'socially attached intelligentsia' (the Church in the Middle Ages is mentioned as constituting a closed social stratum, highly unified internally) in an attempt to differentiate those intellectuals capable of autonomous cognitive activity from those whose function was directly interest bound and thus ideological.

The development of the modern intelligentsia is the result of a broad process of democratisation embracing the professions, education, communications and the cultural institutions of industrial society which effectively liberate the intellectual from patronage and total dependence on state institutions; the modern intelligentsia is thus an open stratum, lacking a unified world view, democratic and sceptical in outlook. Their marginal social position makes the modern intelligentsia highly sensitive to the political and cultural fragmentation of the modern world:

> These unattached intellectuals are the typical advocate-philosophers, *ideologues* who can find arguments in favour of any political cause they may happen to serve. Their own social position does not bind them to any cause, but they have an extraordinarily refined sense for all the political and social currents (Mannheim, 1953, pp. 126–7).

As examples Mannheim cites both Enlightenment philosophy and Romanticism as currents of thought developed by intellectuals acting as the spokesmen for specific social groups. Intellectuals effectively give theoretical expression to the material interests of social groups and classes and in so doing become the allies of such groups and classes without belonging to them. Thus Mannheim describes Kant's critical philosophy as expressing the 'inner nature' of the French Revolution, not because Kant identified with its political aims, but 'because the form of his thought . . . (was) of the same brand as that which was the dynamic force behind the French revolutionaries' (Mannheim, 1953, p. 84).

Mannheim's sociological writings tended to emphasise the essentially passive role played by the intellectual in the formation of styles of thought: at times Mannheim's work approximates to vulgar Marxism especially the formulation of intellectuals as merely expressing the 'appropriate' thought of a specific social group or class. This is especially the case with one of his major studies, 'Conservative Thought' (1925). Here Mannheim distinguished 'Conservative' thought from 'Traditional' thought in terms of the former's reflective structure, arguing that in the wake of the French Revolution and the rise of more open, socially mobile societies, new secular philosophies and the disintegration of the static pre-industrial world view, 'Conservative' thought emerged as a self-conscious mode of opposition both to individualistic capitalism and the collective philosophy of nascent socialism. In particular 'Conservative' thought stressed the organic nature of society, the importance of family and corporations in opposition to the atomistic philosophy of Social Contract philosophy with its stress on the inalienable rights of the individual and values of popular sovereignty. Human life was fundamentally irrational and historical development conceived as an organic not mechanical process. In this way 'Conservative' thought legitimised opposition to industrial capitalism, individualism, liberalism and socialism.

The new industrial society of the early nineteenth century could no longer be legitimised through appeals to traditional values as such: thus the 'unattached intelligentsia', unable to articulate its own distinctive interests and secure an autonomous social position, identified with the conservative reaction against the values of Enlightenment (Mannheim's analysis focuses mainly on Germany with its weak industrial base and fragmented political system). It is precisely because intellectuals are relatively unattached to specific material interests that they lack their own ideology but remain highly sensitive to existing social and political currents: 'By themselves they know nothing. But let them take up and identify themselves with someone else's interests – they will know them better, really better, than those for whom these interests are laid down by the nature of things, by their social condition' (Mannheim, 1953, p. 127).

In Mannheim's later work, intellectuals constitute more than a passive instrument of a specific class. In *Ideology and Utopia* intellectuals have the task of elucidating the category of totality through synthesising different perspectives, a process not bound up with class interests (as with Lukács's proletarian and bourgeois thought concepts for example). Later, in the essay on the intelligentsia, written during the 1930s, although not published until after his death, this emphasis on totality is replaced by empathy. As an open stratum the relatively free intelligentsia participates in historical experience from a variety of different perspectives; reality is multiple and not single centred, the product of increasing social mobility and complexity of modern society. Thus intellectuals empathise with other standpoints and enter a critical dialogue developing an attitude of 'fruitful scepticism'. It is the structural and cognitive openness of the intelligentsia which Mannheim identified as the means of making sense of the many conflicting ideologies that characterise the modern age.

Ideology and Utopia

These arguments find their first formulation in *Ideology and Utopia*. In this work Mannheim distinguished ideology from Utopia by defining ideology as the process whereby the thought of a ruling group becomes so interest bound that it no longer comprehends the existence of facts which might undermine its claim to domination. Ideology implies 'that in certain situations the collective unconscious of certain groups obscures the real condition of society both to itself and to others and thereby stabilises it'. In contrast, Utopian thought reflects the struggles of oppressed groups to seek change thus seeing only 'those elements in the situation which tend to negate it'. Utopian thought is thus incapable of a valid analysis of an existing situation only of grasping the possible negative elements in situations: as examples of Utopian thought Mannheim cites the orgiastic chiliasm of the Anabaptists, Liberal humanitarianism, Communist socialism, all of which are structured around concepts 'incongruous' with the existing state of reality. Only intellectuals, from their privileged vantage point, can provide historically objective knowledge through their ability to synthesise the valid elements from different perspectives. Truth is historical and holistic: neither Utopian nor ideological thought can grasp the historical whole.

In *Ideology and Utopia* Mannheim sketched an evolutionary development of utopian thought beginning with chiliasm and ending with Socialist-Humanism. He noted the difficulties in distinguishing the utopian and ideological modes of action suggesting that the utopias 'of ascendent classes are often . . . permeated with ideological elements'. Thus the world view of the ascendant bourgeoisie embraced the Utopian ideal of human freedom (in opposition to the static corporatist ideal of feudal society) which was ideological in that it was actually realised historically: Mannheim described bourgeois freedom as 'a relative utopia' (Mannheim, 1960, pp. 183–4). His basic argument remained resolutely historicist: 'our ideas and existence are components of a comprehensive evolutionary process (in which) conservative and progressive ideas appear as derivatives of this process' (Mannheim, 1952, p. 146). The result is that the distinction between Utopia and ideology is made *ex post facto* since it was clearly impossible at the time to know if bourgeois freedom could be realised in bourgeois society. Many of Mannheim's arguments have this *ex post facto* character and his sociological theorems on the relation of knowledge and society are couched in such terms as 'appropriate to the situation', 'in accord with the needs of the time', 'never by accident that' (Merton, 1957, pp. 498–9). In effect, the criterion of truth becomes the adequacy of thought to an existing reality, a functionalist rather than an historicist standpoint.

Mannheim's sociology of knowledge thus embraced two distinct theoretical positions: first, a correspondence theory of knowledge in which styles of thought were related to definite social groups and social locations, and secondly, an historicist conception of truth and validity in tension with the functionalist notion of 'appropriateness' and 'needs'.

Knowledge and mass society: Mannheim and the Frankfurt School

Mannheim's historicism led him to develop a sociology of knowledge which lacked a distinctive sociological theory of society. Thus although he discussed the production of knowledge in its relation to social groups, social classes and social location, the links between these components of social structure and forms of thought are untheorised. In his later writings, following exile from Germany in the 1930s, Mannheim developed a theory of mass society which is close to that articulated by the Marxist Frankfurt School.

The school took its name from the Frankfurt Institute for Social Research established in Germany in 1923. Its leading members were Theodore Adorno (1903–70), Max Horkheimer (1895–1973), and Herbert Marcuse (1898–1978). Like Mannheim, they were deeply influenced by German idealism, the pessimistic cultural sociology of Simmel and Weber, and the philosophically oriented Marxism of Lukács and Karl Korsch (1886–1961). Unlike Mannheim, the Frankfurt theorists accepted the broad arguments of Marxism but followed Lukács and Korsch in criticising its tendency towards positivism, evolutionism and scientism. Marxism was predominantly a critique of capitalist society and its forms of knowledge; thus the emphasis was placed on consciousness, *praxis* and human values. But unlike Lukács and Korsch, the Frankfurt School remained aloof from politics believing that the proletariat had become integrated into what they called 'organised capitalism' and thereby lost its revolutionary historical role.

The Frankfurt School's theory of society is profoundly pessimistic. Mannheim, too, adopted a pessimistic standpoint. The rise of totalitarian governments – Communist and Fascist – led him to argue that the historical trend of modern society was one of increasing centralisation and atomism: the social and political institutions, essential for a democratic society, were increasingly losing their autonomy. An inevitable escalation of bureaucratisation, a burgeoning army of technical 'experts', a transformation of knowledge into a commodity to be manipulated in the interests of social order, all these effectively undermined the autonomous role of the intellectual. The relatively free intelligentsia becomes problematic as intellectuals are assimilated by centralised, bureaucratic state institutions. In 'The Problem of the Intelligentsia' Mannheim wrote:

> Free inquiry is . . . losing its social basis through the decline of the independent middle classes from which . . . an older type of the relatively unattached intelligentsia used to recruit itself. No other stratum or alternative plan has arisen to assure the continued existence of independent and uncommitted critics (Mannheim, 1956, p. 169).

There is thus a sharp, unresolved tension in Mannheim's work between his pessimistic theory of the social role of the modern intelligentsia and his optimistic sociological–historical theory of intellectuals, as a relatively free social stratum developed by the processes of industrialisation with its tendency towards secularisation, bureaucratisation and multi-polarity of views. Mannheim's thesis of the necessary rise of modern 'mass society' and the eclipse of a strong, independent civil society led him towards a concept of intellectuals as standing above all class interests and the dehumanising trends of modern society, an élite whose 'proper' function was as moral guardians of society as a whole.

The Frankfurt School, too, advanced a theory of mass society and mass culture: capitalism, they argued, had become increasingly centralised and its social structure progressively 'atomised'. In the nineteenth century the bourgeoisie had enlarged the 'public sphere', institutions separate from the state through which they conducted their business and organised their culture. But with the development of a centralised economy and polity, collectivist ideologies emerge which emphasise conformity to the social system. The public sphere shrivels: the social structure no longer contains strong, independent institutions that guarantee individual values. The autonomous individual disappears. In this process science played an important 'instrumentalist' role: the scientistic, anti-humanist principles of bourgeois science permeate society as a whole and lead inevitably to a new mode of domination centred in technology and bureaucracy. Consciousness and culture become alienated from the realm of human action, values and *praxis*. The relation between individuals increasingly becomes a relation between things.

To combat the threat of scientistic positivism, the Frankfurt School, whose leading theorists worked within an academic context, proposed the concept of 'critical theory'. Like Gramsci's notion of the philosophy of *praxis*, the term critical theory largely implied Marxism. It was a Marxism which emphasised the active role of cognition and rejected the 'copy', or reflection theory of knowledge: theory was defined as an autonomous practice, a critical element in the transformation of society and culture. The leading figures of the Frankfurt School rejected Lukács's historicist identification of the proletariat with historical truth, but followed many of his other arguments such as the universality of reification within capitalism, and the methodological importance of categories such as totality, negativity, dialectics and mediation in the analysis of ideological and cultural forms. The school concentrated on cultural analysis and their substantive studies included problems of aesthetics, literature, art and music ('high' or intellectual culture), the operas of Wagner, the twelve-note music of Berg and Schoenberg and modernist fiction (Proust, Kafka, Beckett). Culture was the realm of humanity's essential being, not economics or politics; humanity defined its goals and purposes and affirmed itself through cultural forms which resisted incorporation into the alienated structure of industrial society. Mass culture was the ultimate denial of affirmative culture, the means whereby the individual is stripped of individuality, creativity and autonomy.

Critical theory concerned itself with truth, with universality and emancipation. Mannheim's argument that knowledge was socially related to specific historical locations was rejected because it undermined the crucial distinction between 'true' and 'false' knowledge. The Frankfurt School were sceptical of the whole notion of the sociology of knowledge since they identified sociology with positivism, agnosticism and relativism. Marxism was not a sociology in this sense, concerned as it was with human *praxis*, meaning and emancipation. To suggest that the partial perspectives opened up by the historical process might be synthesised into truth by free-floating intellectuals was to advance a mechanical *Gestalt* theory of truth and a metaphysical notion of totality. Mannheim's sociology of knowledge assumed the existence of an objective historical reality which was reflected imperfectly in human consciousness: for the Frankfurt School, reality was created through *praxis* in which subject and object were dialectically unified. Underlying the Frankfurt School's epistemology was the Hegelian concept of totality and its expression in the laws of society and history. Critical theory did not relate different forms of thought to particular social groups, but rather sought to 'decipher the general social tendencies which are expressed in these phenomena' and thus bring to consciousness contradictions, negativity and the lack of harmony of individual to society (Adorno, 1967, p. 32).

In his essay, 'Critical and Traditional Theory' (1937), Horkheimer had argued that the goal of bourgeois, positivist science was 'pure' knowledge, not action. Whereas critical theory was based in *praxis*, traditional theory (that is, positivism) separated thought and action, establishing the authority of observation over imagination, and advocating the methods of the natural sciences, especially biology, in the analysis of socio-cultural phenomena. Knowledge was thus 'fetishised' as something standing apart from, and superior to, human action. But this kind of disinterested research was impossible within the framework of capitalist, mass society for it assumed an autonomous individual researcher. In reality, however, the researcher's perception was always mediated through social categories which in the context of modern society meant reification. Bourgeois science, including social science, was linked organically to technical control, technological domination and instrumental rationality. For Horkheimer, only in a non-reified, rational world was prediction – of of the principles of positivist science – possible. The basic distinction, therefore, between critical and traditional theory, was that the former rejected the bourgeois illusion of the autonomous scientist and the goal of a politically neutral objective knowledge. Critical theory postulated an inseparable relation between knowledge and interests. But knowledge was not produced automatically; it required the active intervention of intellectuals. Thus although rejecting Mannheim's sociology of knowledge, the Frankfurt School advanced a modified version of the concept of the free floating intellectual. For only intellectuals can consciously reveal the negative and contradictory forces at work within society through their commitment to critical thought and 'emancipatory interests'.

Methodologically, the Frankfurt School developed a notion of immanent criticism: they argued that the methods of social science should be 'adequate' to its objects. Since objects are neither static nor external but made through human action and mediated by human values and subjectivity, social scientific method must start from the concepts and principles of the object itself and not from its appearances and surface reality. The concepts, however, were not identical with the object because they sought to uncover both the object's immanent tendencies as well as its relation with the wider whole. The objects of social science become known only through practice, through the subject transforming reality. Thus truth constituted a 'moment' of 'correct' practice. But what was correct practice? For Horkheimer, correct action meant action linked with emancipatory interests which were distinguished from class or group interests by their universality and authenticity (Horkheimer, 1976).

In an important sense, therefore, the Frankfurt School's critique of positivism and bourgeois science was less dependent on Marx's class theory than on Lukács's idealist, anti-sociological treatment of alienation and reification in *History and Class Consciousness*, with its assumption of a universal human essence manifestly corrupted by the workings of capitalism and technology. The concept of emancipatory interests is clearly *a priori*, speculative historicism and such phrases as the 'furthering of human emancipation' or the striving of humanity towards the possibilities of utopia (Marcuse, Adorno) sociologically meaningless. Whereas Marx had developed beyond his early philosophical works towards a positive science, the Frankfurt School abandoned empirical sociology in favour of abstract, pessimistic speculation.

12
Democracy, Industrialisation and Sociological Theory

In this book I have argued that sociology originated in eighteenth-century philosophy, political economy and cultural history. Eighteenth-century social theory embraced both a voluntaristic pole – Vico for example – as well as a deterministic, systemic perspective – Montesquieu. The tension between these two approaches to the study of human society dominated the subsequent development of sociological positivism and Marxism. It needs emphasising that although Vico, Montesquieu, Ferguson and Millar laid the foundations for sociological theory their work was not sociology: the complex socio-historical relation between action and structure remained untheorised. Ferguson's concept of the unintended consequences of human action was never integrated with the notion of society as a system: it was Hegelian philosophy which transposed Ferguson's voluntaristic element into an organic part of totality. Later Marx developed these negative and contradictory notions into the dichotomy of the capitalist system, structured in objective laws of change, and class agency, structured in collective consciousness and political organisation. Marx's contemporaries, Comte and Spencer, equally conceived society as an organic whole, its structure determined by specific laws of evolution, but the action element was ultimately subordinated to the system and the whole.

Comte, Marx and Spencer grasped the concept of society as a dynamic system evolving historically and inevitably towards complex industrial structures. Although these writers differed sharply in their analysis of modern capitalist society they shared one common theme: that industrial society constituted a new form of social organisation built around the separation of state and civil society. Industrialism expanded the institutions of industrial society and thus produced the institutional framework that enabled individuals, as members of different social collectivities (associated with education, communications, political organisation, trade unions, etc.), to change society. Nevertheless, the early sociologists were deeply sceptical of bourgeois society: but it was classical sociology, with its themes of alienation, urbanism, anomie, rationalisation, bureaucratisation, reification, mechanisation which advanced a pessimistic theory of bourgeois culture. Durkheim, Tönnies, Weber and Simmel were as concerned with the collapse and disintegration of old, traditional social orders as they were with the rise of a fluid, dynamic industrial and egalitarian democratic society. Industrialisation seemed to lead to a culture hostile to human values. These tensions are nowhere more evident than in Weber's sociology which succeeds in analysing social change both in terms of objective structure and subjective human action, yet concludes pessimistically that the fate of humanity is necessarily one of increasing bureaucratisation and the domination, from above, of specialised élites.

Marxism, industrialism and democracy

The history of sociology and the history of Marxism are directly linked to these developments. At the turn of the century, European sociology engaged in a debate with Marxism which raised precisely the problems of democratic structures within the framework of advancing industrialism. The pessimism of classical sociology largely flowed from its failure to grasp the enormous democratic energies which capitalism in its historical development had, and would continue, to release. One might say that classical sociology lacked a dialectical sense of historical change. The structural complexity of the social formation was frequently assimilated to an abstractly con-

ceived universal process, or universal history – the rationalisation of culture, total reification, functional consensus, mass
society and mass culture.

As with sociology so with Marxism. In some of his writings
Marx had emphasised the crucially significant and creative
role played by the active human subject (*praxis*) in the
formation of an open, decentralised, socialist society. Yet the
basic trend of Marxist thought was away from such libertarian
conceptions towards a deterministic, economic theory of
historical change in which human action is meaningful only in
terms of the emergent social order lying within the womb of
the old society: thus social institutions, social change, culture,
could all be assimilated to the dominant underlying economic
system. Human agents were effectively transformed into passive
objects. The inherent collectivism of Marxism, both its conceptual framework and political ideology, led to the evolutionary,
undemocratic, élitist collectivism of German Social Democracy
(so perceptively analysed by Michels), the centralised party of
Leninist theory and the totalitarian ideology of Stalinism. The
core of Marxist theory lay in its ideology of finalisation (history
has a definite, single meaning) and collectivist political prescriptions (the rising class must organise society as a whole
from the centre in terms of its specific interests). But the
problem is that Marxist political and social finalisation con-
tradicts the historical logic of capitalist industrialism. Modern
industrial societies, far from being structured around a single
dominant centre – contradiction or class force – increasingly
developed open-ended, decentred social structures. Politically,
Marxism leads to the annihilation of civil society as a living and
active force built around democratic institutions. In general,
the main trends of twentieth-century Marxism, the 'humanist'
form that stems from a concern with alienation and dehumanisation of the subject, the so-called 'scientific' form associated
with structuralism, have both denigrated the capacity of the
human subject to democratise, humanise and understand the
necessity for collectivist, democratic change *from below*. Implicit
in both forms is a conception of Marxism as finalised ideology
of both subject and structure.

Yet there is a crucial difference between Marxist finalisation
and the pessimism of classical sociology. Tönnies, Weber and

Simmel described modern industrial society in negative terms but they also grasped the possibilities latent within industrial development. Classical sociology, unlike Marxism, stressed the complex ambiguity of modern society, its open structures – mobility, class relationships, democratisation, increasing dialogic modes of communication – as well as its tendency towards closure – rationalisation of culture, reification, lack of community. Both were present simultaneously. In America, Charles Cooley drew attention precisely to the structural significance of primary groups in industrial society, and although noting that societies built around primary groups were often tyrannical in their assimilation of the individual to collective norms, industrialisation and democratisation nevertheless create the conditions for 'a higher and freer consciousness' enabling the individual to become a rational member and not 'blind agent' of the social whole (Cooley, 1956, p. 116).

For Cooley, modern society was essentially decentred, consisting of a network of strong primary groups within distinctive communities. This structure enabled individuals to create for themselves differing loyalties and ideologies. Cooley's optimism is in sharp contrast to the later, post-classical sociology of the Chicago School of urban studies. Robert Park and his associated, influenced especially by Simmel, interpreted the development of industrialism some-what negatively: society was depicted in a state of ecological disorder, the modern city described as the locus of human isolation in which community has collapsed under population pressure and the 'massness' of the culture. Later American sociologists – a major exception was Talcott Parsons – subscribed uncritically to this gloomy perspective on modern industrial culture. Perhaps one of the major American sociologists to sympathise with this pessimistic theoretical standpoint was C. Wright Mills (1916–62) who, in a series of influential studies – notably, *White Collar* (1952) and *The Power Elite* (1956) – described post-Second World War America as a society lacking an independent middle class, resilient community ties and a strong civil society. For Mills, modern American constituted an atomised mass society, its institutions and culture dominated by a pervasive commercial ideology and values and a military–industrial complex which functioned to integrate individuals passively into a bureaucratised system. Far from expanding popular democratic institutions, capitalist industrialism had produced a society dominated by élites active in industry, culture and politics: as power was concentrated in different élite groups so the mass of the population exercised no influence on the conduct of public life (Mills, 1956, pp. 301–20).

Mills's conclusions, on the inevitable drift towards totalitarianism within American society is broadly similar to Herbert Marcuse's argument, advanced in his *One Dimensional Man*, that modern industrial societies are converging towards systems of total administration. But such pessimism is both historically inaccurate and sociologically naïve. Mills and Marcuse, like the Frankfurt School, abstract one tendency from within the social formation and assume that it constitutes the dominant principle – the centre or essence of the system – in the logic of social development. But as I have argued, the logic of industrialism is both to augment state power through increasing bureaucratic centralisation, and strengthen the autonomous institutions of civil society. Classical sociology laid down the foundations for understanding this highly complex process – in particular the problem of the subject, ideology, consciousness – but both Marxism and Marxist-influenced sociology failed to develop such insights.

Contemporary American critics of the mass society thesis, such as Daniel Bell and Edward Shils, have emphasised the complexity of industrial culture and society, that despite the continued existence of income inequality, status and power, there remains a strong sense of attachment to society as a whole. Industrial society is not a mass society but one structured in pluralistic institutions and democratic processes. Community has survived into the industrial age. Of the three macrosociological theories which have dominated the development of sociology since the 1920s – Marxism, Functionalism, Mass Society – only the mass society argument glances backwards to a mythical past when community and individual autonomy were 'genuinely' resilient, active forces. In opposition to mass society Shils has argued for a consensual society based upon centralised government and administration and independent pressure groups which represent different and often conflicting interests:

> These institutions . . . can exist because a widespread consensus, particularly a consensus of the most active members of the society, legitimises them, and, more fundamentally, because a more general and more amorphous consensus of the less active imposes restraint on the more active . . . The consensus grows in part from an attachment to the centre, to the central institutional system and value order of society (Shils, 1972).

Thus although acknowledging the importance of civil society and the possibility of popular democratic forms, Shils's sociological pluralism follows Functionalism and Marxism in minimising the importance, both to society as a system and the subject as agent, of active, oppositional values and culture. Society is conceived around a central core of values and democratic processes defined in terms of centralised decision making.

As I noted at the end of Chapter 8, Functionalism became the dominant paradigm within Western sociology immediately after the end of the Second World War. At the same time Marxism was widely held to be an ideology, intellectually exhausted and of dubious sociological value. Mass society theory was thus the alternative to Marxism and Functionalism. Although influential during the 1950s and early 1960s, the theory has become increasingly marginal to sociology. New theories of industrial society and culture have emerged. The most significant is the theory of the post-industrial society.

The theory of post-industrial society

During the 1950s a number of eminent sociologists, such as Daniel Bell, S. M. Lipset, Raymond Aron and Ralf Dahrendorf, argued against what they saw as the static, ahistorical bias of Functionalism and the worn-out ideological historicism of Marxism by advancing a concept of post-industrialism (although the term varied from one sociologist to another – 'post-capitalist', 'post-bourgeois society', the 'technological society', the 'knowledge society' – in essentials it suggested the priority of technology, science and culture over private property and class divisions). Post-industrial society was contrasted with nineteenth-century capitalist society and twentieth-century industrial society in terms of the transformation of social structure: post-industrial society constituted a social formation in which private property, class interests and class conflict had lost their centrality as 'axial principles'. The social structure of capitalist and industrial society was largely organised around the axis of private property; post-industrial society is organised around the axis of 'theoretical knowledge'. In *The Coming of Post-Industrial Society* (1973) Bell argues that the 'energising principle' of modern societies will increasingly be centred within the educational, scientific and governmental institutions. The traditional business firm and the entrepreneur are in the process of being replaced by scientists, economists and engineers. The source of innovation and policy-making is no longer the business enterprise but the university.

Bell's general thesis rests on his argument that modern society is organised into three separate although related realms: the economy, the polity and the culture. The polity regulates the distribution of power and the different interests in society; the culture, as the realm of self-realisation, establishes meaning through the expressiveness of art and ritual: the economic realm relates to the social structure. Each is ruled by different axial principles: self-realisation in culture, equality in politics, efficiency in economics. Thus society as a whole is not organised around one dominant element or integrated into a single system. There is always a disjunction between the different realms so that culture, for example, may repudiate the axial principle of economic efficiency and rationality in favour of irrational, hedonistic modernism with its rejection of tradition and established institutions. Similarly, the axial problem of the polity 'is the relation between the desire for popular participation and bureaucracy' (Bell, 1976, p. 115). Each of these spheres has its own inner logic and contradictory nature. Prediction and forecasting generally in the cultural and political realms is thus hazardous and Bell's main emphasis is on the economic sphere. Thus:

The concept of a post-industrial society is not a picture of a complete social order; it is an attempt to describe and explain an axial change in the social structure (defined as the economy, the technology and the stratification system) of the society. But such a change implies no specific determinism between a 'base' and a 'superstructure' . . . it is likely that the various societies that are entering a post-industrial phase will have different political and cultural configurations (Bell, 1976, p. 119).

As with other post-capitalist theses, Bell's concept of post-industrial society assumes the decline of manual labour and the rapid growth of white collar work, service industries, professional groups and greater expenditure on higher education, research and development. As society is transformed from one largely dominated by the production of goods to one dominated by the production of theoretical knowledge a new social structure will emerge. In modern societies, theory dominates empiricism in the areas of science, economics and computer studies. The scientist, the mathematicians, the computer-technologist and the economic theorist rise to prominence to form what Bell calls a distinct 'knowledge class'. At the heart of post-industrial society is a professional class embodying norms of social responsiveness derived from an ethics of service to the community. The profit motive has no place within the burgeoning research institutes and universities. This professional–scientific class will eventually saturate society with its professional values: Bell distinguishes his position from earlier writers such as Saint-Simon by defining the new class as those who apply their knowledge to the organisation of society as a whole. It is not a question of technocrats exercising power, but rather the production of new values and principles of organisation.

Bell's work describes many of the basic changes which are occurring within modern industrial societies, although he exaggerates the significance of the autonomy of theoretical knowledge. In many modern industrial societies, for example, the proportion of Gross National Product devoted to pure science is significantly smaller than that channelled into practical research and research in already established areas. Research and development is not yet dominated by theoretical knowledge. More pertinently, the argument that the new science-based professions generate their own immanent values (universal rather than particular, opposed to profit and for the community) is difficult to sustain in view of the frequent involvement of academic intellectuals in government defence projects and foreign policy objectives. The post-industrial thesis assumes, further, that market forces will eventually disappear as the axis of organisation and change: yet one of the most significant contributions to the development of pure economic theory in the last twenty years, monetarism, has focused both on the centrality of market forces in the formation of a democratic system and the irrelevance of government and centralised authority and bureaucracy to involve itself in economic management.

Many critics of the post-industrial thesis have emphasised the persistence of class inequalities, class conflict, the concentration of economic resources in a few hands, the unskilled nature of white collar work and the tendency towards the professionalisation of all occupations, thus diluting the norm of professionalism itself. But the most important aspect of Bell's theory is its advocacy, as historically inevitable, of a planned, centralised, rationalised and bureaucratised social system. The post-industrial theory thus maintains a continuity with classical sociology. But the logic of industrialism was not, as Bell and others have argued, to separate the economic from the political and cultural spheres and thus enable authority to be centralised and autonomous within the polity: the logic of industrialism was both to centralise society and produce the possibilities of democratic decentralisation. It is this dialectic which Bell assimilates to an élitist and finalised notion of post-industrialism. In Bell's theory the human agent plays no role in the shaping of the culture, the polity or the economy. The planners and the technocrats, basing their policy decisions on theoretical knowledge and a professional ethos, effectively neutralise popular democratic forms and active political institutions. A bureaucratic, administrative relation subsists between rulers and ruled: the logic of post-industrial society is thus to eliminate dialogic modes of communication and the ambiguity of human discourse and action. There is a deep vein of pessimism running through Bell's thesis, a distrust of the institutions of civil society:

His political world is still pluralist, but afflicted by 'populism' and *ressentiment*. The tranquillity of the 1950s élite pluralism seems to have been rudely upset by the political claims of all sorts of non-élite groups (blacks, students, women, workers, etc) . . . No longer vaunting the virtues of America as democracy embodied, Bell clearly prefers rule by the élites (Ross, 1974, p. 346).

The post-industrial thesis shares the élitist standpoint of the Frankfurt School and fits neatly into the general drift of much modern sociology which increasingly neglects the possibilities for democratisation *from below*.

Problems of legitimation

If post-industrial society is to be organised politically *from above* then the problem of democracy is clearly posed. Post-industrial society would remain a democratic system based on consensual values. The disjunction between the economic, cultural and political realms creates contradictions notably those related to cultural values and economic goals. A culture based on hedonistic rather than the values of the Protestant ethic cannot generate the necessary pattern of motivation for sustained economic growth. Bell describes this as perhaps the major crisis in the transition from industrial to post-industrial society. There is, in short, a problem of accumulation (of capital) and a potential crisis of legitimacy (of values). The state must provide both 'a unified direction for the economy' in relation to a notion of the common good, and adjudicate between the differing claims of various competing groups. Bell writes:

> The economic dilemmas confronting Western societies derive from the fact that we have sought to combine bourgeois appetites which resist curbs on acquisitiveness, either morally or by taxation; a democratic polity which, increasingly and understandably, demands more and more social services as entitlements; and an individualist ethos which, at best defends the idea of personal liberty, and at worst evades the necessary social responsibilities and social sacrifices which a communal society demands (Bell, 1979, pp. 248–9).

In the long run the solution lies in the communal ethos of post-industrial culture. And Bell notes ironically that the term post-industrial was employed initially by the utopian-minded followers of William Morris to describe the alternative society to undemocratic individualistic, profit-geared capitalism. Bell's vision, however, is a tough-minded realism: human society must be regulated and ordered by values which originate, not in 'the people' but from the élite of scientists and technologists.

Bell shares with the Frankfurt School the view of modern society as essentially collectivist. The state increasingly acts independently of the economic and cultural spheres. The separation of the economy from the polity and the culture constitutes the basic problem of legitimation in that politics is no longer simply one element of the superstructure of society but is actively involved in securing mass loyalty to the social system and continued economic reproduction. Much of modern sociology and Marxism has become preoccupied with the problem of the state and its relation with other elements of the social formation. To what extent is the state a specific and autonomous structure characterised by its own immanent laws and processes? In the analysis of the state (or the political order) is it necessary to elaborate concepts specific to the political structure? In general, Marxist theory has tended to analyse the state structure in terms of concepts derived from the economic system, that is, the state reproduces the social conditions necessary for capital accumulation and functions in the long-run interests of the dominant class. Bell's work is one example of avoiding such reductionism. Similarly, Jurgen Habermas (1929) has developed a Marxist-inspired sociology addressed to the problems of legitimation and social cohesion within modern industrial society.

Habermas's work owes a great deal to the Frankfurt School theory of state-regulated capitalism. His analysis of modern society incorporates many of the concepts of critical theory – knowledge is interest-bound; the goal of social theory is emancipation not technical control; positivism has long ceased as an emancipatory method as it was during the eighteenth and early nineteenth century when it advanced a critique of metaphysics; science and technology have become increasingly enmeshed with production and administration; social consciousness has become technocratic and structured in instrumental reason.

For Habermas, capitalist society has become a state–capitalist system, highly centralised and regulated. The public sphere, which functioned to mediate society and the state in nineteenth-century capitalism, has been eclipsed with the growth of technology and bureaucracy. Institutions which normally function to articulate and communicate public opinion have become commercialised and depoliticised. An atomised, mass society is the result.

Habermas focuses on the crises tendencies and the legitimation problems of state or 'late' capitalism. In his analysis Habermas employs categories derived from a variety of intellectual sources ranging from modern system theory to Marx, Freud, Mead, Piaget and Parsons. Sociological theory, he argues, must combine an emphasis on both action and system, subject and structure. The study of legitimation involves objective structures such as the state and economy, as well as motivation and patterns of communication. 'From Hegel through Freud to Piaget the idea has developed that subject and object are reciprocally constituted, that the subject can grasp hold of itself only in relation to and by way of the construction of an objective world.' Thus social systems are 'networks of communicative actions' involving socialised personalities and speaking subjects (Habermas, 1979, pp. 98–100). Crisis is defined at the level of the social system and the socialised actor:

A social-scientifically appropriate crisis concept must grasp the connection between system integration and social integration. The two expressions 'social integration' and 'system integration' derive from different theoretical traditions. We speak of social integration in relation to the systems of institutions in which speaking and acting subjects are socially related. Social systems are seen here as *life-worlds* that are symbolically structured. We speak of system integration with a view to the specific steering performances of a self-regulated *system* . . . Both paradigms, life-world and system, are important. The problem is to demonstrate their interconnection (Habermas, 1976, p. 4).

Social system and life-world combines both objective, structural forces with subjective, voluntaristic, psychological motivation. Nevertheless, the general tendency is for Habermas to analyse social institutions and development from the standpoint of system integration.

He identifies three sub-systems – economic, political–administrative, socio-cultural. Crisis tendencies within late capitalism can arise at different points within the social system and they are not simply economic in character. Habermas suggests a typology of four possible crisis tendencies (Habermas, 1976, p. 45):

Point of Origin	System Crisis	Identity Crisis
Economic System	Economic Crisis	—
Political System	Rationality Crisis	Legitimation Crisis
Socio-Cultural System	—	Motivation Crisis

Late capitalism has produced a shift in the pattern of motivation that characterised the historical development of capitalist society. A crisis of motivation occurs when the socio-cultural system (values oriented to labour, etc.) no longer functions to socialise individuals into roles, occupations and cultural institutions. A rationality crisis occurs when the administrative system can no longer reconcile and fulfil the 'imperatives received from the economic system', that is, the allocation of adequate rewards for labour (consumerism) and the necessity for capital accumulation. It is at this stage that a crisis of legitimacy may occur. The social system depends on a widespread acceptance of rules and laws, on patterns of normative integration and social identity thus enabling agents to recognise the 'worthiness' of the political order. But if culture becomes 'privatised' through consumerist ideology, an object of private enjoyment, it runs the danger of becoming separated from the socialisation process and therefore no longer functioning to integrate the personality system with the social system: 'The less the cultural system is capable of producing adequate motivations for politics, the educational system, and the occupational system, the more must scarce meaning be replaced by consumable values.' Legitimation becomes problematical with the development of 'inflexible normative structures that no longer provide the economic–political system with ideological resources, but instead confront it with exorbitant demands' (Habermas, 1976, pp. 91–3).

Habermas's crisis theorems are advanced as tentative hypotheses. Nevertheless, he seeks to describe the broad tendencies of advanced, late capitalist societies and his general theory rests on the Frankfurt School argument of a declining public sphere and a depoliticised public world. Historically bourgeois society was able to generate adequate motivational structures from its socio-cultural system. But with the development of a centralised state system institutions increasingly function to control and plan from the centre. If culture is privatised – or atomised – it leaves the administrative–political system with the task of producing motivational values; and this it cannot do. The state system produces ideological values which justify the existing structures. Thus the problem: the state apparatuses of late capitalism will inevitably encounter 'long-term insoluble problems', for if the state itself is identified as the producer of ideological values – as the source of social integration – a legitimation crisis develops: 'A legitimation crisis . . . must be based on a motivation crisis – that is, a discrepancy between the need for motives declared by the state, the educational system and the occupational system on the one hand, and the motivation supplied by the socio-cultural system on the other' (Habermas, 1976 pp. 74–5).

Ultimately democrary itself is threatened. Industrialisation, far from enriching human society, expanding the realm of the possible, inevitably transforms individuals into passive, private objects whose actions are entirely dependent on the functioning of the social system. Legitimation problems develop because of disjunctions between the various sub-systems, the inability of the socio-cultural sphere to provide adequately for the 'needs' of the economic sphere. Thus Habermas's position is remarkably close to Parsonian functionalism in his assumption that the source of action and change and contradiction and crisis within advanced industrial society is the system and not the subject.

Theory and industrial society: convergence or diversity?

Since the collapse of sociological functionalism as the major paradigm of Western sociology only Marxism, in its various forms, and the mass society thesis have attempted to develop a total theory of industrial society. The theory of post-industrial society constitutes the single exception but it has yet to be developed as a general sociological theory comparable with Parsonian functionalism or Marxism. As I have suggested, Habermas's work advances a totalising conception of social science and is, in many ways, a return to 'grand theory'. Like Parsons, Habermas seeks to assimilate the systemic, holistic approach (drawing on Marxism and Parsonian systems theory) and a dynamic, voluntaristic theory of communicative human action (drawing on the work of Mead, Freud, Piaget, Goldmann and Chomsky). Thus like Parsons in the 1930s, Habermas is arguing for a convergence of sociological theory. But unlike Parsons, Habermas emphasises the 'emancipatory' role of social theory rejecting the scientistic objectivism and acceptance of the status quo characteristic of sociological functionalism and nineteenth-century grand theory. Stressing his continuity with the ideas of the Frankfurt School, Habermas attempts to synthesise systemic structural analysis with *praxis*.

As I have argued throughout this book, sociological theory is concerned both with society as a structure and system, and with the human subject as constituting a theory of action or practice. Much of nineteenth-century sociology diminished the action element in favour of an ongoing evolutionary process. Yet even here the dualism of action and structure was evident constituting an important contradiction within sociology itself. It was the failure of nineteenth-century positivism and Marxism to resolve this contradiction which led to the development of 'voluntaristic' action theory, in its various forms, during the years 1880 to 1920. The human subject was rediscovered: in Weber's theory of social change, Simmel's concept of culture, Gramsci's notion of hegemony, Lukács's theory of consciousness and ideology. During the 1960s many of these ideas became the basis of what was called 'radical' sociology: rejecting functionalism and holistic Marxism, 'new' sociologies were discovered centred on the constituting subject – phenomenology, ethnomethodology, humanist Marxism, 'reflexive sociology'. An artificial distinction emerged between system and action: Comte, Marx and Parsons versus Weber, Mead, Freud and Schutz. A characteristic work was Berger and Luckmann's *The Social Construction of Reality* (1966) which argued for the 'young Marx' and the theory of alienation and dehumanisation, and against the 'old Marx' and the theory of laws of development and large-scale systemic change. A theory which postulated the concept of system and laws, objective structures and processes was deemed anti-humanist. But it was Alvin Gouldner, in his *The Coming Crisis of Western Sociology* (1971), who captured the prevailing mood in his concept of reflexive sociology.

For Gouldner, all social theory 'has both political and personal relevance' and is never simply the product of logic and empirical evidence but of the sociologists' 'whole social existence' (Gouldner, 1973 pp. 148–9). It is this lack of self-awareness on the part of the sociologists which constitutes the fundamental weakness of academic sociology. Gouldner's argument is that sociology, in its historical development, was both radical or critical, and conservative. But with the rise of the modern welfare state and highly centralised industrial systems, sociological theory has become predominantly conservative: sociologists are directly implicated 'as consultants, contractors, and client-recipients' with sociology 'saturated by theories stressing the importance of social order'. Thus:

> One of the central contradictions of modern sociology . . . derives from its role as market researcher for the Welfare State. This role exposes the sociologists to two contradictory . . . experiences: on the one side it limits the sociologist to the reformist solutions of the Welfare State; but, on the other, it exposes him to the failure of this state and of the society with whose problems it seeks to cope (Gouldner, 1971, p. 439).

Increasingly both functionalist and orthodox Marxist theory converge to promote a reified, dehumanised model of the social system which removes all value commitment and emancipatory potential. There is thus a need for both a new sociology and a new society: knowledge of society has to be constructed not discovered and this is possible only within a common community whose members are committed to a common, creative language and culture. The task of radical, reflexive, emancipatory sociology is thus the creation of a new intellectual vanguard whose aim is the reconstruction of society. 'In short', concludes Gouldner, 'it is social organisation, that today provides the key mediation between social theory and social praxis. It is in *this* sense that what sociology needs today is not so much its first Newton and another Karl Marx but, rather, a V. I. Lenin who can formulate its organisational requirements' (Gouldner, 1973, p. 97). In this way sociology contributes to the reconstruction of society and furtherance of human emancipation; and sociological theory is no longer dominated by instrumental values and a spurious scientistic objectivism.

There is, in these formulations, a dangerous subjectivism: it is difficult to understand how an emancipatory social science can wed itself to the totalitarian assumptions of Leninist organisational theory. Truth and objectivity become bound up with organisation and an élite of radical sociologists whose claims to scientific exactitude flow from *a priori* emancipatory values. None of this is genuinely part of the sociological tradition as I have sketched it in this book. The basic assumptions of Marxist thought tend towards centralisation and finalisation, towards a closed, ideological discourse. Emancipatory interests assume a similarly ideological discourse. Thus both Gouldner and Habermas conclude their analyses of academic sociology and industrial society with an appeal (reminiscent of Saint-Simon on the one hand and Lukács on the other) to an intellectual élite of organised social scientists who, through their intuitive grasp of authentic values, offer the only viable, scientific solution to the major social, economic and political problems. This standpoint seems implicit in Habermas's theory of crisis in that it assumes that ordinary persons, passively integrated into modern organised welfare capitalism, can never *actively* constitute the source of legitimacy: rather, the crises of legitimacy flow from the values of the system itself and the complex structural relations between the different sub-systems. Such a closed, ideological notion of social system and the passivity of the 'masses' who comprise it, clearly belongs to the élitist traditions of Frankfurt School Marxism and reflect its failure to theorise the dialogic, contradictory nature of modern industrial society.

As the object of study for sociology, society is both structure and action: and if sociology is emancipatory it is so because it has adequately theorised a real historical development. Gouldner is right to emphasise the contradictory nature of classical sociology, but such contradictions relate to the ability of sociology to theorise a real objective historical movement as society develops from pre-industrial, highly centralised systems to decentred, complex industrial systems, characterised by the growth of autonomous institutions that enable social groups and communities to define and articulate their specific interests in relation to others and enlarge society as a whole.

Sociology is both a humanism and a science conceiving society as an objective structure created through human action. It can never entirely escape the influence of the socio-historical context. But this should not imply subjectivism. Because it deals with the results of social action which, although structured, can never be predicted accurately, sociological theory must remain provisional in its attempts to explain and comprehend the structure and development of human society. But its future as a human science lies with the fate of industrial society, whether Western societies become more centralised and civil society weaker, whether Soviet societies maintain control from their centre or if ideological finalisation collapses and a revitalised civil society emerges. There is, as Gouldner emphasises, a possible convergence between deterministic system theories, such as functionalism and Marxism, which relate to questions of organisation and control; and a convergence, too, between humanist systems theory and social action (such as Habermas, Goldmann). The existence of different sociologies attests to the failure of sociology to theorise its relation to democracy and industrialism and to assimilate the dialogic openness implicit in the notions of active subject and human structure.

Further Reading

1 Origins of Sociology

One of the most thorough works on the history of sociology (Szacki, 1979) traces the development of sociological thought from its intellectual origins in the philosophy of Plato and Aristotle, Renaissance thought and Vico, to modern social theorists such as Mead, Mannheim, Parsons. Mauss (1962), Nisbet (1967), Fletcher (1972, 1973), Hawthorn (1976) offer general histories and idiosyncratic interpretations, while Aron (1965, 1968) examines the major sociological figures from Montesquieu to Weber. Coser (1971) is especially valuable for relating sociological theory to social context and biography.

Shils (1980) offers a wide-ranging interpretation of the main traditions in sociology while a valuable collection of essays on the history of sociology is Bottomore and Nisbet (1979).

The most comprehensive study of Enlightenment philosophy and its relation with social thought and early sociologists such as Montesquieu and Ferguson is Gay (1967, 1970).

Vico's major work has been translated into English (Vico, 1948). A good discussion is Berlin (1976) while Cahnman (1981) examines the relation between Vico, Hobbes and Tönnies.

Montesquieu (1949) includes a penetrating introduction by F. Neumann.

A general overview of the Scottish Enlightenment is Chitnis (1977) while Swingewood (1970) and Therborn (1976) analyse the specifically sociological aspects. Ferguson's *Essay* has been republished (1966) while Millar's *Origin and Distinction of Ranks* is included in Lehmann (1960). For good discussion of Ferguson's contribution to sociology see Kettler (1965), MacRae (1969) while a useful collection of writings, including Ferguson, Kames, Robertson, Millar, is Schneider (1967).

2 Industrialisation and the Rise of Sociological Positivism

Useful histories of positivism include Simon (1963), Giddens (1977, Ch. 1), Halfpenny (1982). The relation of the French Revolution to the development

330

of sociology is discussed by Nisbet (1967) and Gouldner (1971). A critique of Nisbet's thesis identifying sociology with conservative thought is advanced by Giddens (1977, Ch. 6).

Saint-Simon's writings relating to social theory have been translated in two collections (Ionescu, 1976; Taylor, 1975). Saint-Simon's importance to both nineteenth-century sociology and socialism is examined by Durkheim (1958) and his relation with the Enlightenment by Manuel (1962). Hayek (1955) has interpreted the works of Saint-Simon and Comte as laying the foundations for modern totalitarianism and methodological collectivism, while Bell (1976) explores the sources of the concept of industrial society in relation to Saint-Simon.

Comte's work was translated into English during the nineteenth century (Comte, 1896, 1877). His early essays have been recently republished (Fletcher, 1974). Two useful selections of Comte's sociological and philosophical writings are Andreski (1978) and Thompson (1976). Fletcher (1972) advances a sympathetic view while Marcuse (1954) develops a critical Marxist perspective of Comte's sociology. J. S. Mill's study is still worth reading (Mill, 1961). A short, lucid account of Comte's relation with nineteenth-century statistics and social surveys is Halfpenny (1982).

For J. S. Mill see Fletcher (1972), Feuer (1976). Mill's *System of Logic* is widely available: a good, recent edition is edited by Fletcher (Mill, 1976).

The most succinct introduction to Spencer's voluminous works is the popular *Study of Sociology* (Spencer, 1965). Spencer's opposition to collectivism, his advocacy of the organismic analogy in social science is best approached through the essays (Spencer, 1969a). Selections from Spencer's works include Carneiro (1967), Andreski (1971), Peel (1972). The most thorough discussion of Spencer's work which places it within the context of English nonconformity is Peel (1971). The wider debate on evolutionism is examined by Burrow (1966) and critically evaluated by Hirst (1976).

3 Marxism: A Positive Science of Capital Development

Marx and Engels's collected works are currently being published (Marx–Engels, 1975) but there is a useful two-volume edition which includes many of their most important writings including *The Communist Manifesto*, *The Civil War in France*, *The Eighteenth Brumaire of Louis Bonaparte* (Marx and Engels, 1962). The Penguin editions of *Capital* (Marx, 1976–80), *Grundrisse* (Marx, 1973) and the political writings (Marx, 1974–6) are highly recommended.

Selections from Marx's and Engels's writings include Bottomore (1964a) for the early works, Bottomore and Rubel (1961), McLellan (1980a).

The most exhaustive and stimulating study of Marxism is Kolakowski (1981) while a more sympathetic series of essays is McLellan (1983). One of the best defences of the Hegelian, humanist Marx is Avineri (1968). Cohen (1978) rejects the humanist core of Marxism arguing that concepts such as mode of production, rather than alienation, are more central to Marx's scientific project. He emphasises the role of technology in social development minimising the role of ideas and the subject. Other anti-humanist interpretations include Althusser (1969, 1971), Hindess and Hirst (1975). These works should be read in conjunction with Rosdolsky (1977) which contains a thorough analysis of the *Grundrisse* and its relation with the early and later works.

For Marx's relation with sociology see Gouldner (1980), Bottomore and Nisbet (1979), Therborn (1976). Still worth reading is Schumpeter (1961).

4 Critique of Positivism: I Durkheim

The general social and intellectual background to the development of Durkheim's sociology is examined by Lukes (1973) and Clark (1973). Wolff (1964) includes a number of essays dealing with the social and political context that shaped Durkheim's sociology.

Durkheim's most important works have all been translated into English. There is a new edition of *The Rules of Sociological Method* (Durkheim, 1982) which includes some of Durkheim's articles relating to methodology and sociological theory. Other works include the study of suicide (Durkheim, 1952), studies in philosophy and social theory (Durkheim, 1953, 1964, 1965), the study of economic organisation (Durkheim, 1964, new translation forthcoming 1984), professions (Durkheim, 1957), religion (Durkheim, 1961) precursors of sociology (Durkheim, 1958, 1965).

Selections from Durkheim's work include Giddens (1972b), Bellah (1973), Traugott (1978).

The most thorough analysis of Durkheim's relation with nineteenth-century positivism remains Parsons (1961a). Other valuable discussions include Coser (1971), Giddens (1971), Aron (1968). The relation of Durkheim's theory of society to contemporary science has been discussed by Hirst (1975), to contemporary French Marxism by Llobera (1981) and his theory of politics analysed perceptively by Giddens (1977).

Douglas (1967) has advanced a phenomenological critique of Durkheim's use of official French suicide statistics. This argument should be read in conjunction with Pope (1978) and Taylor (1982).

5 Critique of Positivism: II Social Action

For a good, general survey of the *verstehen* tradition in social theory see Rickman (1967) and the stimulating historical and critical account of the reaction to positivism in late nineteenth-century and early twentieth-century social thought by Hughes (1959). Outhwaite (1975) is short, lucid and critical.

Dilthey (1976) is a useful selection and an important essay is included in Gardiner (1959). Rickert's major work is available (1962). For German sociology see Aron (1964). Baumann (1978) surveys the hermeneutic tradition from Dilthey to Parsons.

The development of formal sociology is discussed by Aron (1964), Szacki

(1979, Ch. 12). Tönnies's major work is available (Tönnies, 1963) and there are two good selections from his work (Tönnies, 1971, 1974).

Many of Simmel's works are now available in English translation: the early study of history (Simmel, 1977), studies in interpretative sociology (Simmel, 1980), conflict (Simmel, 1956), the role of money in the development of culture (Simmel, 1978), the theory of modern culture (Simmel, 1957) as well as selections from his essays (Wolff, 1950, 1965). The most recent study of Simmel is Frisby (1981). A negative view is argued by Sorokin (1928), pp. 501–5. Durkheim's assessment is reprinted in Coser (1965).

Weber's major works are all available in English translation: on interpretative sociology (Weber, 1968), the methodological essays (Weber, 1949, 1975, 1977), the specialised histories (Weber, 1923, 1976), the studies of religion (Weber, 1968, 1951, 1952, 1958a). Useful selections from his work include Runciman (1978), Gerth and Mills (1948). General discussions of his work include Bendix (1963), Giddens (1971), MacRae (1974), Stammler (1971), Wrong (1970).

The critical literature on the Protestant ethic is enormous but a good, recent survey is Marshall (1982). A negative argument is advanced by Samuelson (1961).

Pareto's major work has been translated into English in four volumes (Pareto, 1963). The classic account of his relation with Durkheim and Weber is Parsons (1961a), which strives to force Pareto's sociology into a convergence with action theory and voluntarism. Other sympathetic accounts include Sorokin (1928), Lopreato (1975, 1981).

6 The Sociology of Class and Domination

Marx's writings on domination are contained in Marx and Engels (1962, 1971). For Marx's early writing on the state and his critique of Hegel see Bottomore (1964). Marx's comments on Bakunin's *Statism and Anarchy* are included in the Penguin edition of his *Political Writings* (Marx, 1974–6).

There is a good, critical analysis of Marx's concept of centralisation in Kolakowski (1981), Volume I. Also of interest are Therborn (1976) and McLellan (1983).

Weber's writings on class and domination are widely available: Weber (1968) consists of three volumes which includes the important essay, 'Parliament and Government in a Reconstructed Germany'. The essays on 'Socialism' and 'Politics as a Vocation' are in Gerth and Mills (1948).

Weber's politics and concept of domination are ably discussed by Mommsen (1974), Beetham (1974), Giddens (1972). A Marxist critique is presented by Therborn (1976). Weber's relation with Marxism has been widely discussed but see especially Lowith (1982), Aron (1968), Giddens (1971, 1977).

On élites see Mosca (1939) and Michels (1962).

7 Marxism and Sociology

A lucid, critical account of the development of Marxism after Marx is offered by McLellan (1983). Kolakowski (1981) Volume 1 is indispensable. Anderson (1976) is a short, idiosyncratic account.

Bernstein (1963) is the main text for the revisionist debate. Sorel's major theoretical writings are available in English translation (Sorel, 1950, 1969). The important essay on the disintegration of Marxism is included in Horowitz (1961). There is a good selection of his essays on Marxism and the revisionist debate (Sorel, 1976). Labriola's essays have been translated (1967, 1980) and there is a good discussion in Kolakowski (1981) Volume 2, Ch. VIII.

Many of Gramsci's writings have now been translated into English and published in three volumes (Gramsci, 1971, 1977, 1978). The important critique of Bukharin and sociology is in 1971, while the essay on the Southern Question, in which the first formulation of hegemony is advanced, is in 1978.

Lukács's early political writings, including the critique of Bukharin, are available (Lukács, 1972) as well as the difficult essays on dialectics and history (Lukács, 1971).

Gouldner (1973) has discussed the importance of Lukács's concepts for modern sociology although somewhat uncritically. Kilminster (1979) discusses the relation of Gramsci, Lukács and the Frankfurt School to Marx's social thought.

There is a useful selection of writings of the Austro-Marxists (Bottomore and Goode, 1978) and Hilferding's major work is now available in translation (Hilferding, 1980). There is a short, lucid account of the relation between Marxism and sociology, with reference to Lukács, Gramsci and the Austro-Marxists in Bottomore (1975).

8 Functionalism

Functionalist anthropological formulations are represented by Malinowski (1922) and Radcliffe-Brown (1952) while Merton (1957) advances a sociological approach. Gouldner (1973) includes the indispensable essay on reciprocity and autonomy in functionalist theory. Other useful discussions include Cohen (1968), Mulkay (1975), Rex (1961), Strasser (1976), Sztompka (1974).

Parsons's writings are widely available: the difficult study of the social system (1951) is in sharp contrast to the more readable and stimulating essays (Parsons, 1954, 1961b, 1964, 1967). The key article on pattern variables, first published in 1960, is included in Parsons (1967) while a succinct theoretical view of the social system is in Parsons (1961b). Difficult texts which seek to reconcile action with systems theory include Parsons and Shils (1962) and Parsons and Smelser (1956). Parsons and Bales (1955) discusses the relation of the nuclear family to industrialism.

During the 1960s Parsons developed an evolutionary perspective: an early statement on 'evolutionary universals' is reprinted in Parsons (1967) and further argument is in Parsons (1966, 1971). One of his last statements sums up his attempt to develop a systematic and voluntarist social theory and brings out the importance both of Durkheim and Freud (the latter's concept of 'overdetermination') for his thought (Parsons, 1981).

Critical discussions of Parsons's work include Black (1961), Gouldner (1971), Part Two; Menzies (1977), Mills (1959), Rocher (1974).

A valuable collection of essays which discuss functionalism and conflict is Demerath and Peterson (1967). Coser (1956, 1967) attempts to synthesise conflict sociology with functionalism while Lockwood (1964) distinguishes system from social integration in a difficult but rewarding essay.

A classic statement by Aberle *et al.* on the functionalist theory of stratification is reprinted in Demerath and Peterson (1967). Davis's early statement is still available (Davis, 1949). The whole debate is critically discussed by Wrong (1976) and Tumin (1968).

9 Self, Society and the Sociology of Everyday Life

The major statement of action theory is Parsons (1961a): a shorter statement is Parsons (1961b). A more general view is Parsons (1978). For Parsons's attempt to integrate psychology into action theory see his essay on Freud (Parsons, 1971b) and the essays on psychological and social structure (Parsons, 1964). Useful discussions of Parsons's theory of personality includes Rocher (1974), Dawe (1979).

Freud's works are widely available both in the standard edition (1953–) and Penguin edition (1977–). The best introduction to Freud's theories is probably the introductory lectures (Freud, 1977, Vol. 1) and the three essays on sexuality (Freud, 1977, Vol. 7). A sociological discussion is Bocock (1983). A lucid introduction is Brown (1961) and other useful discussions include Wollheim (1971) and Rieff (1965). Marxist interpretation is provided by Marcuse (1962) and the relation between Freud's theories and the Frankfurt school is discussed by Jay (1973) and Held (1980).

Cooley's writings are an important source of social interactionism (Cooley, 1902, 1956) and are ably discussed by Coser (1971). The major study of the polish peasant contains much of value for sociological theory (Thomas and Znaeicki, 1927). Mead's works are widely available (Mead, 1934, 1936, 1938) and a useful selection from them is Mead (1964) which includes an essay on Cooley.

A valuable study which explores the complex relation between Simmel, German Idealism, American Pragmatism and the formation of symbolic interactionism is Rock (1979). Gouldner (1973) Ch. 11 argues that Chicago sociology was largely romantic, intuitive, anti-rationalist. A recent analysis of Mead in relation to Marx is Goff (1980). Blumer (1981) is a succinct summary.

Schutz's major work is available in English (Schutz, 1972). There are three volumes of essays (Schutz, 1962–6) and two studies of the life-world and meaning structures (Schutz, 1974, 1982). A wide-ranging collection of essays includes two by Schutz (Luckmann, 1978). Discussions of phenomenology include Garfinkel (1967), Outhwaite (1975), Heeran (1971).

10 Structuralism

A short, lucid introduction to structuralism is Piaget (1971). Saussure's lectures are widely available (Saussure, 1974). A good account of Saussure's work and its importance for social theory is Culler (1976).

There are English translations of the most significant early structuralist works: Propp (1968), Bakhtin (1968, 1973), Mukarovsky (1970).

Barthes's writings are widely available and include the early analysis of mass culture (Barthes, 1973) and semiology (1967). There is an informative study of Barthes's thought (Culler, 1983). Goldmann's approach to structuralism is best approached through his early study of methodology and theory (Goldmann, 1969) and his substantive study of Racine and Pascal (Goldmann, 1964).

For Althusser see especially his early essays on Marx (Althusser, 1969), the painstaking reading of *Capital* (Althusser, 1970) and the essays on ideology and state apparatuses (Althusser, 1971, 1972, 1976). The most extensive critique of Althusserianism is Thompson (1978) and other analyses include Kolakowski (1981) Vol. 3, Lorraine (1979). Other structuralist works which examine class structure include Poulantzas (1973, 1975), Hindess and Hirst (1975).

The structuralist movement in anthropology is best exemplified by the various writings of Claude Lévi-Strauss especially his essays on Durkheim, Mauss, Saussure and Propp (Lévi-Strauss, 1968, 1977).

11 The Sociology of Knowledge and Culture

For the development of the sociology of knowledge the most lucid account is Merton (1957). A selection of essays, somewhat dated, include important works by Scheler and Speier (Curtis and Petras, 1970).

Durkheim's contribution to the sociology of knowledge is best approached through his analysis of primitive classification (Durkheim and Mauss, 1967) and his study of religion (Durkheim, 1961). A good discussion is Lukes (1973).

For Mannheim the most accessible of his works is the study of ideology (Mannheim, 1960) followed by his essay on conservative thought (Mannheim, 1953). His early essays are available (Mannheim, 1952) and there is a good selection from his work, including his review of Lukács's *Theory of the Novel* in Wolff (1971). The most readable account of his work is Merton (1957) which nevertheless tends to debunk Mannheim's approach as too philosophical and speculative. More subtle critics have emphasised the significance of Mannheim's critique of epistemology (Simmonds, 1978). A hostile view is advanced by Popper (1963) Vol. 2.

Some of Scheler's writings are available in English translation (Curtis and Petras, 1970). A general statement is Scheler (1980).

General accounts of intellectuals include Coser (1970), Shils (1972). A good account of Mannheim's theory of intellectuals is Heeran (1971) and there are useful comments in Simmonds (1978) and Coser (1971). One of Mannheim's first statements on intellectuals (1960) should be read in conjunction with the later essay of 1933 (Mannheim, 1956).

For the Frankfurt School see the accounts in Jay (1973), Slater (1977), Held (1980). A good selection of essays is Connerton (1976). The critique of positivism is developed in Horkheimer (1972, 1976). Mannheim's study of democratisation is worth reading (1956) in conjunction with the mass society theory of the Frankfurt School. A hostile view of the Frankfurt School is advanced by Shils (1972).

12 Democracy, Industrialisation and Sociological Theory

The theory of post-industrial society is developed by Bell (1976) in relation to economic and political structures, technology and science. Bell's book contains a valuable analysis of the concept of industrial society as it emerged in the work of Saint-Simon, Marx, Weber and Sombart. The discussion of culture in post-industrial and industrial society is developed in a later, stimulating volume (Bell, 1979). For criticism see Ross (1974) and Kumar (1978) which includes an excellent bibliography. Other studies of post-industrial society include Touraine (1971) and Dahrendorf (1959).

Habermas's writings are widely available in English translation: they include philosophical and theoretical studies (Habermas, 1971), studies in the theory of the modern state and public sphere (Habermas, 1976, 1974, 1979a), studies in language, communication and historical materialism (Habermas, 1979b). An excellent introduction to Habermas's thought is Held (1980), while Wellmer (1974) discusses the philosophical and epistemological problems of Habermas's reworking of Frankfurt School critical theory. There is a volume of essays discussing all the aspects of Habermas's thought (Thompson and Held, 1982).

Bibliography

Althusser L. (1969) *For Marx* (London: Allen Lane).

Althusser L. (1970) *Reading Capital* (with E. Balibar) (London: New Left Books).

Althusser L. (1971) *Lenin and Philosophy* (London: New Left Books).

Althusser L. (1972) *Politics and History* (London: New Left Books).

Althusser L. (1976) *Essays in Self-Criticism* (London: New Left Books).

Anderson P. (1976) *Considerations on Western Marxism* (London: New Left Books).

Andreski S. (ed) (1971) *Herbert Spencer: Structure, Function and Evolution* (London: Nelson).

Andreski S. (ed) (1978) *The Essential Comte* (London: Croom Helm).

Aron R. (1964) *German Sociology* (New York: Free Press).

Aron R. (1965, 1968) *Main Currents in Sociological Thought* 2 Vols. (London: Weidenfeld & Nicolson).

Avineri S. (1968) *The Social and Political Thought of Karl Marx* (Cambridge: Cambridge University Press).

Bakhtin M.M. (1968) *Rabelais and His World* (London: MIT Press).

Bakhtin M.M. (1973) *Marxism and the Philosophy of Language* (published under the name of V. Volosinov) (London: Academic Press).

Bales R.F. & Shils E. (eds) (1962) *Working Papers in the Theory of Action* (New York: Harper Torchbooks).

Barthes R. (1967) *Elements of Semiology* (London: Cape).

Barthes R. (1973) *Mythologies* (London: Paladin Books).

Baumann Z. (1978) *Hermeneutics and Social Science* (London: Hutchinson).

Beetham D. (1974) *Max Weber and the Theory of Modern Politics* (London: Allen & Unwin).

Bell D. (1976) *The Coming of Post-Industrial Society* (Harmondsworth: Penguin Books).

Bell D. (1979) *The Cultural Contradictions of Capitalism* (London: Heinemann).

Bellah R. (ed) (1973) *Emile Durkheim on Morality and Society* (Chicago: University of Chicago Press).

Bendix R. (1963) *Max Weber: An Intellectual Portrait* (London: Heinemann).

Bendix R. & Roth G. (eds) (1971) *Scholarship and Partisanship: Essays on Max Weber* (Los Angeles: University of California Press).

338

Bibliography

Benton T. (1977) *Philosophical Foundations of the Three Sociologies* (London: Routledge & Kegan Paul).

Berlin I. (1976) *Vico and Herder* (Oxford: Oxford University Press).

Bernstein E. (1963) *Evolutionary Socialism* (New York: Schoken Books).

Black M. (ed) (1961) *The Social Theories of Talcott Parsons* (New Jersey: Prentice-Hall).

Blumer H. (1969) *Symbolic Interactionism* (New Jersey: Prentice-Hall).

Blumer H. (1981) 'George Herbert Mead', in Rhea (1981).

Bocock R. (1976) *Freud and Modern Sociology* (London: Nelson).

Bocock R. (1983) *Sigmund Freud* (London: Methuen).

Bottomore T.B. (ed) (1964) *Marx: Early Writings* (London: Watts).

Bottomore T.B. (1975) *Marxist Sociology* (London: Macmillan).

Bottomore T.B. & Goode P. (eds) (1978) *Austro-Marxism* (Oxford: Oxford University Press).

Bottomore T.B. & Nisbet R. (eds) (1979) *A History of Sociological Analysis* (London: Heinemann).

Bottomore T.B. & Rubel M. (eds) (1961) *Karl Marx: Selected Writings in Sociology and Social Philosophy* (Harmondsworth: Penguin Books).

Boudon R. (1979) *The Crisis in Sociology* (London: Heinemann).

Bramson L. (1961) *The Political Context of Sociology* (Princeton: Princeton University Press).

Brown J.A.C. (1961) *Freud and the Post-Freudians* (Harmondsworth: Penguin Books).

Buci-Glucksmann C. (1981) *Gramsci and the State* (London: Lawrence & Wishart).

Buckley W. (1967) *Sociology and Modern Systems Theory* (New Jersey: Prentice-Hall).

Bukharin N. (1969) *Historical Materialism* (Ann Arbor: University of Michigan Press).

Burrow J.W. (1966) *Evolution and Society* (Cambridge: Cambridge University Press).

Cahnman W. (1973) (ed) *Ferdinand Tönnies: A New Evaluation* (Leiden: Brill).

Cahnman W. (1981) 'Hobbes, Toennies, Vico: Starting Points in Sociology', in Rhea (1981).

Carneiro R.L. (ed) (1967) *Herbert Spencer: The Evolution of Society* (Chicago: University of Chicago Press).

Cassirer E. (1951) *The Philosophy of the Enlightenment* (Boston: Beacon Press).

Chitnis A. (1977) *The Scottish Enlightenment* (London: Croom Helm).

Clarke T.N. (1973) *Prophets and Patrons: The French University and the Emergence of the Social Science* (Cambridge: Harvard University Press).

Cohen G.A. (1978) *Karl Marx's Theory of History: A Defence* (Oxford: Oxford University Press).

Cohen P. (1968) *Modern Social Theory* (London: Heinemann).

Comte A. (1877) *System of Positive Polity* (London: Longmans Green).

Comte A. (1896) *The Positive Philosophy* (London: Bell & Sons).

Connerton P. (ed) (1976) *Critical Sociology* (Harmondsworth: Penguin Books).

Bibliography

Connerton P. (1980) *The Tragedy of Enlightenment: An Essay on the Frankfurt School* (Cambridge: Cambridge University Press).

Cooley C.H. (1902) *Human Nature and the Social Order* (New York: Charles Scribners).

Cooley C.H. (1956) *Social Organisation* (New York: Schocken).

Coser L.A. (1956) *The Functions of Social Conflict* (London: Routledge & Kegan Paul).

Coser L.A. (ed) (1965) *George Simmel* (New Jersey: Prentice-Hall).

Coser L.A. (1967) *Continuities in the Study of Social Conflict* (New York: Free Press).

Coser L.A. (1970) *Men of Ideas* (New York: Free Press).

Coser L.A. (1971) *Masters of Sociological Thought* (New York: Harcourt Brace Jovanovich).

Croce B. (1913) *Historical Materialism and the Economics of Karl Marx* (London: Howard Latimer).

Culler J. (1976) *Saussure* (London: Fontana).

Culler J. (1983) *Barthes* (London: Fontana).

Curtis J.E. & Petras J. (eds) (1970) *The Sociology of Knowledge: A Reader* (London: Duckworth).

Dahrendorf R. (1959) *Class and Class Conflict in Industrial Society* (London: Routledge & Kegan Paul).

Dahrendorf R. (1968) *Essays in the Theory of Society* (London: Routledge & Kegan Paul).

Davis K. (1949) *Human Society* (London: Routledge & Kegan Paul).

Davis K. & Moore W. (1969) 'Some Principles of Stratification', in Heller, C. *Structured Social Inequality* (London: Collier-Macmillan).

Dawe A. (1970) 'The Two Sociologies', *British Journal of Sociology*, XXI, No. 2 (June).

Dawe A. (1979) 'Theories of Social Action', in Bottomore & Nisbet (1979).

Demerath N. & Peterson R. (eds) (1967) *System, Change and Conflict* (New York: Free Press).

Dilthey W. (1976) *Selected Writings* (Cambridge: Cambridge University Press).

Douglas J. (1967) *The Social Meanings of Suicide* (Princeton: Princeton Univeresity Press).

Douglas J. (ed) (1973) *Understanding Everyday Life* (London: Routledge & Kegan Paul).

Durkheim E. (1952) *Suicide* (London: Routledge & Kegan Paul).

Durkheim E. (1953) *Sociology and Philosophy* (London: Cohen & West).

Durkheim E. (1957) *Professional Ethics and Civic Morals* (London: Routledge & Kegan Paul).

Durkheim E. (1958) *Saint-Simon and Socialism* (London: Routledge & Kegan Paul).

Durkheim E. (1961) *The Elementary Forms of the Religious Life* (London: Allen & Unwin).

Durkheim E. (1964) *The Division of Labour* (New York: Free Press).

Durkheim E. (1965) *Montesquieu and Rousseau* (Ann Arbor: University of Michigan Press).

Bibliography

Durkheim E. (1982) *The Rules of Sociological Method* (London: Macmillan).

Durkheim E. & Mauss M. (1967) *Primitive Classification* (London: Routledge & Kegan Paul).

Easton L.D. and Guddatt K. (eds) (1967) *Writings of the Young Marx on Philosophy and Society* (New York: Anchor Books).

Engels F. (1942) *The Origin of the Family, Private Property and State* (New York: International Publishers).

Engels F. (1954) *Anti-Duhring* (London: Lawrence & Wishart).

Ferguson A. (1966) *An Essay on the History of Civil Society* (Edinburgh: Edinburgh University Press).

Feuer L.S. (1976) 'John Stuart Mill as a Sociologist', in Robson J. and Laine M. (eds) *James and John Stuart Mill* (Toronto: University of Toronto Press).

Feuerbach L. (1969) 'Preliminary Theses on the Reform of Philosophy', *Arena*, No. 19.

Finer S.E. (ed) (1966) *Vilfredo Pareto: Sociological Writings* (London: Pall Mall Press).

Fisher B.M. & Strauss A.L. (1979) 'Interactionism', in Bottomore and Nisbet (1979).

Fletcher R. (1972, 1973) *The Making of Sociology* (London: Nelson) 3 Vols.

Fletcher R. (ed) (1974) *The Crisis of Industrial Society: The Early Essays of Comte* (London: Heinemann).

Freud S. (1953–) *Complete Works*, ed Strachey J. (London: Hogarth Press).

Freud S. (1977–) *Selected Works* (Harmondsworth: Penguin Books).

Frisby D. (1981) *Sociological Impressionism: A Reassessment of George Simmel's Social Theory* (London: Heinemann).

Gardiner P. (ed) (1959) *Theories of History* (New York: Free Press).

Garfinkel H. (1967) *Studies in Ethnomethodology* (New Jersey: Prentice-Hall).

Gay P. (1967, 1970) *The Enlightenment: An Interpretation* (London: Weidenfeld & Nicolson).

Gerth H.H. & Mills C.W. (eds) (1948) *From Max Weber* (London: Routledge & Kegan Paul).

Giddens A. (1971) *Capitalism and Modern Social Theory* (Cambridge: Cambridge University Press).

Giddens A. (1972a) *Politics and Sociology in the Thought of Max Weber* (London: Macmillan).

Giddens A. (1972b) *Emile Durkheim: Selected Writings* (Cambridge: Cambridge University Press).

Giddens A. (1977) *Studies in Social and Political Theory* (London: Hutchinson).

Goff T.W. (1980) *Marx and Mead* (London: Routledge & Kegan Paul).

Goldman L. (1964) *The Hidden God* (London: Routledge & Kegan Paul).

Goldman L. (1969) *The Human Sciences and Philosophy* (London: Cape).

Gouldner A. (1971) *The Coming Crisis of Western Sociology* (London: Heinemann).

Gouldner A. (1973) *For Sociology* (London: Allen Lane).

Gouldner A. (1980) *The Two Marxisms* (London: Macmillan).

Gramsci A. (1971) *Selections from the Prison Notebooks* (London: Lawrence & Wishart).

341

Bibliography

Gramsci A. (1977, 1978) *Selections from the Political Writings* (London: Lawrence & Wishart).

Habermas J. (1971) *Knowledge and Human Interests* (London: Heinemann).

Habermas J. (1976) *Legitimation Crisis* (London: Heinemann).

Habermas J. (1979) *Communication and the Evolution of Society* (London: Heinemann).

Halbwachs M. (1970) *The Causes of Suicide* (London: Routledge & Kegan Paul).

Halfpenny P. (1982) *Positivism and Sociology* (London: Allen & Unwin).

Hawthorn G. (1976) *Enlightenment and Despair: A History of Sociology* (Cambridge: Cambridge University Press).

Hayek F. (1955) *The Counter-Revolution of Science* (New York: Free Press).

Heeran J. (1971) 'Karl Mannheim and the Intellectual Elite', *British Journal of Sociology* Vol. 22, No. 1 (March).

Heeran J. (1973) 'Alfred Schutz and the Sociology of Common-sense Knowledge', in Douglas (1973).

Held D. (1980) *Introduction to Critical Theory* (London: Hutchinson).

Hilferding R. (1980) *Finance Capital* (London: Routledge & Kegan Paul).

Hindess B. & Hirst P. (1975) *Pre-Capitalist Economic Formations* (London: Routledge & Kegan Paul).

Hirst P.Q. (1975) *Durkheim, Bernard and Epistemology* (London: Routledge & Kegan Paul).

Hirst P.Q. (1976) *Social Evolution and Sociological Categories* (London: Allen & Unwin).

Horkheimer M. (1972) *Critical Theory* (New York: Seabury Press).

Horkheimer M. (1976) 'Traditional and Critical Theory', in Connerton (1976).

Horowitz I.L. (1961) *Radicalism and the Revolt against Reason* (London: Routledge & Kegan Paul).

Horton J. (1964) 'The De-humanisation of Alienation and Anomie', *British Journal of Sociology* Vol. XV, No. 4 (Dec).

Hughes H.S. (1959) *Consciousness and Society* (London: MacGibbon & Kee).

Ionescu G. (ed) (1976) *The Political Thought of Saint-Simon* (Oxford: Oxford University Press).

Jay M. (1973) *The Dialectical Imagination* (London: Heinemann).

Kahn J.S. & Llobera J. (eds) (1981) *The Anthropology of Pre-Capitalist Societies* (London: Macmillan).

Kautsky K. (1983) *Selected Political Writings* (London: Macmillan).

Kettler D. (1965) *The Social and Political Thought of Adam Ferguson* (Columbus: University of Ohio Press).

Kilminster R. (1979) *Praxis and Method: A Sociological Dialogue with Lukács, Gramsci and the Early Frankfurt School* (London: Routledge & Kegan Paul).

Kolakowski L. (1981) *Main Currents in Marxism* 3 Vols. (Oxford: Oxford University Press).

Kolko G. (1960) 'Max Weber on America', *History and Theory* 1.

Krygier M. (1979) 'Saint-Simon, Marx and the Non-Governed Society', in Brown R. (ed) *Bureaucracy* (London: Arnold).

Kumar K. (1978) *Prophecy and Progress* (Harmondsworth: Penguin Books).

Bibliography

Labriola A. (1967) *Essays on the Materialist Conception of History* (New York: Monthly Review Press).

Labriola A. (1980) *Socialism and Philosophy* (Washington: Telos Press).

Lehmann W. (ed) (1960) *John Millar of Glasgow* (Glasgow: Glasgow University Press).

Levine D. (ed) (1971) *Simmel: On Individuality and Social Forms* (Chicago: University of Chicago Press).

Levine D. (1981) 'Sociology's Quest for the Classics: The Case of Simmel', in Rhea (1981).

Lévi-Strauss C. (1968, 1977) *Structural Anthropology* (London: Allen Lane).

Lively J. (ed) *The Works of Joseph de Maistre* (London: Allen & Unwin).

Llobera J. (1981) 'Durkheim, the Durkheimians and their Collective Misrepresentation of Marx', in Kahn & Llobera (1981).

Lockwood D. 'Social Integration and System Integration', in Zollschan and Hirsch (1964).

Lopreato J. (1975) *The Sociology of Pareto* (Morristown: General Learning Press).

Lopreato J. (1981) 'Vilfredo Pareto: Socio-Biology, System and Revolution', in Rhea (1981).

Lorraine J. (1979) *The Concept of Ideology* (London: Hutchinson).

Lowith K. (1982) *Karl Marx and Max Weber* (London: Allen & Unwin).

Luckmann T. (ed) (1978) *Phenomenology and Sociology* (Harmondsworth: Penguin Books).

Lukács G. (1971) *History and Class Consciousness* (London: Merlin Press).

Lukács G. (1972) *Political Writings: 1919–1929* (London: New Left Books).

Lukes S. (1973) *Emile Durkheim: His Life and Work* (London: Allen Lane).

Lukes S. (1977) *Essays in Social Theory* (London: Macmillan).

MacRae D.G. (1969) 'Adam Ferguson', in Raison (1969).

MacRae D.G. (1974) *Weber* (London: Fontana).

Malinowski E. (1922) *Argonauts of the Western Pacific* (New York: Dutton).

Mannheim K. (1952) *Essays in the Sociology of Knowledge* (London: Routledge & Kegan Paul).

Mannheim K. (1953) *Essays in Sociology and Social Psychology* (London: Routledge & Kegan Paul).

Mannheim K. (1956) *Essays in the Sociology of Culture* (London: Routledge & Kegan Paul).

Mannheim K. (1960) *Ideology and Utopia* (London: Routledge & Kegan Paul).

Mannheim K. (1982) *Structures of Thinking* (London: Routledge & Kegan Paul).

Manuel F. (1962) *The Prophets of Paris* (New York: Harper).

Marcuse H. (1954) *Reason and Revolution* (New York: Humanities Press).

Marcuse H. (1962) *Eros and Civilisation* (New York: Vintage Books).

Marcuse H. (1964) *One Dimensional Man* (London: Routledge & Kegan Paul).

Marshall G. (1982) *In Search of the Spirit of Capitalism* (London: Hutchinson).

Martindale D. (1960) *The Nature and Types of Sociological Theory* (London: Routledge & Kegan Paul).

Marx K. (1957, 1958, 1962) *Capital* (London: Lawrence & Wishart).

Marx K. (1961) *The Poverty of Philosophy* (London: Lawrence & Wishart).

Marx K. (1963) *Economic and Philosophical Manuscripts* (London: Lawrence & Wishart).

Marx K. (1964–72) *Theories of Surplus Value* 3 Vols. (London: Lawrence & Wishart).

Marx K. (1971) *A Contribution to the Critique of Political Economy* (London: Lawrence & Wishart).

Marx K. (1973) *Grundrisse* (Harmondsworth: Penguin Books).

Marx K. (1974–6) *Marx: Political Writings* 3 Vols (Harmondsworth: Penguin Books).

Marx K. (1976–80) *Capital* 3 Vols. (Harmondsworth: Penguin Books).

Marx & Engels (1956) *The Holy Family* (London: Lawrence & Wishart).

Marx & Engels (1962) *Selected Works* (London: Lawrence & Wishart). This is a two volume edition.

Marx & Engels (1964) *The German Ideology* (London: Lawrence & Wishart).

Marx & Engels (1971) *On the Paris Commune* (London: Lawrence & Wishart).

Marx & Engels (1975–) *Collected Works* (London: Lawrence & Wishart). This, the first complete English edition of the complete works of Marx and Engels will include *Capital* and comprise 50 Volumes when complete.

Marx & Engels (n.d.) *Selected Correspondence* (London: Lawrence & Wishart).

Masaryk T. (1970) *Suicide and the Meaning of Civilisation* (Chacago: University of Chicago Press).

Mauss H. (1962) *A Short History of Sociology* (London: Routledge & Kegan Paul).

McLellan D. (1969) *The Young Hegelians and Karl Marx* (London: Macmillan).

McLellan D. (1973) *Karl Marx: His Life and Thought* (London: Macmillan).

McLellan D. (ed) (1980a) *The Thought of Karl Marx* (London: Macmillan).

McLellan D. (1980b) *Marxism after Marx* (London: Macmillan).

McLellan D. (ed) (1983) *Marx: The First Hundred Years* (London: Fontana).

Mead G.H. (1934) *Mind, Self and Society* (Chicago: University of Chicago Press).

Mead G.H. (1936) *Movements of Thought in the Nineteenth Century* (Chicago: University of Chicago Press).

Mead G.H. (1938) *The Philosophy of the Act* (Chicago: University of Chicago Press).

Mead G.H. (1964) *On Social Psychology* (Chicago: University of Chicago Press).

Meisel J.H. (1962) *The Myth of the Ruling Class: Gaetano Mosca and the Elite* (Ann Arbor: University of Michigan Press).

Meisel J.H. (ed) (1965) *Pareto and Mosca* (New Jersey: Prentice-Hall).

Menzies K. (1977) *Talcott Parsons and the Social Image of Man* (London: Routledge & Kegan Paul).

Merton R.K. (1957) *Social Theory and Social Structure* (New York: Free Press).

Michels R. (1962) *Political Parties* (New York: Collier-Macmillan).

Mill J.S. (1961) *Auguste Comte and Positivism* (Ann Arbor: University of Michigan Press).

Mill J.S. (1976) *A System of Logic* (ed Fletcher R.) (London: Nelson).

Mills C.W. (1956) *The Power Elite* (New York: Oxford University Press).

344

Bibliography

Mills C.W. (1959) *The Sociological Imagination* (New York: Oxford University Press).

Montesquieu (1949) *The Spirit of the Laws* (New York: Haffner).

Montesquieu (1965) *Considerations on the Greatness of the Romans and their Decline* (New York: Free Press).

Mommsen W. (1974) *The Age of Bureaucracy: Perspectives on the Political Sociology of Max Weber* (Oxford: Blackwell).

Mosca G. (1939) *The Ruling Class* (New York: McGraw Hill).

Mouffe C. (ed) (1978) *Gramsci and Marxist Theory* (London: Routledge & Kegan Paul).

Mukarovsky J. (1970) *Aesthetic Function, Norm and Value as Social Facts* (Ann Arbor: University of Michigan Press).

Mulkay M. (1975) *Functionalism, Exchange and Theoretical Strategy* (London: Routledge & Kegan Paul).

Nisbet R. (1967) *The Sociological Tradition* (London: Heinemann).

Oberschall A. (ed) (1972) *Empirical Social Research in Germany 1848–1914* (New York: Harper & Row).

Ollman B. (1971) *Alienation: Marx's Theory of Man in Capitalist Society* (Cambridge: Cambridge University Press).

Outhwaite W. (1975) *Understanding Social Life: The Method called Vesthen* (London: Allen & Unwin).

Pareto V. (1963) *The Mind and Society: A Treatise on General Sociology* (New York: Dover).

Pareto V. (1965) *The Rise and Fall of Elites* (Towata: Bedminster Press) (First published in 1901).

Parsons T. (1951) *The Social System* (New York: Free Press).

Parsons T. (1954) *Essays in Sociological Theory* (New York: Free Press).

Parsons T. (1955) *Family, Socialisation and Interaction Process* (with Bales R.F.) (London: Routledge & Kegan Paul).

Parsons T. (1961a) *The Structure of Social Action* (New York: Free Press).

Parsons T. (1961b) *Structure and Process in Modern Societies* (New York: Free Press).

Parsons T. (ed) (1961c) *Theories of Society* (New York: Free Press).

Parsons T. (1961d) 'The Point of View of the Author', in Black (ed) (1961).

Parsons T. (1964) *Social Structure and Personality* (New York: Free Press).

Parsons T. (1966) *Societies: Evolutionary and Comparative Perspectives* (New Jersey: Prentice-Hall).

Parsons T. (1967) *Sociological Theory and Modern Society* (New York: Free Press).

Parsons T. (1971a) *The System of Modern Societies* (New Jersey: Prentice-Hall).

Parsons T. (1971b) 'The Interpretation of Dreams by Sigmund Freud', *Daedalus* Vol. 103, pp. 91–6.

Parsons T. (1978) *Action Theory and the Human Condition* (New York: Free Press).

Parsons T. (1981) 'Revisiting the Classics', in Rhea (ed) (1981).

Parsons T. & Shils E. (1962) *Toward a General Theory of Action* (New York: Harper).

Parsons T. and Smelser N. (1956) *Economy and Society* (New York: Free Press).

345

Peel J.D.Y. (1971) *Herbert Spencer: The Evolution of a Sociologist* (London: Heinemann).

Peel J.D.Y. (ed) (1972) *Herbert Spencer on Social Evolution* (Chicago: University of Chicago Press).

Piaget J. (1971) *Structuralism* (London: Routledge & Kegan Paul).

Pope W. (1978) *Durkheim's Suicide* (Chicago: University of Chicago Press).

Popper K. (1963) *The Open Society and its Enemies* 2 Vols. (London: Routledge & Kegan Paul).

Poulantzas N. (1973) *Political Power and Social Classes* (London: New Left Books).

Poulantzas N. (1975) *Classes in Contemporary Capitalism* (London: New Left Books).

Propp V. (1968) *Morphology of the Fairy Tale* (Austin: University of Texas Press).

Radcliffe-Brown A.R. (1952) *Structure and Function in Primitive Society* (London: Routledge & Kegan Paul).

Raison T. (ed) (1969) *Founding Fathers of Social Science* (Harmondsworth: Penguin Books).

Rex J. (1961) *Key Problems of Sociological Theory* (London: Routledge & Kegan Paul).

Rhea B. (ed) (1981) *The Future of the Sociological Classics* (London: Allen & Unwin).

Rickert H. (1962) *Science and History* (New York: Van Nostrand).

Rickman H.R. (1967) *Understanding and the Human Sciences* (London: Heinemann).

Rieff P. (1965) *Freud: The Mind of a Moralist* (London: Methuen).

Ringer F. (1969) *The Decline of the German Mandarins: The German Academic Community 1890–1933* (Cambridge: Harvard University Press).

Rocher G. (1974) *Talcott Parsons and American Sociology* (London: Nelson).

Rock P. (1979) *The Making of Symbolic Interactionism* (London: Macmillan).

Rosdolsky R. (1977) *The Making of Marx's Capital* (London: Pluto Press).

Ross G. (1974) 'The Second Coming of Daniel Bell', in *The Socialist Register* (ed Miliband R. & Saville J.) (London: Merlin Press).

Runciman W. (ed) (1978) *Weber: A selection* (Cambridge: Cambridge University Press).

Sahay A. (ed) (1971) *Max Weber and Modern Sociology* (London: Routledge & Kegan Paul).

Salamon L. (1981) *The Sociology of Political Praxis* (London: Routledge & Kegan Paul).

Samuelson K. (1961) *Religion and Economic Action* (London: Heinemann).

Saussure F. (1974) *Course in General Linguistics* (London: Fontana).

Sayer D. (1978) *Marx's Method* (Hassocks: Harvester Press).

Scheler M. (1980) *Problems of a Sociology of Knowledge* (London: Routledge & Kegan Paul).

Schneider L. (ed) (1967) *The Scottish Moralists on Human Nature and Society* (Chicago: University of Chicago Press).

Schumpeter J. (1961) *Capitalism, Socialism and Democracy* (London: Allen & Unwin).

Bibliography

Schutz A. (1962–6) *Collected Papers* 3 Vols. (The Hangue: Mouton).

Schutz A. (1972) *Phenomenology of the Social World* (London: Heinemann).

Schutz A. (1974) *The Structures of the Life World* (with T. Luckmann) (London: Heinemann).

Schutz A. (1978) 'Phenomenology and the Social Sciences', 'Some Structures of the Life World', in Luckmann (ed) (1978).

Schutz A. (1982) *Life Forms and Meaning Structures* (London: Routledge & Kegan Paul).

Schwendinger, H. & H. *The Sociologists of the Chair* (New York: Basic Books).

Shils E. (1972) *The Intellectuals and the Powers* (Chicago: University of Chicago Press).

Shils E. (1975) *Centre and Periphery* (Chicago: University of Chicago Press).

Shils E. (1980) *The Calling of Sociology* (Chicago: University of Chicago Press).

Simmel G. (1956) *Conflict and the Web of Group Affiliations* (New York: Free Press).

Simmel G. (1957) *Philosophic Culture* (New York: Putnam).

Simmel G. (1968) *The Conflict in Modern Culture and other Essays* (New York: Columbia University Press).

Simmel G. (1977) *The Problems of a Philosophy of History* (New York: Free Press).

Simmel G. (1978) *The Philosophy of Money* (London: Routledge & Kegan Paul).

Simmel G. (1980) *Essays in Interpretation in the Social Sciences* (Manchester: Manchester University Press).

Simmonds A.P. (1978) *Karl Mannheim's Sociology of Knowledge* (Oxford: Oxford University Press).

Simon W.M. (1963) *European Positivism in the Nineteenth Century* (New York: Cornell University Press).

Slater P. (1977) *The Origin and Significance of the Frankfurt School* (London: Routledge & Kegan Paul).

Smith A. (1976) *Theory of Moral Sentiments* (Glasgow: Glasgow University Press).

Smith A. (1970) *Wealth of Nations* (Harmondsworth: Penguin Books).

Sombart W. (1967) *Luxury and Capitalism* (Ann Arbor: University of Michigan Press).

Sorel G. (1950) *Reflections on Violence* (New York: Free Press).

Sorel G. (1969) *The Illusions of Progress* (New York: Cornell University Press) (Berkeley: University of California Press).

Sorel G. (1976) *From George Sorel: Essays in Socialism and Philosophy* (New York: Oxford University Press).

Sorokin P. (1928) *Contemporary Sociological Theories* (New York: Harper & Row).

Spencer H. (1965) *The Study of Sociology* (New York: Free Press).

Spencer H. (1969a) *Man versus the State* (Harmondsworth: Penguin Books).

Spencer H. (1969b) *Principles of Sociology* (ed Andreski) (New York: Macmillan).

Stammler O. (ed) (1971) *Max Weber and Sociology Today* (Oxford: Blackwell).

Strasser H. (1976) *The Normative Structure of Sociology* (London: Routledge & Kegan Paul).

Bibliography

Swingewood A. (1970) 'The Origins of Sociology: The Case of the Scottish Enlightenment', *British Journal of Sociology* (June).

Szacki J. (1979) *History of Sociological Thought* (London: Aldwych).

Sztompka P. (1974) *System and Function* (New York: Academic Press).

Tagliocozzo G. (1983) *Vico and Marx* (London: Macmillan).

Tawney R.H. (1926) *Religion and the Rise of Capitalism* (London: Allen & Unwin).

Taylor K. (ed) (1975) *Saint-Simon: Selected Writings on Science, Industry and Social Organisation* (London: Croom Helm).

Taylor S. (1982) *Durkheim and the Study of Suicide* (London: Macmillan).

Therborn G. (1976) *Science, Class and Society* (London: New Left Books).

Thomas W. I. & Znaneicki F. (1927) *The Polish Peasant in Europe and America* 2 Vols. (Chicago: University of Chicago Press).

Thompson E. (1978) *The Poverty of Theory* (London: Merlin Press).

Thompson J.B. and Held D. (eds) (1982) *Habermas: Critical Debates* (London: Macmillan).

Thompson K. (ed) (1976) *Auguste Comte: The Foundations of Sociology* (London: Nelson).

Tiryakin A.E. (1979) 'Emile Durkheim', in Bottomore & Nisbet (1979).

Tönnies F. (1963) *Community and Association* (London: Routledge & Kegan Paul).

Tönnies F. (1971) *On Sociology: Pure, Applied and Empirical* ed Cahmann W.J. and Meberle R. (Chicago: University of Chicago Press).

Tönnies F. (1974) *On Social Ideas and Ideologies* (New York: Harper & Row).

Touraine A. (1971) *The Post-Industrial Society* (London: Wildwood House).

Traugott B. (1978) (ed) *Durkheim on Institutional Analysis* (Chicago: University of Chicago Press).

Tucker R.C. (1961) *Philosophy and Myth in Karl Marx* (Oxford: Oxford University Press).

Tumin M. (1968) *Social Stratification: The Forms and Functions of Social Inequality* (New Jersey: Prentice-Hall).

Turner B. (1981) *For Weber* (London: Routledge & Kegan Paul).

Vico G. (1948) *The New Science* ed Bergin T. & Frisch M. (New York: Cornell University Press).

Weber M. (1923) *General Economic History* (London: Allen & Unwin).

Weber M. (1930) *The Protestant Ethic and the Spirit of Capitalism* (London: Allen & Unwin).

Weber M. (1949) *The Methodology of the Social Sciences* (New York: Free Press).

Weber M. (1951) *The Religion of India* (New York: Free Press).

Weber M. (1952) *Ancient Judaism* (New York: Free Press).

Weber M. (1954) *On Law in Economy and Society* (New York: Free Press).

Weber M. (1958a) *The Religion of India* (New York: Free Press).

Weber M. (1958b) *The City* (New York: Free Press).

Weber M. (1963) *The Sociology of Religion* (Boston: Beacon Press).

Weber M. (1964) *The Theory of Social and Economic Organisation* (New York: Free Press).

Weber M. (1968b) *Economy and Society* 3 Vols. (Towata: Bedminster Press).

Bibliography

Weber M. (1975) *Roscher and Knies: The Logical Problems of Historical Economics* (New York: Free Press).

Weber M. (1976) *The Agrarian Sociology of Ancient Civilisations* (London: New Left Books).

Weber M. (1977) *Critique of Stammler* (New York: Free Press).

Wellmer A. (1974) *Critical Theory of Society* (New York: Herder & Herder).

Wesolowski W. (1980) *Classes, Strata and Power* (London: Routledge & Kegan Paul).

Wolff K. (ed) (1950) *The Sociology of Georg Simmel* (New York: Free Press).

Wolff K. (ed) (1964) *Emile Durkheim: Essays on Sociology and Philosophy* (New York: Harper & Row).

Wolff K. (ed) (1965) *Simmel: Essays on Sociology, Philosophy and Aesthetics* (New York: Harper & Row).

Wolff K. (ed) (1971) *From Karl Mannheim* (New York: Oxford University Press).

Wollheim R. (1971) *Freud* (London: Fontana).

Wright E.O. (1978) *Class, Crisis and the State* (London: New Left Books).

Wrong D. (ed) (1970) *Max Weber* (New Jersey: Prentice-Hall).

Wrong D. (1976) *Skeptical Sociology* (London: Heinemann).

Znaneicki F. (1965) *The Social Role of the Man of Knowledge* (New York: Harper & Row).

Zeitlin I. (1968) *Ideology and the Development of Sociological Theory* (New Jersey: Prentice-Hall).

Zollschan G.R. & Hirsch, W. (eds) (1964) *Explorations in Social Change* (London: Routledge & Kegan Paul).

Index

Index

351

Index